GERARD MANLEY HOPKINS
(1844-1889)
New Essays on His Life, Writing, and Place in English Literature

Edited by
Michael E. Allsopp and Michael W. Sundermeier

Studies in British Literature
Volume 1

The Edwin Mellen Press
Lewiston/Lampeter/Queenston

Library of Congress Cataloging-in-Publication Data

Gerard Manley Hopkins (1844-1889) : new essays on his life, writing, and place in English literature / edited by Michael E. Allsopp and Michael W. Sundermeier.
    p. cm. -- (Studies in British literature ; v. 1)
  Bibliography: p.
  Includes index.
  ISBN 0-88946-928-8
  1. Hopkins, Gerard Manley, 1844-1889. 2. Poets, English--19th century--Biography. I. Allsopp, Michael E. II. Sundermeier, Michael W. III. Series.
PR4803.H44Z6443 1989
821' .8--dc20   89-9309
                                                              CIP

> This is volume 1 in the continuing series
> Studies in British Literature
> Volume 1 ISBN 0-88946-928-8
> SBL Series ISBN 0-88946-927-X

A CIP catalog record for this book
is available from the British Library.

© Copyright 1989 The Edwin Mellen Press.

All Rights Reserved. For more information contact

      The Edwin Mellen Press   The Edwin Mellen Press
                  Box 450   Box 67
              Lewiston, NY   Queenston, Ontario
               USA 14092   CANADA L0S 1L0

              The Edwin Mellen Press, Ltd.
                Lampeter, Dyfed, Wales,
            UNITED KINGDOM SA48 7DY

Printed in the United States of America

In Memory of
Alfred Thomas, S.J. and Raymond Schoder, S.J.
Friends and Colleagues

Acknowledgements

Every book owes its existence to many people. This volume is no exception. The decision to publish a collection of studies for the centenary of Hopkins' death took life early in 1986 as the result of conversations at Creighton University. It grew in strength from correspondence with members of the International Hopkins Association who expressed their interest and support. Herbert Richardson, Director of the Edwin Mellen Press, moved the project toward maturity. Mrs. Ruth Seelhammer agreed to contribute. Robert Boyle, S.J., Alan Heuser, and Norman MacKenzie were graciously supportive. Warren Anderson, Todd Bender, James Finn Cotter, David Downes, Joseph Feeney, S.J., Peter Milward, S.J., Michael Moore, Donald Walhout, Kelsey Thornton, and Tom Zaniello generously agreed to provide studies, and have consistently given breath to the enterprise. Raymond Schoder, S.J., sent his paper not long before his death. Alfred Thomas, S.J., unfortunately died when the project was still an idea.

As the collection goes to the publisher, there are others who have made its completion possible: Michael Lawler, Dean of the Graduate School, Creighton University, who supported the project financially; Jan Gines, who transcribed most of the manuscripts onto computer disks; and John Guehlstorff, Robert Guthrie, Don Kimmel, and Bruce Malina, who gave us invaluable advice and assistance.

To all, our sincere thanks.

M.E.A.
M.W.S.

Preface

One hundred years ago Gerard Manley Hopkins came to his last landfall as he went into port on that ship called life. Our lifetimes, in a sense, are spent as recipients of landfall, minor often and various, but as the natural outcome of our departures.

The impact and response to Hopkins' poetry, across the oceans of the world, can be noted by activities directly related to his work, such as this volume of landfall studies collected by the editors to commemorate the poet's centenary. Another evidence of the unflagging interest in Hopkins is shown by voyages to a center of Hopkins studies in America of scholars traveling the seas and the land from as far as Pusan and Tokyo and Bangalore. They come from Sydney, Brisbane and Canberra. Some who come are from Rome, others are from Oxford or from Bremen. Some are Bostonians or have arrived from Ann Arbor. From Canada and from Alaska come people with specific projects concerning the poetry or the prose.

Not all responses to Hopkins are outwardly as lively as those of "Old Possum's" practical cats capering across a stage. Some are as quiet, as controlled as the ship's cat of David Jones in *The Anathemata*:

> Cheerily, cheerily
> > with land to leeward
> known-land, known-shore, home-shore
> home-light.
> > Cheerly, cheerly men
> 'gin to work the ropes.
> And she bears up for it
> > riding her turning shadow.
> The incurving *aphlaston* lanterns high above him
> behind him
> > the plank-built walls converge
> to apse his leaning nave.
> To his left elbow
> > the helmsman
> is quite immobile now
> > by whose stanced feet
> coiled on the drying hemp-coil
> > with one eye open
> the still ship's cat
> > tillers, just perceptibly
> her tip of tail.[*]

The tillers of perceptibility in the landfall here are to be found in the thoughtfully-wrought studies of this book, bringing Hopkins a hundred years home.

Ruth Seelhammer
Gonzaga University
1989

---

[*] Reprinted by permission of Faber and Faber Ltd from *The Anathemata* by David Jones.

Table of Contents

Title	i
Dedication	iii
Acknowledgments	v
Preface	
Ruth Seelhammer	vii
Table of Contents	ix
Introduction	1
The Instress of Action: Action and Contemplation in Hopkins' Poetry	
Donald Walhout	11
Two Views of "The Windhover"	
Peter Milward, S.J.	31
All on Two Spools: Aesthetics, Morals, and Janus-Words in Hopkins	
R.K.R. Thornton	47
Homiletic and Poetic Vocabulary in Hopkins	
Todd K. Bender	67
Dangerous Beauty: Hopkins and Newman	
Michael D. Moore	85
Hopkins and Pindar	
Raymond V. Schoder, S.J.	113
"Freshness Deep Down Things": Hopkins' Dublin Notes on Homer	
Warren Anderson	127
Sounding Alpha and Omega in Dante, Milton, and Hopkins	
James Finn Cotter	147

Hopkins as Teacher, The English Years:
Understanding the Man by Watching Him Work
    Joseph J. Feeney, S.J.   179
Of Miracles, Martyrs, and Prayer Gauges
    Tom Zaniello   223
The Final Act: Hopkins' Last Sonnets
    David Anthony Downes   239
Contributors   267
Index   271

Introduction

The Sea of Faith
Was once, too, at the full, and round earth's shore
Lay like the folds of a bright girdle furled.
But now I only hear
Its melancholy, long, withdrawing roar,
Retreating, to the breath
Of the night wind, down the vast edges drear
And naked shingles of the world.
                    (Matthew Arnold, "Dover Beach," ca. 1851)

And for all this, nature is never spent;
    There lives the dearest freshness deep down things;
And though the last lights off the black West went
    Oh, morning, at the brown brink eastward, springs--
Because the Holy Ghost over the bent
      World broods with warm breast and with ah! bright wings.
                    (G.M. Hopkins, "God's Grandeur," 1877)

Gerard Manley Hopkins died in Dublin on June 8, 1889, the year following the death of the famous Arnold, his countervailing sense of the divine presence virtually unknown to his Victorian peers. In the intervening years he has been enthusiastically brought to the attention of the reading public; as the centenary of his death approaches, we should take note of Wendell Stacy Johnson's observation that Hopkins' poetry "should now be allowed to sustain serious critical examination, rather than being apologized for or extravagantly defended as a whole." The essays in this volume are a contribution toward that goal.

Since 1918, when Robert Bridges published the First Edition of Hopkins' poetry, with his comments about the perversion of human feeling in the verse due to his friend's efforts "to force emotion into theological and sectarian channels," controversies about Hopkins' poetry, his aesthetic and philosophical ideas, and his place in literature, have blazed incessantly throughout the forests of literary criticism. John Wain, for instance, entitled his 1959 Chatterton Lecture, "Gerard Manley Hopkins: An Idiom of Desperation"; *In Extremity* was the title John Robinson gave to his 1978 study of Hopkins' poetic language; and Donald Davie has said that Hopkins "has no respect for language, but gives it Sandow-exercises until it is a muscle-bound monstrosity." On the other hand, Marshall McLuhan, Jacob Korg, and Herbert F. Tucker, have seen vitality and drama in Hopkins' diction, as well as indisputable resemblances to Mallarmé's understanding of the English language; all have seen a richness and compactness that embodies depth rather than shallowness of mind and skill. Still, after one hundred years, the definitive opinion about Hopkins' mastery and theory of language yet awaits us.

Other questions, too, still divide the literary community. Is Hopkins a Victorian? Is Hopkins a major English poet? Although Leavis has drawn attention to his genius and craftsmanship, Eliot, as all know, was reserved in his praise of Hopkins, while Yvor Winters and Geoffrey Hartman consistently disagreed with Leavis' estimates, and argued that Hopkins was a minor poet, limited by the confusion his verse creates, his parochialism and punctillio in matters of craft. They saw weaknesses in Hopkins' mixing of linguistic orders and effects, in the volume of his poetry, his subject matter, and his range of subjects; and Hartman has argued that Hopkins, although the purer talent, often appears narrow and idiosyncratic when placed beside Browning. In Harold Weatherby's judgment, too, Hopkins' poetry fails to achieve the unity and intelligibility requisite for poetic greatness or beauty.

However, in spite of such critics, one hundred years after his death, Hopkins occupies a position among the major Victorian poets, and his right to a place among English poets in general seems assured. "The Wreck of the Deutschland" is generally considered one of the finest odes in the history of English poetry, while "Hurrahing in Harvest," "God's Grandeur," "Pied Beauty," and "Henry Purcell" have permanent places in most recent anthologies of English poetry. Hopkins has been translated into all major languages. His diaries and journals, sermons and devotional writings, as well as three volumes of his correspondence have been published; and Norman MacKenzie, to whom much is owed for his pioneer research and dedication, is in the process of completing the Fifth Edition of the poetry.

Hopkins' interest in Scotus has been a constant subject of research. "Inscape" and "Instress" have become part of the English language. Built upon W.H. Gardner's research, there have been explorations of Hopkins' command of Greek philosophy and natural science, his knowledge of Pindar, Homer, Shakespeare, the Bible, and Ignatian spirituality. Hopkins' debt to John Donne and Dante have been carefully investigated, and his use of Pauline imagery has been analyzed.

Today, Hopkins is considered to be less idiosyncratic than first thought. In his inwardness and self-consciousness, his modernity, he fits our age. Robert Boyle's *Metaphor in Hopkins* (1961) made a significant contribution to our understanding of this. James Finn Cotter, a contributor to this volume, has drawn some of these findings together to provide an original solution to the complexities in Hopkins' language by arguing that Hopkins was a modern Origen, a Victorian gnostic, a view in contrast with James Collins' assessments in *Thought* (1947) that Hopkins was not a philosopher at all, although philosophical themes are present throughout his writing, constituting a "minor but essential strain in his approach to reality."

Theologians such as Joseph Sittler, and Hans Urs von Balthasar have also added to Hopkins' stature as a thinker. Both have praised Hopkins for his contributions to Christology, and his awareness that the "world is charged with the grandeur of God." More than once, Sittler has praised Hopkins for his contributions to theological reflection, and expressed his debt to Hopkins for providing him with insights into the all-enfolding force of God's grace. David Jones, the highly respected Anglo-Welsh painter, engraver and poet, has acknowledged his admiration for Hopkins' feeling for "the dearest freshness deep down things."

Less flatteringly, in recent years, Hopkins' personality has been the subject of intense analysis. Central to Paddy Kitchen's *Gerard Manley Hopkins* (1978) is the assumption that Hopkins suffered serious personality dysfunction and disturbing psycho-sexual ambivalence. Linda Pratt, in an as yet unpublished work which groups Hopkins with the late nineteenth century decadents, also alludes to Hopkins' homosexual tendencies. Bernard Bergonzi closed his survey of Hopkins' Dublin years with the observation, "one has the distinct and disconcerting impression of a powerful, original and wellstocked--indeed, polymathic--mind with so little equilibrium that it could not resist picking up and trying to pursue one random proposal after another." Such literary psychologizing may need to be modified as more is brought to light about Hopkins' life and work at University College.

Current research into the relationship between creativity and desperation may prove valuable here as well. Whatever the impressions of psychological disturbance, Hopkins' ability to compose "To R.B." and "Thou art indeed just, Lord," as well as "That Nature is a Heraclitean Fire" and "Spelt from Sibyl's Leaves," provides lasting evidence that neither Hopkins' poetic skill nor his artistic imagination failed or suffered disintegration from his experiences in Ireland.

In addition to the above-mentioned areas of interest, biographical research undertaken since the studies by Gerald Lahey and John Pick, has fuelled new fires. Such questions as, "Was Hopkins a mystic?" and "Was Hopkins a 'modern'?" have been more extensively explored. Recent research has also provided clearer portraits of Hopkins' youth, his Oxford years, his training and teaching as a Jesuit. Joseph Feeney, a contributor to this collection, has taken our knowledge of Hopkins' Jesuit years beyond the frontiers reached by Alfred Thomas and W.A.M. Peters. Feeney's studies have resolved some of the major questions about Hopkins' appointments, his leaving Wales after his ordination, and his Dublin years. They have complemented the visual studies of Hopkins' life, his ability as an artist and musician, provided by R.K.R. Thornton's *All My Eyes See* (1975). Another contributor to this collection, Tom Zaniello, has added to our knowledge of Hopkins' philosophy studies at Oxford, while Graham Storey's research into Hopkins' undergraduate associations, has added to our understanding of his religious conversion. Hopkins' friendships with Walter Pater and with Bridges and Dixon, have been subjects of rewarding study. At least one biographer has gone counter to the general tendency to expand Hopkins' list of talents: Norman White, who is completing a biography for the Oxford University Press, has recently asked that, now that Hopkins has his place of honor in Poets Corner, Westminster Abbey, he should be allowed to rest peacefully among his true companions, the poets. All efforts to carry Hopkins off to stand with the saints should be resisted; nor, White insists, should Hopkins be fashioned into an English Teilhard de Chardin. He is an English *poet*; let us admire his art rather than venerate his virtue.

But assessments of Hopkins' vision and character continue, especially the problems posed by his Irish years. An epigram in the *Stonyhurst Magazine*, a song from Shakespeare in the *Irish Monthly*, a short biographical note about a friend for the *Manual of English Literature*, do not, as Hopkins himself realized, constitute that outstanding work which every ambitious writer longs to see acclaimed by reviewers. Hopkins did find his years in Ireland difficult. He did not see himself as an impressive or successful Jesuit. Biographers, with some justification, still see these years and what Hopkins accomplished as largely wasted and disappointing, as years of unfinished enterprises, fragments, and the "terrible sonnets." Yet the terrible sonnets are "terrible" only in the sense that Yeats, commenting on another Irish situation in which apparent waste was changed into something quite different, said "a terrible beauty is born." How many poets would trade in their collected works, how many academics would sign away their tenure, to have written them? Still, contemporary and future biographers have the task ahead of them of throwing further light upon this period of Hopkins' life, particularly upon the literary and teaching effort which he then expended, as they have upon his years as a child, at Highgate and Oxford.

Notes on the Essays

The contents of this volume are difficult to categorize, which is a natural consequence, one suspects, of the complexity of Hopkins' poetry. The essays touch upon religion, theology, philosophy, linguistics, aesthetics, literary influences, and biography; often various of these areas of interest overlap in the same essay. For example, Donald Walhout's essay, "The Instress of Action: Action and Contemplation in Hopkins' Poetry," uses a fresh analysis of the essentially theological notion of instress to reexamine certain of Hopkins' poems for the light they throw upon the variety of ways in which human beings can come to contemplation, which for Hopkins is both an aesthetic and a religious experience.

Peter Milward, in "Two Views of 'The Windhover,'" gives us yet another interpretation of that difficult poem, challenging the dominant understanding of its point of view and bringing to bear his own experience as a Jesuit to define Hopkins' use of the word *chevalier*. R.K.R. Thornton, in "All on Two Spools: Aesthetics, Morals, and Janus-Words in Hopkins," draws the reader's attention to the constant tension in Hopkins' poetry between "the secular and the sacred, the aesthetic and the moral," and observes the ways in which that duality is unified in what he refers to as Hopkins' "Janus-Words."

Todd Bender, in "Homiletic and Poetic Vocabulary in Hopkins," notes a similar phenomenon which he identifies as "linguistic turbulence." Furthermore, he suggests that in some instances a proper understanding of the tension between the moral and aesthetic elements in Hopkins' poetry must be rooted in a knowledge of how Hopkins used certain words in his sermons.

Michael D. Moore, in "Dangerous Beauty: Hopkins and Newman," considers a problem closely related to the Bender's, the tension between "sensory-imaginative delight and religious response." Moore sees John Henry Newman's influence in Hopkins' usual handling of this relationship.

Raymond Schoder, whose recent death is sadly noted by the editors, in "Hopkins and Pindar" demonstrates with considerable detail the similarities between Pindar and Hopkins and the extent to which Hopkins was in fact influenced by his study of Pindar.

Warren Anderson, taking a somewhat different approach to Hopkins' interest in the classics, in "'Freshness Deep Down Things': Hopkins' Dublin Notes on Homer," evaluates Hopkins' classical scholarship and concludes that, at bottom, his approach to the reading of Homer was that of a fellow poet using Homer's works as a trigger for his own imagination rather than that of a conventional scholar.

James Finn Cotter, in his "Sounding Alpha and Omega in Dante, Milton, and Hopkins," makes a case for Hopkins having many times used the vowels *A* and *O* as symbols of his Christian belief, a practice which he also finds in Milton and Dante and which ultimately has its roots in Gnostic practices in the early church.

Joseph Feeney, in "Hopkins as Teacher, The English Years: Understanding the Man by Watching Him Work," examines Hopkins' teaching career with particular reference to the effect which the effort of teaching had on his mood and poetic production.

Tom Zaniello, in "Of Miracles, Martyrs, and Prayer Gauges," argues that Hopkins' use of the martyrs Thecla, Winefride, and Margaret Clitheroe as subjects for his poetry was at least in part an effort to counter or at least respond to nineteenth-century religious skepticism, particularly with regard to miracles.

David Downes, in "The Final Act: Hopkins' Last Sonnets," sees these last poems as dramatically appropriate in the development of Hopkins' poetry and as constituting something like a fifth act in which the testing which the poet has undergone is brought to a fitting and positive resolution.

Bibliographical Note

Because of the frequency with which the standard Hopkins sources are consulted, they are identified here rather than repeated in the Works Cited sections appended to each essay. References to Hopkins' poems are by poem number and, in the longer poems, by stanza or other appropriate division. References to other material in *Poems* is by page number. On the first citation of a poem in each essay, the poem number is supplied; thereafter it is omitted.

Abbott, Claude Colleer, ed. *The Correspondence of Gerard Manley Hopkins and Richard Watson Dixon*. 2nd imp. London: Oxford UP, 1955. Hereafter referred to as *D*.

---, ed. *Further Letters of Gerard Manley Hopkins including his Correspondence with Coventry Patmore*. 2nd ed. London: Oxford UP, 1956. Hereafter referred to as *F*.

---, ed. *The Letters of Gerard Manley Hopkins to Robert Bridges*. 2nd imp. London: Oxford UP, 1959. Hereafter referred to as *B*.

Devlin, Christopher, S.J., ed. *The Sermons and Devotional Writings of Gerard Manley Hopkins*. London: Oxford UP, 1959. Hereafter referred to as *S*.

Gardner, W.H., and N.H. MacKenzie, eds. *The Poems of Gerard Manley Hopkins*. 4th ed. London: Oxford UP, 1970. Hereafter referred to as *P*.

House, Humphry, and Graham Storey, eds. *The Journals and Papers of Gerard Manley Hopkins*. London: Oxford UP, 1959. Hereafter referred to as *J*.

The Instress of Action

Action and Contemplation

in Hopkins' Poetry

Donald Walhout

Hopkins' concept of instress is generally discussed in connection with the things of nature, where it is often coupled with the concept of inscape. The two are Hopkins' ways of alluding to the forms and dynamics in nature, but instress is equally applicable, I believe, to human action, where its relevance has perhaps been neglected. My discussion in the present article will focus on this human side of instress.

The particular claim to be made is that instress is the link between action and contemplation. That is, instress has the function of prompting contemplation from action. Instress is what leads a person from actions or a life of action to the act or spirit of contemplation. In this regard some remarks from the Prologue to *The Cloud of Unknowing* are suggestive. The anonymous author says that the beneficiary of his tract will be "one who has for a long time been doing all that he can to come to the contemplative life by virtue of his active life" (43). And again, the book "will mean something to those who, though 'active' according to their outward mode of life, are, by the inner working of the spirit of God . . . disposed toward contemplation" (44). I do not claim that Hopkins was directly influenced by this sentiment or this work. The reference is only a helpful allusion. Influences on Hopkins were, as we know, Ignatian, Scotist, indeed multifarious, as discussed by Jerome Bump in *Gerard Manley Hopkins*. I claim only that the concepts of action and contemplation can help to illuminate the concept of instress. Instress is "the inner working of the spirit of God," and it is present in potentiality throughout the created world. Human beings can at times initiate actions which actualize the instressing activity, and one consequence is the enhancement of contemplation.

Hopkins' nature poems are, of course, replete with innuendoes of instress in nature. But a principal locus, a paradigm instance, of the instress of action is to be found in the opening of "The Wreck of the Deutschland" (28). The action in question is the poet's own act of saying yes ("I did say yes") to the "Lord of living and dead" (st. 2, 1), i.e., his own act of converting or changing allegiance. In this entire action he feels a "fire of stress" (st. 2). This is what we shall take instress to be: the fire of stress that makes an impact on a person through the vehicle of action (or of nature). But Hopkins also testifies that what results is contemplation of God: "I find *thee*" (st. 1, italics mine), he says. So from the divine side, instress is God's immanent power in created things which fires forth at auspicious times to energize the recipient into a contemplative gaze of God.

From the human side, the impact felt is paradigmatically expressed in the second stanza of "Thee, God, I come from" (155):

What I know of thee I bless,
As acknowledging thy stress On my being and as seeing
Something of thy holiness.

The immanent power is felt as a stress on our being, an awakening within our being. And the result is that we are brought into "seeing something of thy holiness." This "seeing something" of God is what we shall take as the central note in contemplation. So the pattern of experience, or instress of action, that we shall explore is this: God's immanent power is latent in the created world; we at times perform actions--a familiar religious act, the practice of a virtue, an ordinary action of daily life--which open us to this power; the power is instressed in our being; and the result is a seeing of something about God and his ways. Action is linked to contemplation by instress. This is one theme, among many others, in Hopkins' poetry, and it is our theme here.

To support this claim, illustrations from the poetry are essential. But before this documentation proceeds, some further remarks and distinctions are in order concerning our two terms, "action" and "contemplation."

The term "action" is used by some philosophers, working today in the philosophy of mind, to mean any intentional occurrence in human life. In this sense practically everything about a human being would be an action except purely involuntary physiological or environmental stimuli and reactions. Thus a mental act like contemplation would be an action in this sense. Such terminology can have utility for philosophical analysis; but it blurs the traditional contrast I wish to emphasize between action and contemplation. In the more traditional usage, an action is any intentional behavior in which a person initiates some change in the world in which the person is present. In contrast, if a person simply thinks or reflects about that world, or one's presence in it, without initiating any alteration in it, that would be a mental occurrence, e.g., contemplation. In this sense we are able to contrast action with contemplation, an active life with a contemplative life. In the one case, a person is concerned with intentional deeds in the world; in the other, one is reflecting, meditating, or the like. Nothing philosophical turns on this stipulation of usage; it merely designates a traditional contrast I wish to make in this article.

The term "contemplation" is also subject to ambiguity. The *New Catholic Encyclopedia* distinguishes five levels of contemplation: an aesthetic concentration on beauty, an intellectual dwelling upon truth, a rational or natural reflection upon God, a theological or supernatural gazing upon God, and a mystical union with God (263). We might consider the first two of these as more or less common human acts, the third as philosophical, and the last two as religious. In this article I shall have in mind mainly the contemplation of God in the third and fourth levels, though not the mystical. I shall not be concerned to emphasize a distinction between the third and fourth levels, e.g., by trying to say which is which in which of Hopkins' poems, for I do not think there is much of a basis in the poetry for doing this. Hopkins is very devoted to the contemplation of God; but how to classify it in categories and divisions is not a poetic concern of his.

Nor do I think that Hopkins was invoking any particular Jesuit doctrine about religious contemplation. The following account by J. Aumann would seem to apply to just about any Christian viewpoint:

> Contemplation . . . is primarily a contact or experience through intimate union with God; it is an immediate awareness of God, not as he is in himself, but as present through his gifts of grace, the divine indwelling, and the infused virtues. . . . Contemplation is . . . a special grace. (*NCE* 261)

This account refers chiefly to religious contemplation conceived of as a form of prayer. I am sure Hopkins would consider this the higher level of contemplation, but I want to include in the discussion the broader understanding that would comprise the kind of reflection on God and his ways that we might call philosophical or natural. Both kinds, philosophical and religious, seem to be intimated in Hopkins' poetry without a sharp distinction always being evident. The Godward gaze is the essential factor, poetically considered, whatever else one might go on to say theologically.

A number of additional distinctions regarding action and contemplation in the present context are worth noting, not because they will be explored in depth in this article, but because they may help to clarify the general theme to be illustrated shortly.

(1) What we shall be illustrating are actions which prompt contemplation, i.e., actions which have contemplation as a consequence of their instress. So one preliminary distinction is that between actions which have this consequence directly and those which prompt it indirectly. Some actions, by their very nature, have contemplation as their typical outcome, for example, certain religious acts or the practice of certain virtues. Other actions, such as routine daily secular pursuits, have other outcomes as typical, but might on occasion have the effect of leading to contemplation as well. One might even put the difference grammatically by referring to direct and indirect objects. One might say, for instance, that a sacrament discloses the presence of God, whereas working in the arts might possibly lead a person to the presence of God. Of course Hopkins would hold that grace, through instress, is operative in both; but one is more normal, the other more occasional, in its effect.

(2) A corresponding distinction is that between actions whose contemplative outcome is intentional and those where such an outcome is inadvertent. This distinction is parallel to the previous one except that the focus is on the subjective act of intentionality. All actions are intentional, of course; but some have consequences that are also intended, and some have additional consequences that are inadvertent. A comparison with

instress in nature can be made: One might survey nature, as in "Pied Beauty" (37) with the deliberate aim of enhancing or expressing contemplation of God; but one might also be simply observing a harvest or a hawk without any such intention and then suddenly be cast into this frame of mind. One can plan a result or be surprised by joy. The instress of action is similar regarding this twofold possibility.

(3) The actions to be considered might be those of oneself, e.g., of a poetic speaker, or those of others, and likewise the effect of contemplation might take place in oneself or in others. In summary, there are actions of one's own that affect oneself, actions of one's own that affect others, actions of others that affect oneself, and actions of others that affect others. We are concerned in this article not with the religious discipline of cultivating contemplation in oneself but with a poetic survey of the general phenomenon of actions that prompt contemplation. For this purpose the widest range of possibilities is relevant.

(4) A further distinction is that between contemplation which focuses on God's being in itself and contemplation which focuses on God's ways of relating to the world. Supernatural religious contemplation centers on the former of these: The enjoyment of God is uppermost; God is the joy of man's desiring. But in mundane life, thought about God is likely to focus just as much, or more, on God's ways of dealing with the world. Certainly this is true in Hopkins' poetry. His is not a poetry of supernatural contemplation as such, let alone of mysticism, but a poetry which probes God in his aspect of superintending the world in ways which are, on the one hand, loving and kind, but which often are, on the other hand, baffling, mysterious, even terrifying. I want to include under contemplation this broader dimension of thought about God, even though it expands perhaps the usual religious meaning of contemplation. Perhaps this is one of the

contributions of Hopkins: to show that this dimension too can be handled in faith.

(5) There is an historical distinction between infused contemplation and acquired contemplation, and with it a controversy as to whether all contemplation is infused by God or whether some levels at least can be acquired by man. This is a theological point into which we need not go. Suffice it to say that, for Hopkins' poetry, in so far as instress abounds in the created world and may well up at many times and places, even unexpectedly, contemplation can be considered to be the product of infusion; but at the same time, one can make decisions, undertake careers, practice virtues, and perform daily actions which make infusion possible, and therefore one can at least acquire the necessary disposition. So I am tempted to say that a Hopkinsian view of the controversy would be that contemplation is both infused *and* acquired. Since this is only a poetic extrapolation, I cannot propose it as anything more, but it may have prospects.

(6) Lastly, we should note the historical distinction between the active life and the contemplative life. Happily, this is not a controversy, but a choice of calling. The distinction is relevant here inasmuch as the active life is one subcase under action that we shall consider. We must also consider hosts of particular actions or types of actions that might prompt contemplation. In addition, we are really proceeding from a presumption of the standpoint of the active life, not as to its superiority, but as to its priority for the bulk of mankind. A separate religious calling is proper for some, but most people on earth must work actively in the world. Hopkins himself, while having the usual retreats, was active as a parish priest and later in teaching. I believe this centrality of worldly action for mankind is also the presumption in Hopkins' poetry. Some of his poems, of course,

such as "Heaven-Haven" (9) or "The Habit of Perfection" (22), admittedly reflect a purely contemplative interest. But for the most part his poems reflect the activity in the world, be it that of farrier or ploughman, porter or prelate, bugler or artist. And so we are, by this factor, predisposed to look, in Hopkins, not for the essence of a detached contemplation, but for contexts in which the normal actions of everyday life can nevertheless prompt contemplation, i.e., a serious reflection upon God.

Now it is time to marshal illustrations of this theme in the poetry of Hopkins:

I shall divide the illustrations into three categories. The first consists of particular actions--just any ordinary actions--which are not normally regarded as contemplation-inducing but which might, on a given occasion, be so. The second category is types of action, or action kinds, which, by their very nature, are predisposed to be contemplation-inducing and are therefore prime candidates to be so on any given occasion. The third category is forms of life, or life kinds, whose entire action components are closely linked to contemplation or are predisposed to induce it.

Let us begin our illustrations of the first category with the simple action of walking; for example, walking home at night. Ordinarily this might be routine, not noteworthy. But in "The Lantern Out of Doors" (40) this action prompts in Hopkins a contemplation of Christ and how he minds the unknowns of the world whereas we cannot.

Or consider the occurrence of speech acts. The action of speaking is so prevalent and so diffuse in the world that one can hardly think of it in contemplative terms. And yet an off-hand speech act by a boy in "The Handsome Heart" (47)--"'Father, what you buy me I like best'"--prompts in Hopkins a contemplation of how God has made creatures with a natural "fine function" which is "self-instressed" as in "carriers," and a petition that the boy be enabled to "run all your race" with the same "high hallowing grace."

A more dramatic instance occurs in "The Wreck of the Deutschland." The cries of the tall nun to the men of the ship, in stanza 19, and especially her call to Christ, in stanza 24, initiate Hopkins' contemplation about the theological significance of the words. This occasion is a special circumstance, to be sure. Nevertheless, it illustrates how speech acts can instress contemplation.

Another routine action in life is that of complaining. One could argue that the action of complaining is as universal as any. But in "The Shepherd's Brow" (75), the complaining in lines 5-12, which refers to mankind and is starting to apply to the poet himself, is suddenly broken off, as indicated by the all-important ellipses in line 13, and the poet is instressed into a flash of enlightenment and a prayerful close to the sonnet. It is a remarkable instance of how complaining can induce contemplation.

A performance of music is generally categorized by such epithets as skillful, entertaining, lively, aesthetically masterful, and the like; but in "On a Piece of Music" (148), the poet is led to reflect, first, on how man must have been made in order to produce such a thing, and then to affirm the need of all to "choose as chieftain one."

The action of voyaging has been regarded as a means of travel, of commerce, of exploration, nowadays of recreation. But the way the sailing turned out for the Deutschland and the Eurydice led, in Hopkins, to profound reflection on God's purposes and his methods of dealing with mankind. A common action triggered, inadvertently for the human agents, profound contemplation.

The action of begging has generally been seen as regrettable, deplorable, or belittling; but in one case, in "Cheery Beggar" (142), Hopkins thinks he notices in the beggar that "the motion of that man's heart is fine." The beggar has been elevated to something higher. But the poem is unfinished.

The action of changing location and thereby distancing oneself from present associates is a common event, especially nowadays, and is seen as a means to an end--changing jobs, improving health, and the like. But in one of Hopkins' later sonnets this action is the occasion for a pensive self-probing in which Hopkins wonders whether God is deliberately banning him from natural achievements. The sonnet is another effort to fathom the ways of God, for "To seem the stranger lies my lot" (66) is apparently how God is using the move to Ireland.

Some particular actions, while still not intrinsically related to contemplation, have an aura of seriousness about them which makes them perhaps more likely than others to have this effect. One example, due to the seriousness of death itself, is comprised of the actions surrounding dying. Many such actions are, of course, routine and quite unprovocative. But the responses of a Felix Randal prompt a serene reflection, in the poem of that name (53), on his life, his acceptance of the sacrament, and the providence over his soul.

Another example is the cry of woe or despair. Again, such cries are frequent in human life and do not necessarily have transforming repercussions. But in many of Hopkins' later sonnets such as "No worst, there is none" (65) or "I wake and feel the fell of dark not day" (67), the cries, probably from Hopkins himself, though they might be from anyone, generate the most heart-rending moments of contemplation in all his poetry. Once again the concern is God's handling of him in particular and this world of sorrow in general.

In a more controlled and less impassioned vein, we might mention the self-disciplined action of containing self-pity and self-indulgence. In "My own heart let me more have pity on" (69), this self-control is sufficient to prompt the acknowledgment that God will deal with an individual in God's own proper means and times. One should therefore "leave comfort root-room; let joy size / At God knows when to God knows what." The poet actually suggests, as we have been doing in this section, that unexpected instresses from unusual quarters are fitting and normative; that one need not force God's smile, but be prepared for "unforeseen times rather" in which his will is wrought.

A final example in this category is the simple action of going out and observing the bounties of nature, such as a harvest. Nature often evokes serious reflection, and of course the inscapes in nature itself are involved in this effect. Nevertheless, the actions of going out and observing must be taken by us and are a necessary condition in the result. In "Hurrahing in Harvest" (38) and in other poems, Hopkins reflects on God's immanence in all this beauty and display. Majesty, rather than baffling mystery, is here the attribute contemplated.

These are but random examples in Hopkins from an infinity of human actions. But they do suggest a theme in Hopkins, namely, that instress can flow from many unpredicted and unlikely human acts.

The second category comprises action kinds, to which our last few examples form a transition. The instances of these action kinds are in general very likely to cause the act of contemplation because of their special suitability to this end.

The most obvious of these action kinds would be religious actions, which are directly and explicitly enacted to enhance spiritual life. One of these to which Hopkins is acutely attentive is that of heeding the call felt within one's being. He begins "The Wreck" with this allusion, and it is clear that this call is not just a one-time conversion but something that happens "over again." Many of the later poems, such as "Carrion Comfort" (64) have this sense of calling as a backdrop, and contemplative reflections are offered accordingly.

The overt actions of public ritual and private devotion are more openly designed to unite actor and God. Here again it is not the baffling and mysterious aspects of God which are stressed, but his benevolence and providence. Such actions are means of grace or devotional aids practiced to bring contemplation in the purely religious sense. Hopkins regularly refers to such actions as instressing God to man. In "The Starlight Night" (32), for instance, he alludes to "prayer, patience, alms, vows" as religious actions. Sacraments are often thematized, as in "Easter Communion" (11) and especially "The Bugler's First Communion" (48). Prayer is often alluded to or actually employed in the poems, as in "Thee, God, I come from" (155). The importance of regular religious actions in enhancing the contemplation of God is an understanding which pervades the entire corpus of Hopkins' poems.

An interesting inversion of this theme is also present, however. Hopkins is concerned not only with approaches to God but with flights from God. As does Francis Thompson in "The Hound of Heaven," so also Hopkins considers attempted escapes as significant. In "Carrion Comfort," he refers to "me frantic to avoid thee and flee." Demands of God may be too great, and avoidance by fleeing may seem best. But the result may be the same as in overt religious acts, for the one fleeing is found, or rather preserved despite oneself. This is the supernatural aspect: to be preserved despite one's worst efforts not to be. Grasp of this truth would be a contemplative moment engendered by the action of flight.

The practice of virtues, moral or theological, in one's conduct is another avenue to a contemplative spirit. For Hopkins these would be, of course, the familiar virtues of natural law and Christian tradition. But two that he has a certain fondness for in the poems are patience and faithfulness in suffering. One entire poem, "Patience, Hard Thing!" (68) is devoted to this virtue, but patience is alluded to elsewhere as well, as in "Peace" (51), where the claim is that patience is always available even when peace is not. An entire poem is also devoted to faithfulness in suffering, namely, "Thou art indeed just, Lord" (74). This virtue is also an implicit theme in many other poems. An excellent definition of it is given in "Patience, Hard Thing!": "to do without, take tosses, and obey." It is clear that the practice of these virtues prompted contemplation in the poet and were thought by him to be able to do so as well for anyone.

Actions that we call good deeds can have a similar function, though not perhaps as overtly since their aim is not to transcend but to benefit the human lot. Still there is something about morally good deeds which often inspires reflection about the ultimate source of right and good. Kant is noteworthy in this regard, but hardly exceptional. A lucid example of this response is found in Hopkins' "In the Valley of the Elwy" (34). It begins with a moral sentiment:

> I remember a house where all were good
> To me, God knows, deserving no such thing:

and ends with a contemplative sentiment:

> God, lover of souls, swaying considerate scales,
> Complete thy creature dear O where he fails,
> Being mighty a master, being a father and fond.

Another type of action which particularly moved Hopkins was martyrdom. A martyr for faith both demonstrates and evokes affinity with God. The story of St. Winefred, for example, intrigued Hopkins. And

"Margaret Clitheroe" (145) is an impassioned meditation on the actions and the significance of one whose "life was bent at God" though it ended in martyrdom.

By contrast, a more joyful kind of action which is well-suited to arouse serious contemplation about ultimate things is the action of wedding. Thus it is for Hopkins in "At the Wedding March" (52), and not only because he views marriage as a sacrament. He uses the occasion to comment not only on the spiritual union of bride and groom, bound in "divine charity," but also on his own, quite different "wonder wedlock" which "deals triumph and immortal years."

The making of beauty artistically or the observing of beauty in nature or in human form is, for Hopkins at least, another natural avenue to the contemplation of divine grace. This is the message of "To what serves Mortal Beauty?" (62). While this view of beauty is obviously not held by everyone, the classical Hopkins always sees a transcendent dimension in beauty and art.

Finally, this may be the place to mention not another class of actions but the class of all classes of action, i.e., the whole human scene of activity on this earth. Hopkins often alludes to man's life or activity collectively, and usually with a philosophical or theological interpretation to express. In "That Nature is a Heraclitean Fire" (72), all human activity is seen as a fleeting episode which "time beats level," only to have its true significance rendered in the triumphant second half of the poem, "The Comfort of the Resurrection." Clearly the whole human scene of action is, for Hopkins, a prime instigator of contemplative reflection on God's ways.

The third category of illustrations comprises lifetimes of action, or kinds of life in their entirety. Here we consider active lives as a whole with their instressing of contemplation. Kinds of life can be classified in many ways, and we shall make no attempt to enumerate all principles of division, but shall only give, as before, some representative examples to be found in Hopkins.

One approach is to think of active lives solely in terms of the individual persons who lived them and the traits they exhibited. One may say that any life like that person's, with the traits indicated, is a life that fosters contemplation in the person living that life and by contagion in others as well. Thus Hopkins honors the church work of the Bishop of Shrewsbury in "The Silver Jubilee" (29). In "In Honour of St. Alphonsus Rodriguez" (73), Hopkins says that God "could crowd career with conquest" in the case of a doorkeeper's devoted service. The life of St. Francis is hailed in stanza 23 of "The Wreck." Duns Scotus (44), Henry Purcell (45), and Margaret Clitheroe are reflected upon in separate poems. In all of these cases, and in other allusions, the lives in question are hailed and interpreted for their significance in fulfilling God's purposes. They either exhibit a contemplative life amid their active life, as sought by *The Cloud of Unknowing*, or they prompt contemplation in others about God's ways.

One could also approach active lives that foster contemplative lives in terms of abstract qualities which they display without reference to individual personalities. Thus saintly lives are of special attraction in this regard to Hopkins, as indeed they are to just about anyone. These are lives especially translucent in supernatural grace. Likewise, a life of good deeds, exhibiting "divine charity," is, in its own way, analogous to a saintly life. A life which endures suffering despite confusion of mind and can still say, "Justus quidem tu es, Domine, si disputem tecum" (74), may exhibit a tortured but genuine contemplation. A quality especially treasured by Hopkins is true selfhood. There is an essential self of everyone in God's mind, according to Hopkins, and the fulfillment of this essential selfhood is life's task. So if anyone "acts in God's eye what in God's eye he is," as expressed in "As Kingfishers Catch Fire" (57), we have a genuine union of active and contemplative life. The self comes to a union with God through becoming in its active life what in essence it is in God's mind.

Another way of classifying active lives would be by careers or vocations pursued. Can some career(s) be said to be more predisposed than others to lead to a contemplative spirit, and could careers be graded in this respect? Traditionally, the religious vocation has been thought to be favored in this regard. But Hopkins, while not dissenting from this traditional belief, is concerned to emphasize that any worthwhile occupation can be divinely blessed to this end. God can be instressed through any commendable vocation. "The Soldier" (63) suggests that many a calling can be called virtuous (he says "manly"), and that the practitioner can be ennobled through the calling, with Christ as a model. "Tom's Garland" (70) deals with working-class toilers and views them as the base of a good commonweal. Various professions--those of teachers, artists, and so on--are praised here and there in the poems. So it seems that any worthwhile occupation can be a vehicle through which one can be instressed into a spiritual awareness.

The last way of classifying lives that I shall mention is chronological. One could speak of various stages of life from birth to death--the life of the child, the youthful life, the life of old age, and so on. In "Morning, Midday, and Evening Sacrifice" (49), Hopkins speaks of youthful life, middle life, and old age. Each of these stages of life has distinct qualities and gifts to offer to God's service. The implication is that instress will be felt in increasingly maturing ways in an ideal development of a life. "On the Portrait of Two Beautiful Young People" (157) is a more intricate commentary on the prospects for youthful life in particular and how it can ideally be entwined with ultimate truth and good. The end of life is also a frequent allusion in Hopkins and is a reminder of the spiritual needs of every stage of life.

With all these examples of each of the categories of action instressing contemplation, I have not had in mind to enumerate some more or less complete classification of subkinds or types, either in general or in Hopkins' slim pouch of poems. I have only been concerned with whether there is a rich enough vein of illustration in the Hopkinsian ore to support the claim that there is a significant theme of this sort in his poetry. I believe the claim is justified. The examples are, in a way, random, reflecting what Hopkins happened to write, but I believe enough has been cited to vindicate the claim that the instress of action--action leading to contemplation--is a theme, among others, in Hopkins.

Nor have I attempted to give a particular theological interpretation: for example, to interpret the instressing experience in relation to a conception of God that is Thomist, Calvinist, Whiteheadian, or something else. I have taken it for granted that Hopkins' theology is broadly Thomist with Scotist variations, and that that would be the background for his thinking about the contemplative life. That is sufficient for an article that is probing poetry, not theology.

A question might arise as to whether Hopkins himself articulated the theme we are studying, or would have done so if interviewed. He did not do so in fact. But that is not a barrier, for poets often express themes of significance which they themselves have not recognized or elaborated explicitly. Does that mean that we can take any old theme and run it through a poet? Certainly not. One must be guided by the poems and by the author's known interests. The basis of interpretation must be in these. Thus you will look in vain in Hopkins' poetry for a policy about nuclear deterrence, or for a theory about infinite numbers, or for a definitive interpretation of the myth of Santa Claus. On the other hand, we do know that Hopkins was keenly interested in the concepts of inscape and instress, and we do know that the poems comment on human action as well as on nature, and we do know that contemplation is a vital part of his religious tradition. These data are adequate to authorize exploring a tie linking instress, action, and contemplation. That is what this article has done.

Works Cited

Bump, Jerome. *Gerard Manley Hopkins*. New York: Twayne, 1982.

The Cloud of Unknowing and Other Works. Trans. Clifton Wolters. London: Penguin, 1961.

New Catholic Encyclopedia. Vol. 4. Ed. David I. Eggenberger et al. New York: McGraw-Hill, 1967.

Two Views of "The Windhover"

Peter Milward, S.J.

I. The Falcon[1]

Almost inevitably the name of Hopkins is associated in our minds with three words invented by him and since his time incorporated in the *OED*: namely, sprung rhythm, instress and inscape. Above all, he may be called the "poet of inscape." But as poet of inscape, he is also a poet of landscape, seeing the one is included in the other, especially if we define "inscape" (for so it demands to be defined) as "the inner form of landscape." For Hopkins landscape is the point of departure, on the level of the senses, for his task of poetic exploration, as he strives to seize with his mind and to convey in fit words the inscape implicit in it.

---

[1] The first part of this essay, The Falcon, was originally given as a lecture at Cupples House, St. Louis University, 25 February 1982. The Falcon was originally published under the title, "Poet of Landscape and Inscape," in *Hopkins Research*, 11 (December, 1982): 1-12; and The Chevalier was published in the same publication under the title "O My Chevalier" (10 (December, 1981): 9-14). Since *Hopkins Research* circulates almost exclusively in Japan and is little known in the United States, the editors felt that the combined work, very slightly edited to suit these new circumstances, was essentially new to the American reader.

This may seem to accord with the scholastic axiom: "Nothing can be in the intellect, unless it was first in the senses." But there is a difference between the common or Thomist understanding of this axiom and that of Scotus, who is here followed by Hopkins. The Thomist movement is from what is individual and concrete in the senses to what is general and abstract in the intellect. Scotus, however, and Hopkins remain on the level of particularity even in the intellect, emphasizing the individuality, the uniqueness, the "thisness" of everything not only in the material but also in the spiritual order. The material world of appearance is for Hopkins merely the setting in which (as Newman says) heart speaks to heart through various forms of particularity.[2]

In this sense, it is even wrong for me to speak of "inscape" in such general terms, seeing it is nothing if not particular. I should rather speak of individual inscapes as they appear in individual landscapes; and that means the landscapes of England, with Wales and Scotland, which were collectively regarded by Hopkins as "wife to my creating thought" (*B* 227).

Here, however, a great problem arises as well for Americans: namely, how is it possible for them to appreciate the poetic inscapes of Hopkins, when they have never experienced the landscapes behind them? To this problem I would like to suggest a few solutions.

The best way might seem to be to go on a literary pilgrimage of England, Scotland and Wales, with special attention to the places about which he writes in his poems: St. Beuno's College and the Valley of the Elwy, Holywell and St. Winefride's shrine, Oxford and Binsey, Stonyhurst and the valley of the Ribble, and Inversnaid with Loch Lomond. Failing that, one can learn a lot about such places from books and films on

---

[2] See O'Connell for a compilation of Cardinal Newman's prayers.

England, particularly from a book entitled *Landscape and Inscape*. Yet a third way is open to those who may know nothing previously about England, and have no books at hand for consultation; and that is the way of analogy. After all, the landscapes of England aren't so completely different from those of America, but that many similarities remain to serve as pointers to the inscapes in the poet's mind.

This third way is, in fact, the very way proposed by the poet himself. For his aim in writing poetry isn't just to say "Look!" (as he does from time to time) but to convey the uniqueness of his experience so far as he can through the uniqueness of his language. For example, in speaking to a man who knows all about the flight of kestrels, it might be enough to say, "I saw a kestrel in flight this morning," in order to evoke the same experience. As St. Augustine says of the experience of divine love, "*Da mihi amantem, et sentit quid dico*"--Give me a lover, and he knows what I mean. But it is the aim of Hopkins to reproduce in his poems the uniqueness of his experience for the benefit even of those who have never shared it. His words themselves serve to convey the experience.

Let us now examine "The Windhover" (36) as a perfect example of what Hopkins means by inscape, as this is developed at some length in the octet of the poem: "I caught this morning morning's minion. . . ." In this first part of the poem everything, the way words are chosen as well for sound as for sense, the rhythm they form in combination, their grammatical and syntactical structure, not to mention their total meaning--everything unites to convey a precise impression, enabling the sensitive reader to feel what the poet felt and even to see what he saw. Not that this impression is necessarily formed the first time one reads the poem. One may well have to read it again and again, preferably aloud (as Hopkins himself advised his friend Bridges), till everything in the poem comes into bright focus for the reader as it first did for the poet. Then the reader can truly say for himself, as his main impression after reading the poem: "I caught this morning morning's minion. . . ."

But now I wish to go on and propose a theory of my own about the poem, though to many ears it may perhaps sound an abominable heresy. For I venture to doubt if in this poem Hopkins was really describing a particular experience of seeing a kestrel in flight one morning. I grant, he seems to be describing such an experience; but seeming, as we know from Shakespeare, isn't the same as being. For a poet or a dramatist like Hopkins or Shakespeare, it isn't necessary to be true to actual or historical fact; probability is quite enough. What the poet or dramatist says doesn't need to be true, so long as it seems to be true. Then, you may ask, isn't the poet telling a lie? No, I answer, he is still telling the truth; but the truth he tells belongs to a higher order than that of temporal or historical fact. It looks to the eternal order as perceived within the things of time by means of the heart and the creative imagination.

Anyhow, what I am going to propose about "The Windhover" isn't a mere opinion of my own; but it has a basis, like the poem itself, on observable and verifiable fact. This fact is no mere momentary observation of a bird in flight, about which we have no record in any of the poet's journals, but a particular stuffed bird which may still be seen, and photographed, at the Jesuit College of Stonyhurst in Lancashire. In Hopkins' time this very bird in its glass cage was to be seen not at Stonyhurst but at St. Beuno's College, where it was (and still is) identified as "The Kestrel or Windhover: The commonest and most conspicuous of British falcons remarkable for its habit of remaining suspended in the air without changing position while it scans the ground for its prey."

A photographic representation of this very bird (in colour) may be seen opposite page 48 of the above-mentioned *Landscape and Inscape*. (A reproduction of this very photograph has appeared on the cover of Graham Storey's recent *Preface to Hopkins*.) For all I know, this may well have been the first photographic representation of this bird. Yet not a few reviewers of the book, so far from expressing their gratitude to the author or his photographer, Father R.V. Schoder, only complained of the stuffed bird and stated their requirement of a kestrel in actual flight, as described in the poem. In my opinion, however--that is to say, my present opinion opposed to the common opinion which I also shared and stated in that book--it was very possibly (I can't say certainly) this stuffed bird that provided the poet with the landscape of his poem. It was very possibly from this seemingly static point in place and time that his poetic imagination took over and created a bird of dynamic beauty. Needless to say, the poet must have often observed the kestrel in flight and admired its performance. But now he may well have been merely looking at the bird in its glass cage, just as in another poem he looks at a caged skylark. There he contrasts the caged bird and "the remembering its free fells": here he may well be contemplating the stuffed bird and finding it as though coming to glorious life in his imaginative vision, "bestriding the air high there."

In particular, we may well imagine the poet passing in front of this glass case during his morning meditation. And there he may have paused, wrapped in meditative thoughts--no doubt, on the Kingdom of Christ, as presented in the *Spiritual Exercises* of St. Ignatius. Then, while thinking of himself in relation to Christ, as a knight to his Lord, he may easily have applied his thoughts to the stuffed bird in front of him; and so he may have been led to imagine the bird, now stuffed, once free and flying in the air. Further, to his thoughts and imaginations he may well have gone on to attach appropriate words and phrases in a precise poetical description, till finally a poem sprang into being. And so he might well say, with literary if not literal truth: "I caught this morning morning's minion. . . ."

In this connection, I would like to draw attention to an important element in Hopkins' idea of inscape, as it appears in this poem. It isn't just something objectively vivid in the bird in flight, as experienced or imagined by the poet in the octet of his poem, with all its magnificent "hurl and gliding." It is also included in the poet's self-identification with the bird, according to another scholastic axiom: "In the act of perceiving the perceiver somehow becomes the thing he perceives." Thus if in this poem the poet so admires the movement of the bird, especially after having conjured it up from the physical appearance of its stuffed form, this is because in it he recognizes something of himself, whether as he is or as he would like to be. In watching it, he feels himself as it were one with the bird, just as the Dauphin feels in *Henry V* when bestriding his horse: "I soar, I am a hawk!" (3.7.16) On the one hand, the stuffed bird represents only too accurately the present situation of the poet as a Jesuit student at St. Beuno's College, one among many students of theology engaged in the dull routine of daily classes and studies. On the other hand, while imagining the bird in flight and investing it with words from his poetic imagination, he thinks of what he would like to be, doing great things in the world for Christ the King, in accordance with his daily prayer, "Thy kingdom come!"

This is precisely why Hopkins isn't content with his poetic evocation of the bird in flight, though not a few of his readers wish he had stopped there, at the end of the octet. Rather, it is his idea of inscape that impels him to draw a conclusion that is at once personal and theological. For he isn't so much interested in the bird for its own sake, as in what Christ is saying to him through the bird. Here precisely is for him the heart of inscape, as he looks to the Heart of Christ present "deep down things" in the world of nature. It is this divine Heart that speaks to the heart of the poet and greets him with the rapturous love he describes so enthusiastically in "Hurrahing in Harvest" (38). He it is who (as we read in "The Wreck of the Deutschland" (28)) "is under the world's splendour and wonder," and who (as we also read in "Hurrahing in Harvest") supports all things with "his world-wielding shoulder." The poet, therefore, feels it incumbent on him to reveal this mystery in his poetry and to stress with his words the instress he discovers in things.

What is it, then, that Christ says to the heart of the poet in "The Windhover"? The answer to this question is to be found not so much in the octet, which is but a prelude or composition of place, as in the following sestet. And again, I must confess, the interpretation I am about to propose is an unusual one, though I am convinced it is the only correct one.

Hitherto the poet has been speaking of his imaginary, or real, experience in the first person: "I caught . . . my heart. . . ." But now in the sestet it is no longer the poet speaking, whether to Christ or to himself or even to the bird: it is Christ speaking to him in his vision of the bird. This is the real reason why his heart in hiding is stirred so deeply at "the achieve of, the mastery of the thing." Whose (we may ask) is the achievement, and whose the mastery, if not his whom he addresses in "The Wreck" as "martyr-master" and "master of the tides," the hero, Christ himself?

He it is, "*Ipse* the only one, Christ, King, head," who now points to the "brute beauty and valour and act" of the windhover, its "air, pride, plume," and bids them all "here buckle"--that is, here bow down in humble surrender--in the heart of the poet. He it is who reminds the poet that "the fire that breaks from thee then," in the sacrifice of himself, is "a billion times told lovelier, more dangerous." He it is who, as Lord and King in St.

Ignatius' meditation on the Kingdom, addresses the Jesuit poet as "O my chevalier"--appealing to him to make his offer all the more valuable by going against himself and his sensuality, and against all attachment to the things and values of this world. Christ himself is not the "chevalier," or knight: he is the King, speaking to his faithful knight as "chevalier," as St. Ignatius suggests.

This is, moreover, what leads the poet to put into the mouth of Christ two parallels or parables for the comfort of his knight. The self-sacrifice of his will in humble obedience renders him "a billion times told lovelier" in the eyes of God, just as 1) a ploughshare driven through a muddy furrow shines all the brighter, and 2) dull embers in a fireplace fall through the grating and disclose the gold of fire within them. What produces this unexpected gleam of light and fire isn't just the outward act of obedience but the inner love behind it, in response to the divine word of endearment, "Ah my dear!"

In other words, what Christ tells the poet in the sestet is not to remain on the mere level of romantic imagination, aroused in him at the sight of a stuffed bird and the memory it evokes, but to return to the seemingly dull reality of his religious life. There he may feel himself little more than a stuffed bird, with his desires for God's glory all stifled within him. But Christ encourages him to remember his real dignity and hidden glory as a Christian--a dignity and a glory that have to be achieved, as Christ himself achieved them, through patient suffering.

In the foregoing interpretation one may notice, I think, an interesting parallel with the Gospel story of the transfiguration of Christ on the holy mountain. The disciples on their way up may be compared to the poet as he meditates on the kingdom of Christ while looking at the stuffed bird. Then, their vision of Christ transfigured in glory may be compared to the poet's enthusiastic imagination of the bird in flight. Finally, when the cloud passes and they see "no one but Jesus," it is as when the poet returns to himself in the sestet and hears the words of Christ exhorting him to "buckle" and accept his humble life as a stuffed bird. What he has experienced in his meditation is neither a dream nor a deception but a kind of vision, making him aware of his "heart in hiding" and the reality of divine grace that has to be revealed in him through suffering.

For Hopkins, moreover, this isn't only a parallel but also a kind of mystical identification. In this perception or imagination of the bird in flight he is granted something of that very revelation which was granted the disciples of Christ at the transfiguration. For, as he declares in another sonnet,

> Christ plays in ten thousand places,
> Lovely in limbs, and lovely in eyes not his
> To the Father through the features of men's faces.
>
> (57)

Every such occasion is indeed unique in itself, as a precious inscape of Christ in the world of nature. Yet they all point backwards to Christ as he was in his earthly life, and upwards to Christ as he is in his heavenly life with the Father.

There is in all this an obvious conclusion for the reader. On the one hand, in the poem we find the poet (according to my present interpretation) meditating on a stuffed bird and imagining the windhover as it might actually be in flight. We also note how he sees Christ present in the bird and speaking to his heart. As he relates this in his poem, he relays the message of Christ to his readers, in much the same way as "the call of the tall nun" in the wreck of the Deutschland served as "a finger of a tender of . . . lovely-felicitous providence," so as to "startle the poor sheep back" to their good Shepherd. On the other hand, as we read this poem and grow in our understanding of it, we find ourselves in turn becoming identified with the poet, and through him with Christ, and through Christ with the heavenly Father. Thus all are united in one, while each preserves his unique identity and inscape, according to that mystery of "pied beauty" by which the infinite variety of creatures points to the infinite simplicity of the Creator. Thus, too, the reading of the poem is not merely a literary, but a deeply religious experience, revealing--as all the poems of Hopkins tend to reveal--the intrinsic connection between great literature and true religion.

II. The Chevalier

In the innumerable interpretations of "The Windhover" too much stress has, I fear, been placed on the precise meaning of "buckle." Yet, considering the characteristic tendency of the poet to include many meanings in one word, it seems unnecessary to limit this rich word to one meaning. Rather, so long as the suggested meaning fits in with the context, I would like to say, "The more, the merrier!"

Of greater importance than the meaning of this one word is, I submit, the meaning of the sonnet as a whole. From this point of view it seems to me that the central word is "chevalier" in line 11, involving as it does the identification of "here" and "thee," as well as "ah my dear." Here is the main line of the poet's meaning, at least in the sestet, in comparison with which "buckle" is of but secondary significance.

Seeing that the poem was subsequently dedicated by the poet "To Christ our Lord," many critics have assumed that it was also addressed to Christ. They see the bird as an analogue or symbol of Christ, as Son of the eternal Father, and they conclude that in the sestet the poet goes on to speak directly (in what is called colloquy) to the person symbolized. They note that the bird is described as "kingdom of daylight's dauphin" who rides on the air, and they conclude that the parallel word in the sestet, "chevalier," has reference to Christ.

Such (among many instances) is the recent interpretation of Michael Sprinker who explains the word as "an indication of Christ as soldier / knight, a commonplace in Jesuit spirituality instilled in Hopkins by his making the Spiritual Exercises" (10). This interpretation has, moreover, received the magisterial approval of Norman MacKenzie who understands the sonnet as "a poem to Christ," envisaged by the poet as "the great chevalier whose splendour is a billion times greater than from a created being." The only other interpretation he recognizes is the possible reference "to the windhover, not to the Christ of the title" (76-84).

There is, however, one other interpretation, not uncommon among Jesuit critics, which is (in my opinion, as a Jesuit) not only possible, as I have argued in the first part of this essay, but primary--though in accordance with my above mentioned principle I do not regard it as exclusive. This is the interpretation which identifies the "chevalier," in its primary reference, not with Christ, still less with the bird, but with the poet himself, as a continuation of "my heart in hiding." The reference to Christ may indeed be present, but only in an indirect, oblique sense. It is acceptable only so long as the primary reference is to the poet. As for the bird, I would suggest that he has already flown away, having fulfilled his function in the octet and left but a parting shadow on the opening of the sestet.

In this interpretation, however, what is the point of "To Christ our Lord"? Is it to be regarded as no more than a dedication? No, I would say it is more than just a dedication: it is also an indication of the primary source of the poem, which is entirely overlooked by Norman MacKenzie in his nine page commentary on this poem, though it is mentioned somewhat perfunctorily by Michael Sprinker. I mean the *Spiritual Exercises* of St.

Ignatius, and more precisely the central meditation on the Kingdom of Christ. In this meditation it is significant that Christ is referred to as "our Lord" no less than five times, and as "King" three times.

From this point of view, it may well be doubted if the windhover is meant as an analogue or symbol of Christ at all. It may even be interpreted, as Alison Sulloway does, with reference to "Satan and Lucifer, Isaiah's 'son of the morning'" (110). For the bird is presented not as king but merely as "kingdom of daylight's dauphin." It may perhaps be urged that Christ is Son of God and that, according to St. Paul, he will finally "hand over the kingdom to God the Father" (1 Cor. xv. 24). In the meantime, however, there is no doubt that both St. Ignatius and Hopkins see Christ not just as dauphin, or crown prince, but as eternal King, "*Ipse*, the only one, Christ, King, Head." At the same time, in his meditation on the Kingdom St. Ignatius encourages the exercitant (such as Hopkins) to see himself as "knight, or soldier" (*Spiritual Exercises* 110-15).

In the sestet of the poem Hopkins follows the general advice of St. Ignatius in making an application of the foregoing consideration of the bird in flight to his own situation. Here the point of his application is not, as one might naturally think, that he should do his best to emulate the bird in "the achieve of, the mastery of the thing." This is rather what he regards as a temptation of Lucifer, indicating the standard of Satan, not of Christ. No, he tells himself, as a follower of Christ and of St. Ignatius, he has to aim at something that may seem less impressive but is, in fact, far greater, "a billion times told lovelier, more dangerous." Such precisely is the application made by St. Ignatius, who is not content with the zealous offering of cooperation but goes on to propose another "of greater value and greater importance," involving self-denial and abnegation.

Here is the very point of "buckle," whatever its precise nuance of meaning may be. All the qualities which the poet admires in the "brute beauty and valour and act" of the bird must be subordinated and subdued to the praise, reverence and service of Christ our Lord. This is the task not of the bird, who is unaware of the need, nor of Christ, who is above the need and the object of the service, but of the poet, who is both aware of the need and the subject of the service. Thus it is that he addresses himself, or perhaps Christ his Lord addresses him, as "O my chevalier!" For he is the knight who must now go forth, as St. Ignatius tells him, and help to conquer all the world and all the enemies of Christ.

Here, too, is the point of the connection, otherwise difficult to explain, between "the fire that breaks from thee" and the "sheer plod" of the ploughman. As for "the fire," it is, of course, the spiritual fire of love, the generous ardour of the knights mentioned in the meditation "who will want to be more devoted and signalize themselves in all service of their eternal King and universal Lord" (111-12). On the other hand, the "sheer plod" refers to the material circumstances of the poet, as he pursues his theological studies and other occupations day in day out, without realizing their relevance to his future apostolate. In this he has to bear in mind the second of the "Rules for Scholastics": "Let them persuade themselves that they will do nothing more acceptable to God in the colleges than if they give themselves diligently to their studies with that intention which has been spoken of above" (*Constitutions* 183). He therefore reminds himself both that "sheer plod makes plough down sillion shine" and that "blue-bleak embers . . . fall, gall themselves, and gash gold-vermilion." This is what St. Ignatius means when he goes on to say, in the above-mentioned rule, that "the labour of study, when undertaken out of obedience and charity, is a work of great merit in the sight of the divine and supreme majesty" (183).

It is perhaps with this in mind that he takes the words of George Herbert, "Ah my dear," ("Love") and addresses them not (as Herbert does) to Christ but to himself. For the personal love of Christ for him, implied in these words, is the inner motive enabling him to accept the humdrum of daily routine.

Thus, I maintain, the interpretation of the "chevalier" as referring to the poet himself puts everything in the poem in satisfactory perspective. Nor is it only within the poem that this makes sense, but also with regard to the particular circumstances of the poet as a Jesuit scholastic engaged in the often (especially to him) frustrating study of theology at St. Beuno's College.

At the same time, as I have said, I am quite prepared to admit, once this primary reference is accepted, that there may well be a secondary reference to Christ as King. For whatever hardships and sufferings He expects of His followers, He has already himself endured in even greater measure. His appeal is, indeed, phrased by St. Ignatius in this sense: that "whoever would like to come with me is to labour with me, that following me in the pain, he may also follow me in the glory" (*Spiritual Exercises* 111). Christ, too, has endured the "sheer plod" of His daily life as a carpenter at Nazareth; and in the Passion He has experienced the "blue-bleak embers" of life falling and galling themselves, only to "gash gold-vermilion" in the Resurrection. It is precisely to such a life of faith and hope that He calls his dear knight, or "chevalier," Gerard Manley Hopkins.

As for the proposed application to the bird, that is (I submit) rather ridiculous--save in so far as he is identified with the heart of the poet, in the act of buckling.

Works Cited

Herbert, George. *Poems*. London: Oxford UP, 1907.

Loyola, Ignatius. *The Constitutions of the Society of Jesus*. George E. Ganss, Trans. St. Louis: Institute of Jesuit Sources, 1970.

---. *Manresa or The Spiritual Exercises of St. Ignatius*. London: Westminster Press, 1924.

MacKenzie, Norman. *Reader's Guide to Gerard Manley Hopkins*. Ithaca: Cornell UP, 1981.

Milward, Peter, and Raymond Schoder. *Landscape and Inscape*. Grand Rapids: Eerdmans, 1975.

O'Connell, Daniel M., S.J., Comp. *Heart to Heart: A Cardinal Newman Prayerbook*. New York: America Press, 1938.

Sprinker, Michael. *A Counterpoint of Dissonance: The Aesthetics and Poetry of Gerard Manley Hopkins*. Baltimore: Johns Hopkins UP, 1980.

Storey, Graham. *Preface to Hopkins*. Preface Books. London: Longmans, 1981.

Sulloway, Alison. *Gerard Manley Hopkins and the Victorian Temper*. New York: Columbia UP, 1972.

All on Two Spools

Aesthetics, Morals, and Janus-Words

in Hopkins

R.K.R. Thornton

When the International Hopkins Association held its conference in Dublin, I gave a paper on "Dublin in the 1880s"[1] in which I glanced at some of the ways in which Hopkins struggled to find how to unify the surface of his existence with his sense of the significances "deep down things." His daily life and activities and his delight in the look of things (he was very fond of weighting the meaning of the word "thing") often seemed to be at odds with his higher aspirations. I wish to expand on some of the hints I gave there, and to suggest how Hopkins uses the movement between the two different interpretations of what he saw, the secular and the sacred, the aesthetic and the moral.

Hopkins' sense of the divergence between beauty and the better beauty of moral excellence was established early. His undergraduate essay

---

[1] To be published by IHA in 1988. I have been helped in developing this paper by discussions with Kaye Kossick, some of whose ideas have been incorporated into the text. Thanks.

48 G. M. Hopkins: New Essays

for Walter Pater on "The Origin of Our Moral Ideas" (*J* 80 ff.) dates from about 1865 and makes a comparison between beauty as a relationship "of the parts of a sensuous thing to each other" whether in space or time, and morality which may lie in the "relation between acts"; but he goes on to say that the "analogy may be followed to a point of divergence." It is this point of divergence which is most suggestive, and his conclusion is a central statement for understanding his lifelong attitude. I shall quote it at some length:

> All thought is of course in a sense an effort [towards] unity. . . . In art it is essential to recognise and strive to realise on a more or less wide basis this unity in some shape or other. It seems also that the desire for unity, for an ideal, is the only definition which will satisfy the historical phenomena of morality. There is an important difference to be noted here. In art we strive to realise not only unity, permanence of law, likeness, but also, with it, difference, variety, contrast: it is rhyme we like, not echo, and not unison but harmony. But in morality the highest consistency is the highest excellence. The reason of this seems to be that the desire of unity is prior to that of difference and whereas in art both are in our power, in moral action our utmost efforts never result in its perfect realisation, in perfect consistency. But why do we desire unity? The first answer would be that the ideal, the one, is our only means of recognising successfully our being to ourselves; it unifies us, while vice destroys the sense of being by dissipating thought. ἔστι γὰρ ἡ κακία φθαρτικὴ ἀρχῆς,[2] wickedness breaks up unity of principle. (*J* 83)

---

[2] From Aristotle's *Nichomachean Ethics* vi.v.6.

Many of Hopkins' favourite topics find expression here: his sense of the relationship, sometimes the identity, of disunity and vice; his sense of an ideal one as essential to a recognition of ourselves; his placing of morality on a higher plane than art. His making of the desire for unity prior to a desire for difference also helps to underpin his attitude to children, uncorrupted by a sense of difference or breaking up of unity of principle (earlier in the essay he had written that "when the innocent eye of the uneducated or of children is spoken of in art it is understood that their sense is correct, that is that they are free from fallacies implying some education").

In Hopkins' search for some way of facing the attractions of both art and morality, he discovered what I call his Janus-words which themselves unify disparate ideas. I wish to focus on some of the ways in which he moved between rhyme and echo, the aesthetic desire for difference in unity and the moral desire for unity in difference, in order to arrive at these crucial centres.

First, of course, there is the direct statement of an ultimate unity. In "Pied Beauty" (37) the pleasure in all the variety is taken back directly to the one "whose beauty is past change," a simple statement equivalent to the sense of delight in the Journal of 1874, in an entry significantly following a comment about the innocence of children: "As we drove home the stars came out thick: I leant back to look at them and my heart opening more than usual praised our Lord to and in whom all that beauty comes home" (*J* 254). In the "Wreck" (28) the stability of God is both directly stated and established in the metaphorical boundaries of motion. The "sides," the "wharf," the "wall," the "ground," the "granite," all encompass the motion and variety; and the search for final solidity goes through the prepositions ("past," "behind") to the verbs ("outrides") to the comparative "lower" and the superlative "uttermost" to conclude in the "Father compassionate," just as at the height of her ecstasy the nun perceives "the only one, Christ," and just as the poem ends by penetrating through possessives to the final "Lord."

More important, and artistically more effective as having less palpable design on us, is the making the unity something toward which the language itself is working. Here all of Hopkins' characteristic word-patternings come in. We are all familiar with the way he will unify opposites in alliteration: "flint-flake," "swift-slow," and so on. In "Hurrahing in Harvest" (38), "silk-sack" reconciles the fine and rough of texture and cost, while "moulded ever and melted" brings together the making and unmaking of the clouds; the contradictory elements are united on a plane of sound which suggests their fundamental unity. This is why Hopkins was so interested in the "onomatopoetic theory" of language; it allowed the implication of a divine order. As James Milroy notes in his *The Language of Gerard Manley Hopkins*, Hopkins was much influenced by Max Müller, who considered language as a physical science which thus "deals with the works of God" (52).

Rhyme too can have the effect of reinforcing identity: "the goal was a shoal," "bell rung finds tongue" and so on. Curiously in this connection, over-repetition without variation becomes a negative rather than a positive quality: "Generations have trod, have trod, have trod, / And all is seared with trade, bleared, smeared with toil," though even here the modulation from "trod" to "trade" infers secret workings. This latter type of modulation is typically used to transform one word into another, suggesting their fundamental connection, rather as Lewis Carroll would invent the puzzle of "Doublets" for *Vanity Fair* in 1879 to transform one word into another in the least possible moves. The mysterious links in Carroll's game are emphasised by some of the choices of doublets: "Change CAIN into ABEL,"

"Change BLACK to WHITE," "Evolve MAN from APE," or "Save LAMB from LION"; and even some of the links are suggestive of Hopkins' poems (this last one, for example, goes LION, limn, limb, LAMB) (Fisher 130-39).[3] Hopkins means more than entertainment by his modulations. In lines "On St. Winefred" (139), the line "Sweet soul! Not scorning honest sweat" redeems Hopkins' favourite and rather over-used "sweet" by making the sound-association of beauty and labour. "Spelt from Sibyl's Leaves" (61) is the culmination of this manipulation, being a whole orchestra of modulations sliding down a scale from aesthetic variety to moral singularity, in language as well as subject.

Linkages of this sort have been noticed before and I need not dwell on them. Here I wish to elaborate on two sets of linkages which have not been pointed out and to suggest a motive behind them. The first is a complex set of linkages which goes beyond the individual line and even beyond the individual poem in its effect, and is first seen in one of those linguistic notes which Milroy wonders why writers on Hopkins have made so little use of (45). The entry I am thinking of is this one, dating from 1863:

> *Grind, gride, gird, grit, groat, grate, greet,* κρούειν, *crush, crash,* κροτεῖν, etc.
>
> Original meaning to *strike, rub,* particularly *together.* That which is produced by such means is the *grit,* the *groats* or crumbs,

---

[3] Much is to be written about the similarities of Hopkins and Carroll, two celibate religious men writing in Oxford in the mid-century, fascinated by language, mathematics, the innocence of children, manipulation of words (including Carrollian rhymes like "inexpressi-(Ble), confess he, Jessie"), and united in their hatred of Gladstone. Of course, Hopkins told his mother in January 1885 that *Alice in Wonderland* was "a book I never admired, indeed never read much of; I hold it is not funny" (*F* 167); but he does name it "of course" as the first book to recommend to a "young countess of fifteen or eighteen." It is not influence which is important here but their similar responses to their context.

> like *fragmentum* from *frangere*, *bit* from *bite*. *Crumb, crumble* perhaps akin. To *greet*, to strike the hands together (?). *Greet*, grief, wearing, *tribulation*. *Grief* possibly connected. *Gruff*, with a sound as of two things rubbing together. I believe these words to be onomatopoetic. *Gr* common to them all representing a particular sound. In fact I think the onomatopoetic theory has not had a fair chance. Cf. *Crack, creak, croak, crake, graculus, crackle*. (*J* 5)

This entry is an alternative grouping for the derivation of *granum* and *grain* which Hopkins had earlier associated with *horn* (and through that *crown* and *grow*), and the diary goes on with the next entry to consider words associated with *crook*. After the parodic story of the Scout, Hopkins goes back to consider "*Grando*. meaning splinters, fragments, little pieces detached in grinding, hence applied to hail" and then on to *Grunt*. In other words, Hopkins is well aware of this alliterative pattern of associated words at least from 1863 and pursues the ramifications in many directions.

What I want to argue is a little outrageous. I want to suggest that Hopkins maintained his fascination with this group of words, and built on it until it became a complex associated with the whole of his Christian understanding. I want to assert that the *cr/gr* words provide an undercurrent of Christian coherence through all of Hopkins' poetry; that they occur with a frequency which cannot be random in contexts where Hopkins' interpretation of life is being celebrated or questioned; and that each one of these words is resonant with the whole complex and thus recalls its connections with the associated group. Let me try to indicate their pervasiveness: *Chr*ist is of course at the centre and is associated with a God who is "past all / *Gr*asp God" and is the "*gr*ound of being and *gr*anite of it" ("Wreck" st. 32). It is "God's *Gr*andeur" (31) which "gathers to a *gr*eatness," and if we recognise the function of mortal beauty we recognise "God's better beauty, grace." The greatness is not always apparent and often needs to be brought out "like the ooze of oil / Crushed"; just as in the case of the suffering passengers in the Deutschland ("crushed them"), or Margaret Clitheroe (145) who was "crushed out flat," ("Just like Jesus crucified"). Curiously the one word missing from the eighth stanza of the "Wreck"--lash, plush, gush, flush, flash--is the word "crush," which is what the bursting of the sloe is all about. Christ's story is begun with the "warm-laid grave of a womb-life grey" and climaxes in Christ crucified or sacrificed. The central image is, of course, the cross which the nun in the "Wreck" calls to her in stanza 24 as she "christens her wild-worst Best" (which might be thought to mean that she "cried for the crown"). Mankind, God's creature, can be identified with Christ by being "so grafted on his wood" ("Barnfloor and Winepress"), and can see the atoning blood running "in crimsonings down the cross-wood" ("*Rosa Mystica*" 27). The sufferings involved in the stress of God's message are similarly connected. Those patiently waiting for a sign "hear our hearts grate on themselves" ("Patience" 68), or worse "thoughts against thoughts in groans grind." In the storm where the Euridyce ("Euridyce" 41) is lost "Hailropes. . . grind their / Heavengravel." The result of confrontation of this stress is grief or grieving, but the sense of loss and sin and the crushing and grinding of experience are balanced by the sense of purpose in the understanding that tempest might "carry the grain for thee" ("Wreck" st. 31), and that it will make "my grain lie, sheer and clear" ("Carrion Comfort" 64). Grapes too are crushed and in "New Readings" (7), "Grapes grew" on the thorns on Christ's head and he shed "grains" on them. Recognition of this benevolent aspect of stress causes the poet to "greet him the days I meet him" ("Wreck" st. 5). sometimes with "Rapturous love's greeting" as in "Hurrahing in Harvest;" the recognition may also involve conversion "as once at a crash Paul" ("Wreck" st. 10), or the human may become the Christ-like "at a trumpet-*cr*ash" as in "That Nature is a Heraclitean Fire" (72). The positives of the world which Hopkins sees frustrated can be associated with this pattern: the "*gr*owing *gr*een" of "Binsey Poplars" (43) or the "*cr*eating thought" of "To seem the stranger" (66). A neat summary of some of the stages in the story are to be found in the second version of "Ashboughs" (149) with its upward movement:

> But more cheer is when May
> Mells blue with snowwhite through their fringe and fray
> Of *gr*eenery and old earth *gr*opes for, *gr*asps at steep
> Heaven with it whom she childs things by.

This upward movement is almost a towering "from the *gr*ace to the *gr*ace" ("Wreck" st. 3), and *gr*ace is the Christ-like quality of man. All of these associations, of which I have followed the expression through the poetry, reach out also through the prose. In particular the writings on grace are relevant. The sermon for October 5, 1879, at Bedford Leigh, talks of "giving a special meaning to the words of the Hail Mary, as *Full of grace*" and considers Mary as a medium for God's graces (*S* 29-30). Or take Hopkins' spiritual writing, "On Personality, Grace and Free Will" where he writes of God moving the creature into a possible world of consent:

> It is into that possible world that God for the moment moves his creature out of this one or it is from that possible world that he brings his creature into this, shewing it to itself gracious and consenting; nay more, clothing its old self for the moment with a gracious and consenting self. This shift is grace. For grace is any action, activity on God's part by which, in creating or after creating, he carries the creature to or towards the end of its being, which is its selfsacrifice to God and its salvation. (*S* 154)

In both of these prose extracts I am interested not only in the grouping of sound and idea, but also in the Godlike activity of reading the secret meaning, which will be relevant later.

Since I am likely to be already suspected of making a mystery out of a simple alliterative curiosity, I may as well add that of the few people that Hopkins mentions in his poetry, G*r*egory (62) is one who understands the use of mortal beauty and thus presumably wishes for grace; the name of St. Winefred's attacker is varied from Caradoc to C*r*adock, and the girl who is "g*r*ieving / Over Goldeng*r*ove" is called Ma*r*ga*r*et.

My point can be made in a strong form or a weak form. The strong form would assert that Hopkins chose a consonant group to signal the mysterious connectedness of all aspects of the Christian story so that, even where the immediate appearance was painful, the sound would carry the hint of redemptive possibilities. The weak form (and the more likely one I must admit) would say that Hopkins, having become used to a group of associated words, tended to find them ready to his mind and pen when he considered the mysteries of the world, the relation of suffering to redemption, and the whole Christian story. Although the words seem various and even contradictory (just as in the Virgin Mary "met things that are thought to be and even are opposite and incompatible" (*S* 57)), they tend toward the one root and express the variety of art moving toward the consistency of morality.

Hopkins used other methods to unite words and ideas which work in a way quite opposite to those I have been describing. In "Thou art indeed just, Lord" (74) the syntactic balance of "Wert thou my enemy, O thou my friend" emphasised the puzzling identity of supposedly opposite concepts. In the same way in "To seem the stranger," "dear" seems to be the equivalent of "stranger," while the baffling appearance is that "dear" and "not near" are both rhyme and contradiction, and "peace" the equivalent of "parting." In "Patience, hard thing" the division has been collapsed into the word itself, and the irony of the poem lies in the definition of what it means to be patient, namely, to fight and be wounded. The same ironical opposition lies at the root of "In honour of St. Alphonsus Rodriguez" (73) whose eventless life was crowded with conquest. Seeming and being, appearance and reality, word and meaning, obviously do not correspond.

I have been writing of oppositions united by sound, but there are also unities of sound divided by meaning; and it is here that we come to Hopkins' Janus-words, words which face more than one direction and unite in one sound a dual or perhaps multiple relevance. Words of this type can be crucial in understanding a poet. John Clare, whose poem "I am" Hopkins copied into an early diary, used the word "poesy" to mean both a small bunch of flowers (what we would spell "posy") and poetry, indicating by the identity the inseparability for him of nature and his art. Hopkins uses "dear" in this way on some occasions, signifying both "well-loved" and "costing much expense or effort." So of our hearts in "Patience, hard thing," "it kills / To bruise them dearer." Our hearts are killed by further bruising in the patient war, but it also makes them more precious although it may cost much effort. In "The Leaden Echo and the Golden Echo" (59) the transient part of us is "dearly and dangerously sweet," attractive and yet costly. Colloquial interjections are also treated in this way. In "My own heart" (69) the line "At God knows when to God knows what" allows the usually casual phrase "God knows" to move from dismissive ignorance to positive assertion. Similarly "my God" in "Carrion Comfort" moves from an expression of surprise to a recognition of the real cause of that surprise. Perhaps Hopkins had practised this in the last line of "Let me be to Thee as the circling bird" (19): "Love, O my God, to call thee Love and Love." And there is still a flavor of ambiguity in the second stanza of the "Wreck": "Thou heardst me truer than tongue confess / Thy terror, O Christ, O God;"

and perhaps also in "In the Valley of the Elwy" (34): "I remember a house where all were good / To me, God knows, deserving no such thing." Appropriately in "In Honour of St. Alphonsus Rodriguez" (appropriate since the appearance is contradicted by the interior truth) the word "hew" means both to cut and to create, suggesting as Hopkins explained to Bridges, both increment and decrement (*B* 297).

In some of these cases (like "my God, my God"), the emphasis on the deeper meaning is made by a repetition of the word with an enhanced meaning. So in "That Nature is a Heraclitean Fire" the mess of various elements is purified into the final "immortal diamond." Slight modulation has a similar effect in "Boughs being pruned" (96. vii), where "who pare, repair" suggests the mysterious identity of the two actions and reminds us that Herbert's example is important (especially in poems like "Paradise" (Herbert 24)).

Some words can be more problematic. "Bent," for example, seems to mean both "perverted" and "bent in prayer or tending toward God" in "God's Grandeur" where "the Holy Ghost over the bent / World broods," while in "Harry Ploughman" (71) there is a simple positive litheness in "Harry bends," and no sense of perversion in "we do bid God bend to him" in "Patience, hard thing." Perhaps less usefully "fast" is variously associated with stability and its opposite: "first, fast, last friend" as opposed to "everything that's fresh and fast flying of us." "Strange" also has elements of positive individuality ("all things counter, original, spare, strange"), and negative alienation ("To seem the stranger") which coalesce in "On the Portrait of Two Beautiful Young People" (157) where the essential identity of the individual is described as "The selfless self of self, most strange, most still."

There are occasions where the identity is an identity of sound rather than spelling, where it is a homophone rather than the same word; Hopkins did, after all, often indicate that he wished to be read by the ear. The Victorian love of the pun was strong in him (as in Lewis Carroll) and it is no surprise to find play on the word "not/knot." This is most powerful in "Carrion Comfort" where the collocation "Not untwist" sounds like a complete antithesis, and the six "nots" in the first four lines of the poem ring like an argument diametrically opposed to the untwisting of the strands, until the schoolboy point that two negatives make a positive settles Hopkins' and Hamlet's question--"not choose not to be." Again, Hopkins had practised this many years before in "It was a hard thing to undo this knot" (91).

A more intriguing dilemma is posed by the word "buckle" in the tenth line of "The Windhover" (36). There is a continuing disagreement as to the meaning; whether it means "secure together" or "collapse and fall apart," apparently incompatible opposites. The first meaning seems to be reinforced by the apparent wish to find what makes up the total of the kestrel's inscape, and by the conjunctions which climax in the capital AND; while the second meaning seems to be reinforced by the images of breaking, ploughing and gashing in the final lines. If the parallels offered in the last three lines are to explain the non-wondrousness of the event, they presumably do so by saying that, as breaking the earth causes the plough to shine and breaking the embers causes them to glow, so the breaking of the thing causes Christ's dangerous fire to be revealed. He can then report that he "caught," implying "caught fire." James Milroy, to take one example, prefers the "collapse, bend under stress" interpretation (234), while MacKenzie (81-84) and Catherine Phillips (352) prefer the "come together" interpretation. I shall defer my opinion for the moment.

My last example of a Janus-word is the most interesting, especially since it comes in that most astounding of poems "Spelt from Sibyl's Leaves." It is the word "stained':

> Let life, waned, ah let life wind
> Off her once skeined stained veined variety upon, all on two spools.

It is obvious from all Hopkins' early poems and notebooks that the colours of the world had been attractive in their diversity and their changeability. "Pied Beauty" had delighted in the "freckled" world, and the various colours staining the world were a source of delight. But Hopkins was anxious about colour. In telling Baillie of his abandonment of a wish to be a painter, Hopkins is probably referring primarily to colour: "You know I once wanted to be a painter. But even if I could I wd. not I think, now, for the fact is that the higher and more attractive parts of the art put a strain upon the passions which I shd. think it unsafe to encounter" (*F* 231). "Stain" was to become a word which moved away from colourfulness to moral condemnation. Just before he sent Bridges a copy of "Spelt from Sibyl's Leaves" in December 1886, he had sent in October his translation of Bridges' lines:

> She hath the intelligence of heavenly things
> Unsullied by man's mortal overthrow.

This problem of sullying by mortal overthrow is a central issue of "Spelt from Sibyl's Leaves" and the movement from positive view of "stain" to negative is an encapsulation of the movement of the poem from the variety of day ("her dapple is at end") to the monochrome black on black of the ultimate choice.

I wish to argue that the movement between meanings, the ambiguity of interpretation, is a part of the poetry, another example of Hopkins' love of counterpoint but this time a counterpoint of interpretation. I mean that "stained" functions as a moving meaning, and that "buckle" shifts as we read, and I would like to make three points in support of this.

First, it appears that Hopkins himself moved from a position of certainty to one of doubt looking for certainty. The movement is clearest in his descriptions of perception and images of the eye (with all its implications for the "I"). In "The earth and heaven" of 1866, Hopkins had written of his own stability:

> The unchanging register of change
> My all-accepting fixed eye,
> While all things else may stir and range,
> All else may whirl or dive or fly.
> (130)

This he sets against the impermanent world where the clouds are seen as "skeins" that are gone when "you look again." So in "The Alchemist in the City" (15) again, "The whole world passes; I stand by." He seems to lose this sense of stability in himself and to transfer it to God and Christ, and then to seek stability in God's eye. As he had noted in 1865, "The ideal, the one, is our only means of recognising successfully our being to ourselves" (J 83) The just man "Acts in God's eye," and while Hopkins' eye is associated with movement ("wind / What most I may eye after") (40), Christ "eyes them" and thus establishes their identity. Hopkins gets nearest to his old stability in perceiving the correctness of the nun's perception--"There was single eye" ("Wreck" st. 29)--and in the clearness of St. Winefred's perceptions. Although the speaker is Caradoc, Winefred's beheader, he can see the beauty of her eyes:

> In all her body, I say, no place was like her eyes,
> No piece matched those eyes kept most part cast down
> But being lifted, immortal, of immortal brightness.
> (152.II.25-27)

The variety that had been a source of delight to the secure eye of the youthful observer had become a source of moral anxiety to the mature poet who was looking for the single ideal through which he could recognise his own being to himself.

Second, Hopkins is himself fascinated by the idea of incorrect and correct interpretation. Interpretation is part of his business as a maker of sermons, but it is also an essential part of his poetry. The process of argument in the "Wreck" in both parts is to present an event and offer two incorrect interpretations or answers before settling on the right one. Stanza 6 tells us it was "Not out of his bliss . . . Nor first from heaven" that the stress comes, before stanza 7 gives the true source: "It dates from day / Of his going in Galilee"; stanza 25 offers two alternative answers to the question, "What did she mean?" both of which are denied by stanza 27 ("It was not these"), before stanza 28 gropes for and grasps the single truth. And amid the many repetitions of the "Wreck" one must remember that *Deutschland* is "double a desperate name" and *Mary* a "double-natured name." The same movement of two reasons denied before a final one is offered can be seen in "O Deus, ego amo te":

>Then I, why should not I love thee,
>Jesu so much in love with me?
>Not for heaven's sake; not to be
>Out of hell by loving thee;
>Not for any gains I see;
>But just the way that thou didst me
>I do love and I will love thee.
>   (170)

"Easter Communion" is specifically about interpretation, explaining how the criss-cross marks of the whips may be read:

> Those crooked rough-scored chequers may be pieced
> To crosses meant for Jesu's.
>
> (11)

(The *cr*ookedness may be re-read as the *cr*oss!) "Nondum" (23) describes the soul casting "its searching sight / On being's dread and vacant maze," which cannot be understood until man is given "that sense beyond." In "Let me be to Thee as the circling bird" the poet finds his "music in a common word" and learns to interpret the meaning of "Love. "In "The Leaden Echo and the Golden Echo" the same sound is read either as "despair" or as "Spare," revealing the need to have a receiving eye and ear and mind as well as the thing to be interpreted. Even the echo, which had been Hopkins' image of the identity of things, is subject to variety of interpretation.

The climax of many of Hopkins' poems is this moment of interpretation, often signalled with the ejaculation of "oh" or "ah," and Hopkins obviously considered this process of recognition as twofold. As Wordsworth had written in "Tintern Abbey" of "All the mighty world / Of eye, and ear,--both what they half create, / And what perceive," so Hopkins was to write in "Floris in Italy":

> Say beauty lies but in the meet of lines,
> In careful-spaced sequences of sound.
> These rather are the arc where beauty shines,
> The temper'd soil where only her flower is found.
> Allow at least it has one term and part
> Beyond, and one within the looker's eye.
>
> (102)

He makes the same point in another little poem, suggesting the subjective quality of experience:

> It was a hard thing to undo this knot.
> The rainbow shines, but only in the thought
> Of him that looks. Yet not in that alone,
> For who makes rainbows by invention?
> And many standing round a waterfall
> See one bow each, yet not the same to all,
> But each a hand's breadth further than the next.
> The sun on falling waters writes the text
> Which yet is in the eye or in the thought.
> It was a hard thing to undo this knot.
>
> (91)

What goes for the observer and the rainbow applies also to the reader and the text: the meaning may not be the same to each one but the text is not an invention of the reader. The reader's experience is to struggle with possible interpretations of the text, to be conscious that "buckle" means diversely, that "stained" is part of the world's fleeting beauty *and* of its sinful nature.

Hopkins is well on his way to a "Reader response criticism," and my third point can most simply be summarised be referring to a reader response critic, Stanley Fish, whose article, "Interpreting the *Variorum*," deals with some similar ground. Fish is arguing about the controversy of meaning in Milton's sonnets (curiously the first problem he discusses centres on the meaning of the word "spare"), and he suggests that the problem is not the meaning of the word but rather the meaning of our inability to agree about its meaning. "The lines first generate a pressure for judgment," says Fish, "and then decline to deliver it; the pressure, however, still exists, and is transferred from the words on the page to the reader . . . who comes away from the poem not with a statement, but with a responsibility . . . of deciding." Fish then goes on to discuss the processes of interpretation and revision of interpretation that go on through the reading of a poem, and the way in which these revisions function as part of the meaning of a poem even though they may be rejected.[4]

This is what I am suggesting is at work in Hopkins. Conscious of the necessity of both the sign and the reader of the sign, he presents signs of whose ambiguity he is aware and whose interpretation is crucial to his ideas. In his early poetry, he had often failed to resist the temptation to interpret, to make specific and unambiguous the meaning he wished his audience to derive from his poems. Rhetorical questions often give these moments away: "What is all this juice and all this joy?"; "What did she mean?"; "Buy then! bid then!--What?". The answers are too pat and pre-planned. In his later work the reader must come to the poem as Hopkins himself came to experience, prepared to contribute to the way in which the poem means. The most striking example of the relationship between interpreter and sign is in "Hurrahing in Harvest," where wisely Hopkins avoids answering his own questions. The disunities within unity which I have already mentioned in this poem climax at the point when the interpretation occurs:

> These things, these things were here and but the beholder
> Wanting; which two when they once meet
> The heart rears wings bold and bolder
> And hurls for him, O half hurls earth for him off under his feet.

Interpretation is not forced on the reader however. One must encounter the poems with a sense of their need for the reader to contribute to the process. Thus one must confront the word "buckle" with an awareness that it does face in two directions. One must confront the word "stained" with

---

[4] Reprinted from *Critical Inquiry* in Rylance (155-71).

a sense of its contradictory possibilities. The puzzle, the pressure, the delight, are the reader's.

If we as readers follow the aesthetic line only, the difference, variety, and contrast will be delightful. If we insist on the single moral interpretation, that will help perhaps in "recognising successfully our being to ourselves." "Wickedness," as Hopkins found Aristotle saying, "breaks up unity of principle" (*J* 83) and in "Spelt from Sibyl's Leaves" he portrays the strain of recognising the move from variety to singularity. In finding a tongue in which to spell out things past telling of tongue, Hopkins uses words whose meanings no longer remain static and single things. Meaning comes packed on two spools, and the pressure to decide is left with the reader. Thoughts may well grind against themselves, but the meaning? "O which one? is it each one?"

Works Cited

Fisher, John, ed. *The Magic of Lewis Carroll*. London: Nelson, 1973.

MacKenzie, Norman H. *A Readers' Guide to Gerard Manley Hopkins*. Ithaca: Cornell UP, 1981.

Milroy, James. *The Language of Gerard Manley Hopkins*. The Language Library. London: Andre Deutsch, 1977.

Phillips, Catherine, ed. *Gerard Manley Hopkins*. The Oxford Authors. Oxford: Oxford UP, 1986.

Rylance, Rick, ed. *Debating Texts*. Toronto: University of Toronto Press, 1987.

Herbert, George. *Poems*. Ed. Arthur Waugh. Oxford Edition. 1907. New York: AMS Press, Inc., 1976.

Homiletic and Poetic Vocabulary in Hopkins

Todd K. Bender

One of the most recurrent critical observations concerning the poetry of Hopkins is that his language demonstrates a creative, generative force which renews and makes fresh again dull and commonplace expressions. His poems are like the grand scheme of nature in which there is a deep down freshness to be found in the midst of toil and mire, if we have but the eyes to see the diamond delves, elves eyes, and sparkling citadels of stars hidden in our darkling world. Many of the ways Hopkins makes language sparkle and flash can be described and catalogued. He forces the reader to become aware of etymological resonances. For example, when the speaker of his sonnet 67 awakes and feels "the fell of dark, not day," he evokes an ominous animal clothed in a tactile skin, hide, pelt, or *fell* which intrudes from the shadowy linguistic past of Old High German *fel* and Latin *pellis*. So the speaker stretches forth his hand to feel the skin of an ancient beast there in the dark. But such precision disarms. If we know that it is a beast's skin, our certainty reassures us. It may be that the texture of the night is like a hide or it may be like a cliff, "a standing fell," as the poet says in poem 112, meaning a mountainous cliff. Combined in feeling, the fell of dark is the implied comparison of both touching a rude beast and standing on the edge of a vertiginous drop in the dark. The poet exploits not only the resonant etymology, but also the homographic ambiguity, making the metaphor contain two vehicles, both effective, in one word.

Fell is the past tense of *fall*, and in the terror of the speaker's situation there echoes the dreadful *fall* of man from Eden, which *befell*, or happened, at the beginning of man's mortal state which has *fallen* on us all as an inheritance. Eve's fall, vulgar Latin *fallitus*, her falling, has become our universal *fault*, which can be projected metaphorically as the touch of a terrible beast's skin or a vertiginous cliff yawning before us, but only *felt* on rare occasions, in the dark of night, alone. At such times, the *felon*, the villainous evildoer, feels the *fell* situation, the fierce, cruel, deadly, condition into which he has fallen. In such a case, the word *fell* must be forced out of its expected grammatical role as a noun and construed as another part of speech, an adjective used substantively, parallel to Hopkins' usage in poem 41, where the loss of the ship Eurydice is described as a "fell capsize" (st. 10). All fallen men are in such a fell strait. In each material loss, in every destruction, in each death, we can see the blight of the original fall reflected, whether the Binsey poplars "All felled, felled, are all felled" as lamented in poem 43, or the passengers on the Deutschland perishing in the storm, dropping from the rigging, exhausted as they "fell to the deck / (Crushed them) or water (and drowned them) or rolled / With a sea-romp over the wreck" (28, st. 17). To cut down, fell, quell, or kill reflects the death and destruction brought into the creation by man's first fell disobedience, so the material world must "fall to the residuary worm; world's wildfire, leave but ash" in poem 72. But embedded in the fall is the spark of hope, the counter movement springing upward in resurrection when ashes "fall, gall themselves, and gash gold-vermillion" in poem 36. The fall, or autumnal decay, is answered by the spring tide of Easter, a *felicity* counterpoised against man's *fell* situation, as the "Spring and Fall" in poem 55 of that name opposes youth versus old age, innocence versus experience, death versus resurrection, the Fall of man and the felicity of redemption.

The process described in the paragraphs above, as the reader encounters the text of Hopkins' poems, is the creation of linguistic "turbulence" through etymological resonance, homographic ambiguity, grammatical deviation, multivalent metaphor, reference to specialized symbolic systems, and multilingual puns. It creates a condition of "defamiliarization," forcing the reader to look more closely than usual at the reference of the words written and the "texture" of the language. A simple garden tool, perhaps a common shovel, might become "defamiliarized" if taken from its work-a-day setting and exhibited in a museum. There, in an unfamiliar context, a viewer might note the graceful shape of the handle or the "richly" work-worn texture of the blade of the artifact, which he had not appreciated in the normal context of the tool. No longer seeing the shovel merely as an instrument, the viewer is forced to appreciate its aesthetic qualities, its intrinsic nature. Hopkins' poetry functions in a similar way with many ordinary words, forcing the reader to focus on the language rather than to look through the language as if through a transparent screen to some referential meaning standing apart from the words themselves.

"Turbulence" occurs when the reader finds that he must "struggle" with the text. We can imagine the text, the marks on the page, as a code. The reader brings to such a code his grammar, or set of rules for establishing relationships among the signs of the code, and his lexicon, or list of values to be assigned to those signs. Sometimes the reader's grammar and lexicon are completely adequate to map a satisfactory meaning onto the signs of the code, but frequently the code is so complex that the reader is forced to adjust his grammar and his lexicon to fit the requirements of the code. Especially in cases where the code evokes value-laden and deeply ingrained cultural attitudes, the reader will feel a conflict or struggle as the text requires him to reformulate his lexicon, to reshape his values. For example, in Ford Madox Ford's novel, *The Good Soldier*, most readers approach the text with a highly eulogistic value in their lexicons for the sign *good soldier*. Over the course of reading the novel, however, time after time the author forces the reader to attach a dyslogistic value to that sign, showing that what we call *good soldier* is destructive, ignorant, self-centered, suicidal, and so on. Many other novels proceed by inverting similar common signs, like *good girl, patriot,* or *patriarch*. In such cases, the process of reading is a struggle between the text and the reader to reformulate the reader's lexicon, to reform his initial expectation of what the language signifies, and to reshape his values. Intuitively we appreciate such texts, saying they broaden our knowledge, expand our understanding, or stimulate our thinking.

The reader brings a lexicon to the text. Some texts force the reader to modify his initial lexicon. It is not that the dictionary tells us what the text means, but that the texts tell us what the dictionary must mean. There are two quite different ways to construct a dictionary. The first way is to begin with an arbitrary list of words for which an editor draws on his mental lexicon of possible meanings and sends readers out to look for examples demonstrating that range of meaning in printed sources. Since the advent of large computers in the last thirty years, however, a second possible way to make a dictionary has appeared: It is now possible to begin with a text, perhaps the complete prose and poetry of Hopkins, or Conrad's novels, or the complete fiction of James. Using the computer, it is relatively simple to generate a concordance and summary vocabulary listing all the words actually used by the author and giving the context for each occurrence of each word. The editor of the dictionary can then examine these contexts and create "dictionary slips," or lists of the range of denotation and connotation for each word as it is used by that particular author. Such a dictionary, rather than telling the reader what Hopkins or Conrad or James ought to mean, simply describes what words actually occur in that author's work, how often they occur, and what the range of meaning is for each keyword as it appears in each context.

The first step toward the production of such a modern research tool for Hopkins was begun in 1967 at the University of Wisconsin-Madison with the production of the *Concordance to the English Poetry of Gerard Manley Hopkins* (Dilligan and Bender). The Dilligan/Bender Concordance to Hopkins, although still quite usable, displays the technical limitations of a previous generation of computer technology, such as all upper case type font, and eventually it should be reprinted to conform to contemporary standards for computer generated research tools.

In the 1960's most pioneers in computer applications to literary problems saw the computer as merely a tool to help in traditional tasks of book production. Unfortunately, often researchers at that time discarded their initial data once the desired concordance or other tabulation had been printed in book form. Fortunately, however, in the Dilligan/Bender production of the concordance to Hopkins, we foresaw that any printed concordance was merely a by-product of the much more important computer archive of information standing behind it, and we planned from the beginning to maintain and expand our computer archive to include all of Hopkins' published texts and those of other writers as well. Over a quarter of a century at the University of Wisconsin-Madison, we have steadily expanded the library of literary texts available as computer input and the power of analytic programs applied to that electronic library. In this way, we are now able to generate concordances, dictionary slips, collations of texts, and similar tables of information on demand to fit the specification desired by individual scholars. In commemoration of the one hundredth anniversary of his death, the publication of systematic concordances to the prose texts of Hopkins is now planned.

Eventually a Hopkins dictionary could be produced from these data. Recent developments in laser disk technology indicate, moreover, that such banks of information as concordances and systematic dictionary slips derived from concordances will in the coming decades best circulate in the form of electronic files, rather than bulky printed books.

In the library of the future, a scholar sitting before a computer screen will be able to call up the text of a poem like "Spring and Fall" (55). The reader sees the formal symmetry of the poem in its rhyme scheme (aa bb cc ddd ee ff gg),seven lines turning on the eighth line,"Though worlds of wanwood leafmeal lie," followed by seven more lines. The "shape" of the poem indicated in its rhyme scheme displays bilateral symmetry, like a baroque emblem, perhaps a heart-shaped structure. The formal, poised balance on the eighth line, the middle of the triplet, the middle of the poem, may suggest that there may be some parallel "movement" in the reference of the title: To spring upward and fall downward, the springtide of rebirth and the autumnal approach to death, innocence confronting experience.

If the reader wants to explore the lexicon of this deceptively simple text further, to measure the values the reader brings to the text against those that assuredly Hopkins possessed for his words, a few simple commands to the computer can create a concordance for this poem, showing that it is built of only 70 words, mostly very ordinary and commonplace lexical items. In working with English language concordances, it is usually useful to distinguish between two classes of words, the so-called "high frequency" words versus the "low frequency" words. High frequency words are prepositions, articles, pronouns, certain forms of *to be* and *to have*, and a few other words of limited denotation.

High Frequency Words in "Spring and Fall"

A	1	It	3	Though	1
Ah	1	Like	1	To	1
And	4	No	2	Was	1
Are	2	Nor	3	What	1
As	1	Now	1	Why	1
By	2	Of	3	Will	2
Can	1	Over	1	With	1
For	3	Same	1	Yet	1
Had	1	Such	1	You	5
Is	2	The	5	Your	1

High frequency words are very important in the definition of style, but they require a different treatment from the low frequency words and are best examined in fairly large samples of text. Questions such as how frequently does an author use *for* compared to his use of *by* in two thousand sentences can reveal much about prose style, but the sample,"Spring and Fall," does not provide a large enough field of reference for such statistical inquiries.

The low frequency words are usually dominated by the general topic under discussion, whereas the high frequency words tend to be independent of the particular subject. When we consider the list of low frequency words in "Spring and Fall," the vocabulary seems to be very commonplace and everyday indeed, with the exception of *Goldengrove, Leafmeal, Unleaving*, and *Wanwood*. No word occurs more than once, except the double occurrences of *Man, Margaret,* and *Heart*. Most of the words are monosyllabic, with only three words stretching to three syllables in length, *Unleaving*, *Margaret*, and *Goldengrove*.

"Spring and Fall" is firmly dated in the A MS as completed September 7, 1880. It is not likely to have been composed much before this date. Hopkins' published sermons are dated from July 6, 1879 to June 26, 1881. The poem "Spring and Fall" must have been composed approximately in the middle of the two year period when Hopkins was writing his published sermons.

The Low Frequency words in "Spring and Fall"

Blight	1	Heard	1	Sigh	1
Born	1	Heart	2	Sights	1
Care	1	Know	1	Sorrows	1
Child	1	Leafmeal	1	Spare	1
Colder	1	Leaves	1	Spring	1
Come	1	Lie	1	Springs	1
Expressed	1	Man	2	Things	1
Fall	1	Margaret	2	Thoughts	1
Fresh	1	Matter	1	Unleaving	1
Ghost	1	Mind	1	Wanwood	1
Goldengrove	1	Mourn	1	Weep	1
Grieving	1	Mouth	1	Worlds	1
Grows	1	Name	1		
Guessed	1	Older	1		

If we create a concordance to the collected sermons of Hopkins and look for lexical recurrence in his prose of the low frequency words in "Spring and Fall," defining a word as the string of letters occurring between two blank spaces in the text, we find that all but eight words in the poem appear in his sermons, and six of these eight words form some part of related words in the sermons. For example, *colder* in the poem does not recur in the sermons, but we find *cold* in five occurrences in the prose. The only two words from the poem which do not appear at all in the sermons are *wanwood* and *weep*.

**Low Frequency Words in "Spring and Fall"
which also appear in Hopkins' Sermons:**

Blight	1	Guessed	1	Mourn	0
Born	20	Heard	20	Mourner	1
Unborn	1	Hear	42	Mouth	13
Care	18	Hearing	5	Mouths	1
Cared	1	Hears	3	Name	30
Careful	1	Heart	106	Named	5
Cares	6	Hearts	27	Names	1
Child	12	Heart's	1	Older	1
Childhood	4	Heartache	1	Old	13
Children	32	Heartbeat	1	Sigh	1
Children's	1	Heartless	1	Sighs	1
Colder	0	Heartscald	1	Sight	11
Cold	5	Heartwhole	1	Sights	1
Come	0	Hearty	1	Insight	2
Comes	25	Sweetheart	3	Shortsighted	3
Expressed	1	Know	55	Sorrow	9
Express	1	Knowing	6	Sorrows	6
Expresses	3	Knowledge	10	Sorrowful	2
Expressions	1	Known	21	Spare	0
Fall	27	Knows	8	Spares	1
Befall	4	Unknown	1	Spared	1
Fallen	13	Leafmeal	0	Spring	2
Falling	4	Leaf	1	Springing	1
Falls	5	Leave	25	Dayspring	1
Unfallen	1	Leaving	1	Mainspring	1
Fresh	10	Meal	4	Offspring	1
Fresher	1	Leaves	3	Springs	0
Refreshment	1	Lie	2	Things	99
Ghost	58	Lies	11	Thing	31
Ghosts	1	Man	196	Thoughts	16
Goldengrove	0	Man's	17	Thought	45
Gold	6	Manhood	4	Unleaving	0
Golden	2	Manliness	1	Leaving	1
Grieving	0	Mankind	8	Wanwood	0
Griefs	1	Margaret	4	Wan	0
Grievous	3	Matter	10	Wood	0
Grows	3	Matters	1	Weep	0
Grow	4	Mind	28	Worlds	0
Growing	3	Minds	24	World	94
Grown	3	Mind's	2	Worldly	5
Growth	3			World's	12

The total number of individual words or tokens in the Sermons is approximately 17,925. These tokens fall into 4,342 types or key-words. It is quite unusual to find low frequency words in a sample the size of the collected sermons recurring more than, say, ten times. Frequency of recurrence more often than 10 suggests a thematic or topical concern. For example, we can understand that the word *butterfly* might occur more than 10 times in a collection of essays about Puccini, but it is rather less likely to occur so often in a set of studies about Wagner. One reason for the word's recurrence lies in the particular topic under discussion. It is noteworthy that nearly all the words in "Spring and Fall," although in themselves common, recur so frequently in the sermons as to be thematic: see *Heart* 106 exact recurrences plus various nearly-related forms; *Man* 196 plus; *World* 94 in the singular; *Ghost* 58 plus; or *Fall* 27 plus. Of course, the subject of the sermons necessarily is theological and we must take care not to jump to conclusions based on such limited evidence. Nevertheless, it appears that Hopkins selected his vocabulary for "Spring and Fall" from the lexicon of words he most commonly used to explicate matters of faith.

The high frequency of occurrence of *Heart* in the sermons results mainly from Hopkins' thematic or topical concern with the *Sacred Heart*. More than half of his uses of the word occur in the five pages of printed text which contain his sermon for June 26, 1881, "being the Sunday . . . nearest the feast of the Sacred Heart . . . at St. Francis Xavier's Liverpool--on *the Sacred Heart*" (*S* 100-104). This sermon reads strikingly like a dictionary "slip" for the word *heart*. It also provides one of the four recurrences of the word *Margaret* from "Spring and Fall."

In poem 55, the speaker addresses *Margaret* as an otherwise unidentified dramatic audience:

> Margaret are you grieving
> Over Goldengrove unleaving
> . . . .
> It is the blight man was born for,
> It is Margaret you mourn for.

In the sermon, Hopkins begins with a brief history of "the worship of the Sacred Heart," noting that certain people opposed it as a dangerous or foolish innovation, "when the Bd. Margaret Mary said that our Lord himself had revealed it to her" (*S* 100). As we see from the footnotes to the printed sermon, the feast of the Sacred Heart was first extended to the whole Church in 1856, and at the time of Hopkins' sermon had two divergent aspects: "one stemming from St. John Eudes at the beginning of the 17th century, stressing its joyous aspect, the other from St. Margaret Mary at the end of the 17th century with the stress on compassionate reparation" (*S* 281). St. Margaret Mary Alacoque (1647-90) was a nun of the Visitation Order at Paray-le-Monial, whose heavenly visitations led her to spread the devotion to the Sacred Heart despite opposition. The remaining references to Margaret in the sermons refer to the martyr Margaret Clitheroe, pressed to death in York in 1586 for maintaining the Catholic faith, cited in Hopkins' sermons as an example of joyful sacrifice (*S* 48), and the use of the name twice as a generic common name, "Long before John or Edward, Margaret or Elizabeth ever said / I love our Lord Jesus Christ / he said / I love John, I love Edward, I love Margaret . . ." (*S* 49). Etymologically, the word *Margaret* reaches back in time to the pearl of great price in Greek *Margere*.

The word *heart* occurs twice in "Spring and Fall," once in each symmetrical half of the text. The speaker observes to grieving Margaret that "as the heart grows older / It will come to such sights colder," in the first half. In the concluding half of the poem, "heart heard of, ghost guessed: / It is the blight man was born for, / It is Margaret you mourn for." Although the *OED* dovotes more than four pages to its entry for *heart*, it scarcely prepares the reader for Hopkins' poem 55. In the sermon, Hopkins observes that "There are some perhaps among those who hear me, Protestants and others, to whom the name of the Sacred Heart has a strange sound, an amusing sound. . . . For the sake of such persons I shall . . . say what it is exactly that the Sacred Heart means" (*S* 101). He might well be addressing the lexicon of the *OED* as registering the name of *heart* with an unmeaning sound. The main categories of the *OED* definition all are covered in Hopkins' argument: the bodily organ and seat of life; the seat of inmost thought, feeling, love, and affection; the term of endearment, as in *sweetheart*; the central part or core; and the shape of the heart. Hopkins generates a long catalogue of common usages of the word (*S* 103), concluding "the heart is of all the members of the body the one which most strongly and most of its own accord sympathises with and expresses in itself what goes on within the soul" (*S* 103). Note how like a dictionary entry this sermon is. Hopkins struggles for control of the lexicon. The word *heart* does not merely designate a "blood vessel," but reaches out to include in the metaphoric vessel of everyday speech much more, and points ultimately toward the Sacred Heart which registered the joy and sorrow of Christ's life among us. The preacher enters the battle, like a knight entering the lists, for mastery of the word. In the light of the sermon, the reader is ill-advised to skim past the two references to *heart* in "Spring and Fall" as he might in an everyday context. These words challenge the common, non-technical lexicon and open a whole range of signification often unnoted.

Since the word *spring* elsewhere in Hopkins' poetry very frequently refers to the spring season, the title "Spring and Fall" naturally suggests the opposition of springtide to autumn, perhaps reflected in the dramatic situation of the poem, when the voice of experience addresses the child Margaret, creating a commonplace Post-romantic situation. The child, trailing clouds of glory, has some intuitive feelings which are not found in the adult, more ratiocinative speaker. The adult, understanding, wondering at the fresh feeling of the child, knows that sympathy and affection grow colder as the "heart grows older," and asks if the child can grieve merely for the falling leaves in an autumnal wood. Such a view of the meaning of *spring* is well-documented by the concordance entries from other poetic texts by Hopkins, but the concordance to the sermons casts an unexpected darkening connotation over the word.

Seven references to *spring* occur in the sermons; *spring* (S 44, 93); *springing* (S 70); *dayspring* (S 40); *mainspring* (S 44); and *offspring* (S 60, 67). *Spring* (S 93) designates the spring time in establishing the circumstances surrounding the event described in John 4.34, as a text chosen at random for the sermon. *Springing* (S 70) refers to the figurative leap or spring of a good man to follow the Paraclete, to do God's will, The word is quite eulogistic here, a good impulse or movement. *Offspring* (S 60, 67), children, are also presented as just rewards, a good. The remaining three references to *spring*, however, are more ominous. *Dayspring* (S 40) refers to the dawn of the second coming, "there is no dawn, no dayspring, to tell of the day coming, no morning twilight, the sunrise will be sudden, will be lightning, we are told, will overtake us without warning, will entrap us, will come as a snare upon all that are on the face of the earth." Even darker are the references to *mainspring* and *spring* (S 44): "A watch wound up but kept from going has the spring always on the strain though no motion comes of it. Such a mainspring of evil in us is the concupiscence that comes in with original sin and lasts even when original sin has been taken away by baptism." Such a mainspring of evil, the offspring of the original sin, the proclivity to sin, the wellspring of mortal woe, is very different from the innocent, carefree, culturally primitive figure of a childish Margaret. Here *spring* is not the opposite of *fall*, but the cause of it, concupiscent desire. The lexicon of the sermons challenges in this instance the connotation, as well as the denotation, of the word. Should we feel that *spring* is a commendable or fearful, eulogistic or dyslogistic word? The concordance certainly shows that Hopkins was not always lighthearted in his use of this term.

In the poetry, there is a clear indication that Hopkins used the word *fall* to refer to the autumnal season, the time of falling leaves, although this meaning is not common in his texts, for example, see "A Voice from the World," (81) "When skies are hard as any stone / The fall is o'er, told off the leaves." This seasonal denotation does not recur in the sermons. The 49 occurrences of *fall, fallen, falling,* and *falls* in the sermons show a uniformly negative connotation, meaning simply to fall to the ground in three cases, to fall down drunk or to fall into sin in approximately six cases, but in almost all other cases the reference is to The Fall in its various manifestations. There are a few combined formations involving *fall*, but they too almost uniformly have a negative connotation: to fall short; to fall into doing something sinful; to fall on evil ways; night fall. I do not see a single case in which *fall* is desirable or comfortable. The concordance to the poetry, on the other hand, shows many cases in which *fall* is associated with good, for example, the "fall-gold mercies" in Stanza 23 of "The Wreck of the Deutschland," The single reference to *blight* in the sermons signifies one of the characteristics separating our fallen world from Paradise before The Fall (*S* 60). "The blight man was born for" is a consequence of The Fall.

The effect of defining the connotation of *spring* and *fall* by the concordances to the sermons is to unbalance the symmetry of the title. The two words are seldom used to designate opposite seasons, or youth versus age. Nor are they used to oppose pure, youthful joy to care-ridden old age. Both are rather dark, pessimistic words in the sermons. *Fall* is totally bleak. *Spring* is sometimes positive, but carries a strong strand of the *spring*, or source, of the *fall* within itself, like a sinister mainspring filled with potential energy, straining toward evil.

To read the poem in the light of the recurrence of its lexicon in the sermons shifts the aesthetic balance of its structure. Although the rhyme scheme sets up a perfectly balanced aa bb cc ddd ee ff gg structure, the argument is not an evenhanded or balanced confrontation of good versus evil, innocence versus experience, child versus adult. The positive elements of *spring* struggle lamely against the overwhelmingly negative *fall*. Perhaps in this poem Hopkins is carrying out yet another experiment with the problem of aesthetic balance in artistic structure of the sort he explored in his sonnets.

Normally, in the Petrarchan sonnet the rhyme scheme gives an octave to the exposition of the situation, and the sestet in merely six lines must counterbalance or "overpower" the octave in its witty commentary. In his "Author's Preface" and his letters, Hopkins argues that the essence of the sonnet is not the formula of octave plus sestet. There is nothing essential about the numbers eight and six. The key to the sonnet is its proportion. So he writes curtail or shortened sonnets, and sonnets running longer than 14 lines, maintaining that "proportion" of exposition to commentary, but changing the actual length of the structure. The artistic vitality subsists in the struggle for balance in an unsymmetrical "space" where the argument or content must struggle to balance the two uneven parts of the text. In

"Spring and Fall," however, the "space" is divided evenly, bilaterally, seven lines plus the turn in line eight, plus seven more lines. It is the content that is asymmetrical, not the space. The content pits an overpowering fall against whatever virtues spring up in countermovement.

Each text, and the corpus of the works by every author has its particular lexicon: the list of words used in the text, the range of denotation for each word, and the connotations generated by each context in which each word occurs. Every reader, too, has a lexicon built from his experience with the language. When the reader approaches the text, he tries to apply his lexicon to the author's code. If the code is so complex that the reader must modify his lexicon in the light of what the text requires, the reader senses a struggle. The text is a terrain in which a conflict is taking place. The production of "secondary" literary works, books of explication, commentary, or "theory" can be seen as the external manifestation of the turbulent struggle between the reader's lexicon and that demanded by the text.

In the century since the death of Hopkins, his works have been rescued from obscurity and have become the subject of extensive and ingenious study, often controversial and heated debate. Who can doubt that this activity, even when apparently misguided, shows that the readers appreciate the challenge that the texts of Hopkins provide to their accepted values and everyday concepts. Certainly the failure to build a lexicon from the author's own corpus can result in blind spots and plain mistakes as to denotation, to insensitivity to connotation, and finally failure to grasp large issues of artistic form and ideology, as well as individual significations of words, but few readers have the span of memory and the mental agility to recognize and adjust to all the demands of an author's texts.

Now, as we enter the second century of the study of Hopkins, much challenging work remains to be done. With the assistance of new technology, lexicographical studies of a power and scope undreamed of in the Victorian era are possible. The concordance to all of Hopkins' printed works should be available to scholars for this commemorative year.[1] What young scholars will step forward to build from these concordances, to make Hopkins the subject for the first descriptive dictionary, perhaps the first step in the great English dictionary of the future, before the second anniversary of Hopkins' death?

---

[1] Peter Lang Publishing, Inc., of New York, plans the publication of concordances to the collected prose writings of Gerard Manley Hopkins to initiate a series of commemorative volumes on the poet and the circle of writers about him.

Work Cited

Dilligan, Robert J., and Todd K. Bender. *A Concordance to the English Poetry of Gerard Manley Hopkins*. Madison: University of Wisconsin Press, 1970.

Dangerous Beauty

Hopkins and Newman

Michael D. Moore

Ever since Robert Bridges's observation that Hopkins' poems about natural beauty reveal a "naked encounter between sensualism and asceticism," critics and scholars have been renewing in one form or another the "divided-self" debate. At issue in this ongoing (and much wider-ranging) discussion is the significance of an apparent tension--personal or artistic--within those famous verses on the divine principle in nature. The history and varied terms of the learned debate are so familiar to Hopkinseans as to require little summary here. For one authoritative critical tradition, the poems do seamlessly evoke a poet-priest's ecstatic sense of the mystical unity between "earth's sweet being" and its Creator. The other dominant tendency in interpretation has been to trace in those same texts a symptomatic discontinuity or "friction" between sensory-imaginative delight and religious response.

Today, as we observe the Hopkins centenary year, the subject remains a central one in Hopkins studies, with opinion about equally divided. The following essay is by no means another attempt to resolve, or even to review, the twists and turns of this divergence. Rather, I would like to suggest one new perspective on how the question itself may be applied to an evidently multivalent poetry. For there does seem to be a kind of systematic dissonance--something registered as provisional--in the conduct of the intimational nature poems. An overt concern in later pieces, it is subtly present even in the more joyous poems of the 1870's *annus mirabilis*. By one means or another, they invite a qualified or restrained or deferred assurance as regards their own "reading" of this world's brilliant testimony to its Creator. The claims of natural beauty and of religion are poised in ambiguous relation, though not actually at odds. Both are enthusiastically affirmed, but rarely if ever are the orders of grace and of nature fully coalesced even at the rhetorical level. As has so frequently been pointed out, for example, the typical strategy of a Hopkins nature poem is to transfer or *convert* its own exuberant naturalistic inscaping to something religiously definite, to apply it with no little urgency to the blessings or obligations of Christian faith. The tactic is sometimes an abrupt transition ("What is all this juice and all this joy?"; "Ah well! it is all a purchase, all is a prize"), sometimes a passing proviso (at best the pious beholder's heart only "half hurls" earth off), sometimes the veriest hint (nature is never spent because the Holy Ghost broods "*over*" a bent world). Even "Pied Beauty" makes the point: for all the tribute Hopkins pays there to the delightfully "dappled" variety of God's world, in the end we are exhorted to "Praise" instead a higher principle, a Creator whose own "beauty" is quite otherwise: "past change."

But if the perceptual rhetoric is in this sense divided, the imaginative or sacramental synthesis of earth and heaven incompletely established, it must be consciously so. The intense (and I do think unequivocal) excitement of having "divined" some splendor in the objective world is being tempered-- not renounced--by a qualifying gesture. The poet lightly curbs himself, resists affirming that nature leads us directly to God, even though his own experience, and Catholic philosophical tradition, presumably provided sufficient warrant for believing it can. What Hopkins does seem determined to signal in this way is that an ardent religious instressing of mortal beauty may be much, and yet withal "dangerous."

Why is this? What is lacking? What was at stake here? Do criteria and language influenced by the Bridges dichotomy accurately describe the transmuting or deftly withholding procedures of these particular texts? Why is so otherwise assured and fervently Christian (even sectarian) a spiritualizing vision of Nature nevertheless touched by disquietudes, by self-qualifying acknowledgements of "danger"? If the poet's "sacramental view of nature" is as unproblematic as so many commentators say, why the caution, and why the falling away from confidence in later poems that address more and more directly the question "To what serves mortal beauty?" And, finally, is it in any case at all certain that such caveats are "confessional" on Hopkins' part, an inadvertent disclosure of unreconciled impulses within himself?

In this essay I wish to introduce one kind of evidence for reassessing this aspect of Hopkins' religious response to nature: the remarkable similarity of some of the poet's thought and phrasing to passages in works by John Henry Newman. I mean to illustrate, in a preliminary way, two things: first, that elements of thought and language in some of Hopkins' most acclaimed and apparently original verse may actually have been inspired by corresponding passages in Newman; second, that these affinities with Newman's eloquent treatments of similar motifs and issues may clarify the theological scruple that informs these poems.[1]

---

[1] Cf. Moore, "Newman and the 'Second Spring'" and Moore, "Newman and the Motif."

As we are so often reminded, much of Hopkins' ebullient poetry and other writings about natural beauty and power memorably credit the visible universe with being, in some sense, God's sign or utterance of Himself: "This world then is word, expression, news of God" (*S* 129). The poet-priest's spiritualizing vision of the world was likewise his exhortation to a "fast foundering" nineteenth century: "All things therefore are charged with love, are charged with God and *if we know how to touch them* give off sparks and take fire, yield drops and flow, ring and tell of him" (*S* 195). As I shall suggest, the conditional clause at the heart of that famous quotation evinces more circumspection than commentators usually admit, but otherwise the poet's own enthusiasm for the vital divine stress in "things" is unmixed. Hopkins was also always fascinated by art and by music and by the "lovely manly mould," "favoured make and mind"--and here too sought to articulate the always ambivalent power of those "dearly and dangerously sweet" attractions.

Hence it is, altogether, that the impetus--what Yvor Winters in another context termed the "generating concept"--of Hopkins' nature poetry is perhaps expressed in the title and argument of one of them: "To what serves Mortal Beauty?"(62). The possible influence in these respects of the poet's familiarity with similar ideas and motifs in Newman is in itself of literary-historical interest. But the note of self-qualification in so many of these poems is, I think, initially and ultimately a theoretical rather than personal hesitancy. This counterpointing may be illuminated through comparison with the dogmatic emphasis in Newman's attitude towards contemporary religious admiration for the wonders of nature. Caution in that regard does not develop primarily as a moral qualm but as a considered philosophical recognition of a greater peril in his time: the fundamental threat to dogmatic religion implicit in *natural theology*. This was a context in which, to adopt phrasing from "The Wreck of the Deutschland" (28), "the faithful waver, the faithless fable and miss."

Let me introduce the Newman connection by recalling the key phrase in one of his most memorable passages, lines best known today, perhaps, for the ironic use made of them by James Joyce in *A Portrait of the Artist as a Young Man*. At the end of a Catholic discourse on "The Glories of Mary," Newman declares that the serene loveliness of the Blessed Virgin breathes purity and infuses peace and is "not like earthly beauty, *dangerous* to look upon" (*Discourses* 358). Although few nineteenth-century English writers were more appreciative than Newman of natural beauty, this remark is entirely consistent with his habit, in eloquent sermons and elsewhere, of representing this world as either an inadequate guide to Christian faith or as a trial to it. The philosophical basis for this view can be found throughout Newman's writings, from first to last, notably in the Oxford University Sermons (*Fifteen Sermons*), *The Idea of a University*, and the *Apologia Pro Vita Sua*. The "danger" is almost always intellectual, not moral. The temptation is that of a vague deism or of natural theology in its various forms, consistently assailed by Newman as liberal-rationalist usurpations that dissolve orthodox Christian belief and tend ultimately to atheism. As both Hopkins and Newman averred, there is no "half-way house." Ingenious arguments about "design" or "analogy" or "evidences" or miracles never interested Newman, and such abstract and complacent theories of divine superintendence in the natural world are not what we find in his writings, or in Hopkins'. Newman terms Paley's assumptions "dangerous," adding ominously, "It is indeed a great question whether Atheism is not as philosophically consistent with the phenomena of the physical world, taken by themselves, as the doctrine of a creative and governing Power." In a footnote equally alert to the opposite risk, that of skepticism, in his own argument, he asks further "whether physical phenomena logically *teach* us, or on the other hand logically *remind* us of the Being of a God" (*Fifteen Sermons* 194). Another of the University Sermons, significantly entitled "Contest Between Faith and Sight" (VII), opens by referring directly to "The *danger* to which Christians are exposed from the influence of the visible course of things."

The contemporary ethos of Nature, the benign religion of "wonder," the legacy not only of Paley or Butler, for example, but also--we must assume--of the Lake Poets' (or Carlyle's) natural supernaturalism, had tacitly become a respectable rival to the whole system of dogmatic faith. The threat was not (or not yet) atheism, but pseudo-religion. Gentlemen's religion. Part of the entire tendency to liberalism, "the one great mischief" against which Newman would finally say he had dedicated his whole life.[2] And, ecclesiastical politics aside, it was this "danger"--not any alarm about sin or frank apostasy--that had provoked and nerved the Oxford Movement and that thereby carried both Newman and Hopkins beyond Tractarianism into the Roman Catholic Church.

This persistent vein in Newman's thought, and in particular his tendency to use the word "dangerous" to connote intellectual rather than moral risk, can perhaps be briefly represented in a couple of key texts. "The Powers of Nature" is an early Anglican sermon resisting "the *danger* of many (so called) philosophical pursuits, now in fashion." In particular, Newman connects contemplation of the "beautiful and wonderful objects" of Creation with "the *danger*, that is, of resting in things seen, and forgetting unseen things, and our ignorance about them." He also warns that if we

---

[2] The famous "biglietto speech" of 1879 in which Newman acknowledged his elevation to the cardinalate is reprinted in *Sayings*, 17-21. Cf. appendix "Liberalism" in *Apologia*.

"make the contemplation of them a mere feeling, and a sort of luxury of the imagination. . . . they become but a snare of our enemy." It is our duty instead to "refer" the partial revelations in the natural world to formal religious observance, for "many a man can write and talk beautifully about them, who is not at all better or nearer heaven for all his excellent words."[3] A very significant later locus in Newman for this same concern and usage is the fifth chapter of the *Apologia*, "The Position of My Mind Since 1845." Newman again adduces the dominant tendencies of philosophical and religious thought in England, and the threat they represent for belief in revealed truth. The section features his famous admission, in the "aboriginal calamity" passage, that, but for God's voice speaking in his conscience and heart, contemplation of this world would make him an atheist, or a pantheist, or a polytheist. Inductive evidences of God's existence "do not warm me or enlighten me; they do not take away the winter of my desolation, or make the buds unfold and the leaves grow within me, and my moral being rejoice." But the main concern of this whole part of the *Apologia* is "the *danger* of being led away into a bottomless liberalism of thought." Liberalism is "not very dangerous in itself, though dangerous as opening the door to evils which it did not itself either anticipate or comprehend." Only the Catholic Church suffices to refine "the raw material of human nature, so excellent, so *dangerous*, so capable of divine purposes." Ideas in religious controversy can be "erroneous or *dangerous*."[4] Altogether, then, Newman typically finds the age's prepossessing "danger" not in sin or

---

[3] *Parochial and Plain Sermons*, 358-367. Cf. Newman's mockery of nature-philosophy in "The Tamworth Reading Room," *Discussions and Arguments on Various Subjects*, 302.

[4] *Apologia Pro Vita Sua*, 214-253.

gross materialism or even (since he is not addressing atheists) in irreligion. The real threat for which he usually reserves this word is a disposition of mind he considers hostile not to religiosity and morality but, rather, to dogmatic principle.

I'm suggesting, then, that if Newman--and Hopkins--mistrusted created beauty it was for the sake of religious orthodoxy rather than moral scruple. Wordsworthian "beauteous forms," for example, may indeed cultivate "natural piety" and "moral being," but these are not Christianity, and certainly not Catholicism. Notions of faith and worship deducible from the heart's response to merely worldly things are at best vague, at worst positively prejudicial to revealed truth. As Pascal had said, and as Newman freely reaffirmed in his Oxford sermons, the physical world declares the glory of God and Christ only to Christians already disposed to find it there in fact or in symbol. And even then a divinely infused and sanctioned mortal beauty does not by any means tell people their religious duty. Unless this ambivalent or incomplete signifying of the visible creation's powerful noumena is recognized, they become blurrings of or obstacles to belief in the unseen verities. When the relatively vague inducements to piety engendered by nature-philosophy or enthusiastic Romantic theopathy are preferred to what Hopkins termed "God's better beauty, grace," they are positively dangerous.

Hopkins too uses the word "dangerous" in this virtually sectarian context in letters about the temptations of a merely liberal Christianity, of preferring virtue to truth. As early as 1864, while still a Tractarian Anglican, he could exhort his friend E.H. Coleridge in the following terms:

> Beware of doing what I once thought I could do, adopt an enlightened Christianity, I may say, horrible as it is, be a credit to religion. This fatal state of mind leads to infidelity, if consistently

and logically developed. The great aid to belief and object of belief is the doctrine of the Real Presence in the Blessed Sacrament of the Altar. Religion without that is sombre, *dangerous*, illogical, with that it is--not to speak of its grand consistency and certainty--loveable. Hold that and you will gain all Catholic truth. (*F* 17)

The issue is clearly one of orthodox faith, not moral jeopardy. The immediate "danger" lies in not being "Catholic" enough, in resting with the deceptively reassuring appearances of a creditable religiosity. Entreating letters written later to E.W. Urquhart after Hopkins' conversion, again describe doctrinal laxity as "*dangerous* and likely to mislead" (*F* 47), and specifically invoke Newman's authority on the "dangerousness" of relying complacently on "the outer world" in matters of religious duty:

> I know that living a moral life, with the ordinances of religion and yourself a minister of them, with work to do and the interest of a catholicwards movement to support you, it is most natural to say all things continue as they were and most hard to realise the silence and severity of God, *as Dr. Newman very eloquently and persuasively has said in a passage of the Anglican Difficulties*; but this plea or way of thinking--all things continuing as they were--is the very character of infidelity. *The difference between a state of grace and a state of reprobation, that difference to which all other differences of humanity are as the splitting of straws, makes no change in the outer world*; faces, streets, and sunlight look just the same: it is therefore the more *dangerous* and terrible. (*F* 51)[5]

---

[5] See Newman, *Certain Difficulties* 123, and Newman, *Discourses* 34.

Admittedly, in these instances the threat to religion (there is no threat to virtue) is not solely that posed by fascination with natural beauty *per se*. I mean only to point out that the word finds its way into Hopkins' discourse in the sense indicated here. And that this habit of associating it with doctrinal looseness in otherwise religious persons may have both a general and a particular relation to Newman's thought.

The most famous "dangerousness" in Hopkins' poetry itself is of course that of the windhover (36). And perhaps, without some contextual framework, it is the most mysterious. In what sense is the "fire" of the bird "a million times told lovelier, more dangerous"? Again, we have the explicit conjunction of loveliness and danger, in a poem that nearly all commentators find deeply (if not self-evidently) religious. In this case a massive threat or risk is apparently presented by the dazzle of merely "brute beauty." But the poem's argument is surely not reducible to an ascetic's startled qualm of conscience at having been surprised by worldly joy. After all, the sestet proceeds in the perceptual mode without any other trace of anxiety or regret. And despite decades of ingenious critical exegesis, any moral or religious alarm the poem may suggest (apart from the subtitle "To Christ our Lord," an afterthought) remains very indirect. Indeed, it does not seem to be emphasizing alarm. That almost off-hand acknowledgement of the inevitable confluence of beauty and danger in spectacular natural display would seem to be, were it not so excited, more like a passing theoretical caveat. Why might this be?

Hopkins' journal records a process of imaginative association similar to that presented in "The Windhover." The beauty "caught" in the "shine" and "glare" of bluebells is frankly pagan (it has "Greek rightness"), and is "gracious" only in a colloquial sense (*J* 231). Nevertheless, in a different journal entry Hopkins writes, "I do not think I have ever seen anything more beautiful than the bluebell I have been looking at. I know the beauty of our Lord by it" (*J* 199). Together, these observations indicate the movement of thought also so typical of many Hopkins poems. As in "The Windhover," the essentially aesthetic excitement of "catching" the selving inscape of merely natural beauty is followed up by an active instressing of the definite supernatural meaning it suggests to the religious imagination. In that meaning alone is its value and its claim to Christian implication. Elsewhere in the journal the same process of association is also indicated with regard to stars. "As we drove home," he records, "the stars came out thick: I leant back to look at them and my heart opening more than usual praised our Lord to and in whom all that beauty comes home" (*J* 254).

In fact, the splendor of starry skies seems to have particularly impressed Hopkins as an instance of the divinity capable of being symbolically discerned in (or through) natural beauty. In two other very important poems of the Welsh years, "The Wreck of the Deutschland" and "The Starlight Night" (32), stars are celebrated in inductive relation to Catholic doctrine and practice. The most elliptically theological section of "The Wreck" (stanzas 6-10) are, for example, introduced by these well-known lines:

> I kiss my hand
> To the stars, lovely-asunder
> Starlight, wafting him out of it; and
> Glow, glory in thunder;
> Kiss my hand to the dappled-with-damson west
> Since, tho he is under the world's splendour and wonder,
> His mystery must be instressed, stressed;
> For I greet him the days I meet him, and bless when I understand.

The mystery is that of God's immanence beneath natural beauty ("lovely-asunder . . . splendour")--a hidden truth needing to be instressed and "understood" and calling up an instinctive blessing from the rightly-disposed beholder. Although there is something peculiarly Hopkinsean (and Scotist?) about the recondite Incarnational theory that follows, the fifth stanza's general principle corresponds to Newman's continual reference to "a supernatural system going on *under* this visible scene" (*Parochial* VI, xviii). Newman also affirms in "the Mysteries of Divine Condescension" (*Discourses* XIV) that the "grace and splendour" of natural beauty is an occasion for delight and praise. The material world reflects a divine "glory" which is "ever able to draw us off from ourselves in admiration, which moves our affections, which wins from us a disinterested *homage*." Again, in "Love the Safeguard of Faith against Superstition" (*Fifteen Sermons* XII), Newman describes the "spontaneous movement" of heart by which religious persons go out of themselves to *meet Him* who is unseen and . . . discern Him in such symbols of Him as they find ready provided for them." This eager, albeit qualified, affirmation is reminiscent of Hopkins' "I greet him the days I *meet* him, and bless when I understand." And in "The Infinitude of the Divine Attributes" (*Discourses* XV) Newman explains that "the *mysteries* of nature and of grace are nothing else than the modes in which His infinitude *encounters us and is brought home to our minds*," and he especially emphasizes natural beauty as an instance of such "economies."

But it is exactly there, I think, that Newman indicates the limit that he, and Hopkins, would finally impose on identifying God with the world's betokenings of His attributes. An "economy"--a doctrinal term especially associated with Newman and Tractarian thought--is a use of gradual, partial, and cautious forms (such as parables) to disclose truths that would be, in their fullness, disturbing or unintelligible to simple minds. In an appendix to the *Apologia* (299-301) Newman felt obliged to defend the practice (for example, "elementary information given to the heathen or catechumen") enough, he admits there that the principle is "dangerous" in being liable to abuse or misunderstanding (See footnote 5). It is no surprise, then, that in a Catholic sermon entitled "Omnipotence in Bonds," Newman draws the same sharp distinction Hopkins' stanza does between God's ubiquity and His essence:

> And, while He thus intermingles His presence and His operations with an ineffable intimacy of union in every place, in every substance, in every act, everywhere, He is at the same time, as I have said, infinitely separated from everything, and absolutely incommunicable and unapproachable, and self-dependent in His own glorious Essence.[6]

For Newman this is, as Hopkins also emphasizes in "The Wreck" and elsewhere, a "mystery," but not necessarily a trial to a faith satisfied with whatever momentary glimpses of the unseen are vouchsafed to it in this world. Indeed, as Newman explains in the same sermon, the attempt to associate the pattern of worldly things with that of revelation can be for believers a great comfort in times of spiritual distress--a point perhaps related to Hopkins' concern in the sixth stanza of the "Wreck" for the faithful who "waver." It is of the fifth stanza, however, that Newman's careful conclusion is reminiscent:

> I see here the silent operation, *beneath the surface*, of a great *principle*, which is *not seen until it is investigated* . I *adore* a truth, which, though patent to all who look for it, yet, to be seen in its consistency and symmetry, *has to be looked for.* And further, I *glory in it*, for I see in it the most awful antagonism to the very idea and essence of sin.

---

[6] *Sermons Preached on Various Occasions*, 79.

This passage is as notable for its circumspection as for its devotional feeling. And the final clause is of course Newman's habitual referral of the "great principle" to definite (and unpoetical) religious implications beyond itself.

It may be no coincidence that all Newman's language here about encountering God in nature and rendering Him responsive homage reminds us too of the tenor of Hopkins' sonnet "Hurrahing in Harvest" (38). In this poem, even a "barbarous" beauty in nature's external "glory"--akin to the kestrel's "brute beauty"--moves the beholder to "lift up . . . lift up heart, eyes" to "glean" from it the "majestic" attributes of its Creator, stirring an admiration that "half hurls earth for him off." The poem's wider suggestiveness is perhaps illuminated by its verbal and thematic similarities to yet another passage in Newman, from a sermon already quoted, about the relation of nature to revelation:

> [L]*ift up your eyes, look around,* . . . [W]e are so constituted by our Maker as to be *able to love Him ardently and He has given us the means* of doing so. . . . And we have *eyes* to see much more than the difficulties of His Essence; and the great consolatory disclosures of Him, which Nature begins, Revelation brings to perfection. *Lift up your eyes, I say, and look out even upon the material world.* . . . He has traced out many of His attributes upon it, His immensity, His wisdom, His power, His loving-kindness, and His skill; *but more than all, its very face is illuminated with the glory and beauty of His external excellence.*
> (*Discourses* XIV)

The effect of meditating upon the beauty and splendor of this world, Newman says, is that "your heart kindles, and your voice is full of praise and worship." Even these mere externals, "so bright, so *majestic,* are enough for love and joy because "even in sights of this earth, the pomp and ceremonial alone of royalty is sufficient for the *beholder*." Similarly, in "Hurrahing in Harvest" the poet says "I walk, I lift up, I lift up heart, eyes" to "glean" Christ from the natural world. For both writers, however, this is a only gleaning rather than a harvesting because, as Newman carefully explains, even the noblest earthly beauty is so partial a reflection of the real glory (the "Essence") of its Maker.

But in Hopkins' sonnet "The Starlight Night" it is again the instressed beauty of stars to which an ecclesiastically specific transferral of significance is finally ascribed. And again the reader is exhorted to "look, look up at the skies!" The octave inscapes the glorious night sky with typically Hopkinsean exuberance, visual precision, and metaphorical audacity. But it is the sestet that resolves that complex of delight into religious terms perhaps indebted to Newman. One textual parallel is especially striking. Hopkins interprets the night sky as a "piece-bright paling" (a wall with chinks in it) concealing almost entirely "Christ and his mother and all his hallows" in heaven. The sky and its lights "are indeed the barn," he says, in which are enclosed the bright holiness of those Persons. This conceit seems to be an adaptation of Newman's description of the Church, in "The Visible Church an Encouragement to Faith" (*Parochial* III, xvii), as "a vision of Heaven," the whole surface of which seems illuminated, "though *the light really streams from apertures* which might be numbered. The scattered witnesses thus become, in the language of the text, 'a cloud,' *like the Milky Way in the heavens*." The "witnesses" especially mentioned by Newman throughout this sermon are in fact the saints of the Church who have labored before us for "the *prize* we are seeking." Hopkins' poem similarly has it that the stars are a desirable "prize" and light gleaming through chinks in the heavenly "paling" behind which abide Christ's "hallows." There is a vehement sectarian orthodoxy in the poem's religious "reading" of the sky. The starry heaven is home to Christ, who is specifically the mystical "spouse" of a Church venerating the Blessed Virgin and the Saints, and understanding it should move us beyond enthusiasm to the observance of definite ordinances: to "Prayer, patience, alms, vows." The worth of this world's attractiveness is in its prompting the affective will into action. As Newman says in "The Powers of Nature," already quoted above, it is a duty to interpret nature supernaturally and to discern the unseen world in that which is seen; to indulge otherwise one's feelings for the beauty of the world is to make them "but a snare of our enemy."

A similarly religious transmutation of nature's beauty can be found in the sonnet entitled "Spring" (33). Here too the distinctive theme and phrasing appear to have been modelled even more directly on motifs Hopkins would have met with in Newman. Because of the pervasive verbal and conceptual echoes, it is worth quoting the poem extensively here:

>   Nothing is so beautiful as Spring--
>   When weeds, in wheels, shoot long and lovely and lush;
> . . . .
>   The glassy peartree leaves and blooms, they brush
>   The descending blue; that blue is all in a rush
>   With richness; . . .
>   What is all this juice and all this joy?
>   A strain of the earth's sweet being in the beginning
>   In Eden garden.--Have, get, before it cloy,
>   Before it cloud, Christ, lord, and sour with sinning,
>   Innocent mind and Mayday in girl and boy,
>   Most, O maid's child, thy choice and worthy the winning.

Newman's splendid sermon "The Second Spring" (*Sermons . . . Various* X) opens with a strikingly similar analogy between vernal vitality (including "the blossoms of May") and the attractiveness of merely natural beauty and virtue. This consideration leads Newman to contemplate man's transience in terms (and words) just like those of Hopkins' poem:

> We look at the *bloom of youth* with interest, yet with pity; and the more graceful and sweet it is, with pity so much the more; for, whatever be its excellence and its glory, soon it begins to be *deformed and dishonoured* by the very force of its living on. . . . *How beautiful is the human heart, when it puts forth its first leaves, and opens and rejoices in its spring-tide.* Fair as may be the bodily form, fairer far, in its *green foliage and bright blossoms*, is natural virtue. It *blooms* in the young, like some *rich* flower, so delicate, so fragrant, and so dazzling. . . . --are not these beautiful?

Yet, Newman reminds us, beauty and innocence in Nature and in humankind are insufficient. The cautionary turn of the sermon is the same as the sonnet's. If not cut off early, "the bright soul" is corrupted and transformed. "For moroseness, and misanthropy, and selfishness, is the ordinary winter of that spring." And in both the sole antidote is said to be a timely recourse to dogmatic religion.

In "The Invisible World" (*Parochial* IV, xiii) Newman readily acknowledges "the power and virtue hidden in things which are seen," to be momentarily manifested at God's will. The following excerpt particularly resembles the thought and expression of Hopkins' "Spring," including the Catholic terms of the final typological deferring of Nature's active beauty to its decidedly *non*-natural counterpart:

> Let these be your thoughts my brethren, *especially in the spring season*, when the whole face of nature is *so rich and beautiful*. . . . Then the leaves come out, and the *blossoms on the fruit trees and flowers*; and the grass and corn spring up. There is a *sudden rush* and *burst outwardly* of that hidden life which God

> has lodged in the material world. Well, that shows you, as by a sample, what it can do at God's command, when He gives the word. This earth, which now buds forth in leaves and blossoms, will one day burst forth into a new world of light and glory, in which, we shall see Saints and Angels dwelling. . . .

Besides the distinct verbal parallels, the style of this whole section of the sermon shares Hopkins' emphasis on the suddenness, the bursting *springiness*, with which the secret meaning of natural beauty discloses itself. Still, for both writers, nature's best is but nature, is but an encouraging analogy for another "new world" evoked in orthodox Christian terms.

In all these examples, then, Hopkins fully "meets" and "greets" the worldly beauty to which his poet's eye and mind were so extraordinarily attuned, going on to "bless" experiences "understood" by the theological mind as God's gracious addenda to revealed doctrine. He must also have felt that Newman's writings were an authoritative encouragement to persevere with this poetry of impulse and devotion. Still, the attitude of Newman was always more subdued than what we have seen so far in Hopkins. Newman rarely fails to insist that joy in natural objects and in legitimate religious inferences from them are riskier and less reliable means of real spiritual apprehension than are chastened meditation on religious doctrine, assent to the inner voice of conscience, and resort to the prescribed ordinances of the Catholic Church. With time, however, the poetry of Hopkins did draw closer to Newman's more sober view and towards a less oblique acknowledgement of the moral ambiguity, the practical and theoretical hazards of merely earthly beauty. Not accidentally, a gradual shift in his subject matter was occurring at the same time.

There is in the poems of Hopkins' middle period a greater preoccupation with human beauty, juxtaposed even more with gestures of corrective dogmatic scrupulosity. The anxiety Hopkins acknowledges in "Henry Purcell"

(45) or "The Loss of the Eurydice" (41) about the beauty that has "listed to a heresy," and the theories by which he seeks to excuse it, are paradigmatic. "The Soldier" (63) gently disparages our (merely natural?) inclination to associate beauty with goodness and heroism: the heart "gives a guess . . . hopes . . . makesbelieve . . . fancies, feigns, deems, dears . . . And fain will find as sterling all as all is smart." Instead, the same poem continues, we should "Mark Christ our King"--turn to a better example of both heroism and judgement. Even in "Ribblesdale" (58)--a poem more distinctly about "sweet Earth" itself--we find that although the natural world still looks "rich" and "lovely" and "strong," in fact it "canst but only be." Silent, inert, and fragile, the world's "appeal" (in this case an appearance of "care and dear concern") is for better or worse just a mirroring or echoing back of the mind of the beholder ("dear and dogged man"). In general, then, Hopkins' intimations of divinity in nature are increasingly bemused ones, dwelling on such themes as the transience and unreliability--almost never the moral threat--of earthly beauty. What is implicit in the more joyous nature poems of the earlier period becomes explicit, delight subsumed by concern, beauty by truth. The visible universe of things is less and less in the foreground. Instead, the service nature renders to God simply by virtue of being is now set over against human obligation. This can also be seen earlier, as in "The Sea and the Skylark" (35) or "In the Valley of the Elwy" (34), but now--in "Ribblesdale" or "Kingfishers" (57), for example--it is the primary concern. It is as if the poet finds himself turning inexorably to the radical implications of the question he asks Margaret in "Spring and Fall" (55):

> Leaves, like the things of man, you
> With your fresh thought care for, can you?

The paradox pressed itself more and more upon Hopkins, though still declared in image patterns that had long been habitual. Here are lines from "On the Portrait of Two Beautiful Young People" (157), a fragment rehearsing more severely a situation, language, and theme developed years before in "Spring":

> A juice rides rich through bluebells, in vine leaves,
> And beauty's dearest veriest vein is tears.
> . . .
> But ah, bright forelock, cluster that you are
> Of favoured make and mind and health and youth,
> Where lies your landmark, seamark, or soul's star?
> There's none but truth can stead you. Christ is truth.
> . . .
> None good but God--a warning waved. . . .
> Worst will the best.

The full scope of this tonal amplification in Hopkins' later nature poetry is undoubtedly anticipated in the sinister "Spelt from Sibyl's Leaves" (61), where "earth her being has unbound; her dapple is at end." Now the heart's only response is to make the ending of natural beauty a cautionary analogy for the stark moral dichotomy of "black, white ǀ right wrong" and of another "world" hereafter where "but these ǀ two tell." Abandonment by nature is "Our tale, O our oracle," and its lesson is, to borrow terms from a much lighter-hearted verse, "*Im*mortal beauty is death with duty."

Yet in Hopkins' own sterner, more Newmanesque juxtaposition of natural beauty and supernatural grace I don't find what many other readers have considered a debilitating conflict of desires, a tension between vision and dogma. But we undoubtedly do see a change from the poet's earlier concentration on what his supernaturalizing mind's eye perceives as blessed and sanctioned by God. His focus of attention has gradually shifted from the religious meaning of natural beauty to the proper human *use* of it. He did not so much renounce his earlier vein as change his concerns to matters of beauty far more subtle and problematic in their moral bearings. To human beauty alone is the moral and spiritual consideration applicable because, as Hopkins and Newman both contended, man alone was created in God's own image with a duty to give God glory (and to do so knowingly). Man is to do this by adding the beauties of grace within to those of nature without. Brute beauty is but dim glory after all.

As mentioned above, one of Newman's best-known Catholic sermons--in a collection very familiar to Hopkins--contrasts the pure loveliness of the Blessed Virgin with earthly beauty ("dangerous to look upon"). "The Glories of Mary for the Sake of Her Son" (*Discourses* XVII) is directed to Protestants (and "wavering faithful"?), its apologetic theme indicated well enough by the second part of the title. Here is the context of the particular remark about dangerous beauty:

> In thee, O Mary, is fulfilled, as we can bear it, an original purpose of the Most High. *He once had meant to come on earth in heavenly glory*, but we sinned, and then he could not safely visit us, except with a *shrouded radiance* and a *bedimmed Majesty*, for He was God. So He came in weakness, not in power; and He sent thee, a creature, in His stead, *with a creature's comeliness and lustre suited to our state. . . . not like earthly beauty, dangerous to look upon*, but like the morning star, which is thy emblem, bright and musical, breathing purity and telling of heaven, and infusing peace. O harbinger of day! O hope of the pilgrim! lead us still as thou hast led; in the dark night, across the bleak wilderness, guide us on to our Lord Jesus, *guide us home.*

Features of Newman's thought and language in this sermon are interestingly similar to details in a poem by Hopkins on much the same subject. In "The Blessed Virgin Compared to the Air We Breathe" (60), the poet too praises her fairness while defining her mediatory role between God and mankind.

The poet likens it in this respect to the function of our earth's atmosphere. As part of a considerate divine dispensation, her "one work" serves to "Let God's *glory* through," to "transmit" light ("sifted to suit our sight') that would otherwise have been the blinding "glory bare" that obtained when "God was god *of* old." A closing prayer begs her to "Fold *home*, fast fold thy child." Even so, this role is ancillary and subordinate:

> Yet no part but what will
> Be Christ our Saviour still.

Hence Hopkins' insistence, and Newman's, that while a natural or creaturely mediation is "dear" and "does no prejudice" it is not provided for its own sake. As we have seen, this qualification is typical of Hopkins' nature verse; indeed, his behest in this poem that the Blessed Virgin

> Stir in my ears, speak there
> Of God's love, O live air,
> Of *patience, penance, prayer,*

is a gesture quite like the ending of "The Starlight Night." But an equally striking affinity between the Marian poem and a text by Newman is the vivid conceit of diffusive atmosphere employed by both writers to illustrate God's use of this world as a means of enhancing His glory and mitigating His otherwise dazzling power. Hopkins' version of the motif is epitomized in these lines:

> Whereas did air not make
> This bath of blue and slake
> His fire, *the sun would shake,*
> *A blear and blinding ball*
> *With blackness bound, and all*
> *The thick stars round him roll*
> *Flashing like flecks of coal,*
> *Quartz-fret, or sparks of salt,*

> *In grimy vasty vault.*
>
> . . .
>
> Through her we may see him
> Made sweeter, not made dim,
> And *her hand leaves his light
> Sifted to suit our sight.*

In an Anglican sermon, "Infant Baptism" (*Parochial* 3, 20), Newman had used an almost identical analogy to explain the necessity of sacraments to "bring home" God's grace to His people:

> What an inactive useless world this would be, *if the sun's light did not diffuse itself through the air* and fall on all objects around us, enabling us to see earth and sky as well as the sun itself. *Cannot we conceive nature so constituted that the sun appeared as a bright spot in the heavens, while the heavens themselves were black as in the starlight, and the earth dark as night?* Such would have been our religious state, had not our Lord applied and diversified and poured to and fro, in heat and light, those *heavenly glories* which are concentrated in Him. He should shine upon us from above in all His high attributes and offices, as the Prophet, Priest, and King of His elect; but how should we bring *home* His grace to ourselves?

Besides the remarkable textual parallelism here, we find implied again in both the theory of "economy" by which alone this world's valid but "sifted" communication of God is to be appreciated. Of course Hopkins shares Newman's perception of the different effects on man of Mary's and nature's mediations. In this poem she is said to allay "The deathdance in his blood," whereas, in another, merely mortal beauty is "dangerous; does *set* dancing blood."

"The Leaden Echo and the Golden Echo" (59) is Hopkins' own version of a dialogue of self and soul, or of two inner voices. The pagan

Leaden Echo advances the counsel of despair, lamenting the fleetingness of mortal beauty, whereas the Golden Echo claims there is one way to preserve it. Ephemeral human beauty, so "dearly and dangerously sweet", can indeed be "fastened with the tenderest truth/ To its own best being," but only if we "freely forfeit" it and prefer "beauty-in-the-ghost." What we "resign" will be kept for us "yonder" by God with a "fonder" and "finer" care than we are capable of.

> Give beauty back, beauty, beauty, beauty, back to God,
> beauty's self and beauty's giver.

Plainly, then, the danger in mortal beauty is not in itself but in our tendency to rely on it or to become preoccupied with its loss or possession. Instead, one must realize that man's best self, sweetest beauty, cannot be or depend on that which fades. The thought and language of both parts of this dramatic poem corresponds to some of Newman's writings more fully than can be illustrated here, but the thought and language of one parallel passage is worth citing. In "Scripture a Record of Human Sorrow" (*Parochial* I, xxv), Newman does direct the lesson of human infirmity towards the resolution uttered by Hopkins' "Golden Echo." The sermon refers to all of this world's pleasures (not exclusively to beauty) in pointing out that "our *danger* is on the side, not of undervaluing, but of overvaluing them, . . ." Sorrow, Newman says, is "a gracious *gift from God* sent to us, as a remedy for all *dangerous* overflowing joy in present blessing, in order to save us far greater pain (if we use the lesson well), the pain of actual disappointment, such as the overthrow of vainly cherished hopes of lasting good upon earth, will certainly occasion."

> The true Christian rejoices in those earthly things which give joy, but in such a way as not to care much for them when they go. *For no blessing does he care much, except those which are immortal*, knowing that he shall receive all such again *in the*

> *world to come.* But the least and the most *fleeting,* he is too religious to condemn, considering them *God's gift;* and the least and most fleeting, *thus received,* yield *a purer and deeper, though a less tumultuous joy.*

This is the attitude of Hopkins in "The Golden Echo" and, to one extent or another, in the deference that touches most of his otherwise "tumultuous" nature poems.

We come finally to the poem actually named "To what serves Mortal Beauty?" It is informed by much the same conclusion as "The Golden Echo." Even such "lovely" things as do serve divine ends and advance Catholic faith in this world should nevertheless be subordinated to a "better beauty." In this case the beauty instanced is again chiefly that of persons, but the worth of all natural loveliness is implied. And its bright force is, Hopkins declares, "*dangerous*; does set dancing blood." It has a use: "See: it does this: keeps warm/Men's wits to the things that are; what good means." Indeed, in glancing at the idolatries fostered in simple religiously-disposed heathens, this poem specifically brings together beauty, danger, and false religion. And I think the historical illustration, England's conversion to Roman Catholicism, is one that Hopkins borrows from Newman. According to a legend that Newman was particularly fond of citing in his more hortatory works, Britain was originally converted to Christianity after Pope Gregory became so charmed by the physical beauty of Anglo-Saxon prisoners in Rome that he sent missionaries to the island. Here are Hopkins' lines:

> Those lovely lads once, wet-fresh | windfalls of war's storm,
> How then should Gregory, a father, | have gleaned else from swarm-
> ed Rome? But God to a nation | dealt that day's dear chance.
> To man, that needs would worship | block or barren stone....

So it is, Hopkins says, that mortal beauty, though "dangerous," is also "heaven's sweet gift," and can serve at least to promote the fulfillment here on earth of divine purposes. Newman refers often to this story of Gregory's resolution and to the beauty in God's own eyes of the Anglo-Saxon people. For example, in "Christ upon the Waters" (*Sermons... Various* IX) Newman remarks that because the *idol-worshipping* English were "too fair to be heathen," God "looked once again" and "determined in this instance in His free mercy to unite what was beautiful in nature with what was radiant in grace." The historical circumstances of the great conversion of the Anglo-Saxons were a result of "the love of justice, manly bearing, and tenderness of heart, *which Gregory saw in their very faces*." In "The Second Spring" (*Sermons... Various* X) Newman speaks of the transience of human beauty, but he ends that sermon too by referring to the "fair bright haired Saxon youths" at Rome. "What do then?" asks Hopkins' poem; "how meet beauty?" The ready answer, perhaps by now predictably, is:

> Merely meet it; own,
> Home at heart, heaven's sweet gift; | then leave, leave that alone.
> Yea, wish that though, wish all, | God's better beauty, grace.

Here is the resolution upon which was based Hopkins' whole intellectual and poetic practice with regard to the dangerous splendors of the "World's loveliest." This poem's language of natural "flashing" and "selving," and of the heart's legitimate "meeting" and "gleaning" phenomena that are indeed "heaven's sweet gift," makes it continuous with Hopkins' earlier work. What also persists, though more frankly, is the glancing at "danger" and "Mastery" and at the duty of "merely" acknowledging the intimation and "*then*" desiring to "leave" aside all attachment to natural beauty in favor of supernatural "better beauty, grace." Nor is this a friction or an ascetic repudiation:

Our law says: Love what are | love's worthiest, *were all known*;

The "law"--Catholic, Hopkinsean, and Newmanesque--is that we are entirely free to "greet" and "bless" natural beauty "*when*" we do "understand" the relation of good to better: "what good means . . . were all known."

That "law" is also, I think, the informing principle of Hopkins' nature poetry. If it is a poetry of tension, the strain comes not of a conflict between imagination and religion, between impulse and conscience. Rather, it lies in the poet's resolution to dissociate the glowing rhetoric of his verse from the Romantic nature-worship or deistic natural theology it might otherwise resemble. In resisting, even recoiling from, those tendencies in contemporary literature and thought, Hopkins has no doubt employed strategies and left textual traces of strain or pressure that many readers ascribe instead to a repressive self-regulation. Effects of the sort that Bridges, again, assumed came of efforts on his friend's part to "force emotion into theological or sectarian channels." And of course such interpretations are at least partially right, and quite natural. But if Hopkins' religious transmutation of mortal beauty, as expressed in the verse, is finally somewhat provisional or deferential, it may be less a "forcing" of one set of religious assumptions than a dexterous eschewing of another. The analogy and probable influence of Newman's works in this regard may confirm, moreover, that the literary conduct of Hopkins' nature poetry is rather more "sermonic" and dramatic than personally "confessional," its caveats more monitory or punctilious than self-estranged.

Works Cited

Moore, Michael D. "Newman and the Motif of Intellectual Pain in Hopkins's 'Terrible Sonnets.'" *Mosaic* 12.4 (1979): 29-46.

---. "Newman and the 'Second Spring' of Hopkins's Poetry." *Hopkins Quarterly* 6.3 (1979): 119-137.

Newman, John Henry. *Apologia Pro Vita Sua*. Ed. Martin J. Svaglic. Oxford: Clarendon Press, 1967.

---. *Certain Difficulties Felt by Anglicans in Catholic Teaching*. London: Longmans, Green and Co., 1850.

---. *Discourses Addressed to Mixed Congregations*. London: Longmans, Green and Co., 1849.

---. *Discussions and Arguments on Various Subjects*. London: Longmans, Green and Co., 1918.

---. *Fifteen Sermons Preached Before the University of Oxford*. London: Rivingtons, 1871.

---. *Parochial and Plain Sermons*. London: Rivingtons, 1868.

---. *Sayings of Cardinal Newman*. Dublin: Carraig Books, 1976.

---. *Sermons Preached on Various Occasions*. London: Burns and Oates, 1857.

Hopkins and Pindar

Raymond V. Schoder, S.J.

There is no one in Greek literature quite like Pindar in concept and style, though there are many resemblances to him in Aeschylus. No English poet is a close parallel to Hopkins in his remarkable combination of qualities. Yet these two, Pindar and Hopkins, are strikingly like one another in many aspects of their style, thought, and use of language. Each is essentially unique and extraordinary, characterized by literary features that are "counter, original, spare, strange" (37), the distinctive marks of original and dynamic minds, dealing "out that being indoors each one dwells" (57). Hopkins and Pindar were essentially kindred spirits and the artistic expression of their inner visions and emotions therefore ended up in styles of language that are also cognate. I wish to analyze here some of these shared aspects of self-expression and look into the soil and roots from which they spring. The results will not be wholly original; they have not passed entirely unnoticed by others; but their collocation may be of use toward appreciating more fully the special merits and delightful genius of these towering poetic giants.

Pindar's fame is based on many aspects of his work. Down the ages there has been awed amazement at the virtuosity of his fancy, his language, and his rhythm. Quintilian (10.1.61) rated Pindar far ahead of the other Greek lyric poets for grandeur of spirit, striking expressions and imagery, and an unrivalled abundance of thought and words in a veritable flood of eloquence so great that Horace justifiably believed that no one could imitate him. Horace's own praise (*Odes* 4.2.1-27) compares Pindar to an over-flowing mountain torrent seething and rushing in a vast flood of deep speech, or to a swan soaring aloft on strong blasts of inspiration as he drives upward to the clouds where he is, as Merlet adds (131), sometimes lost to our sight. Gray, in *The Progress of Poesy*, sketches Pindar's genius in similar terms as that

... ample pinion
That the Theban eagle bare,
Sailing with supreme dominion
Through the azure deep of air.

Jebb (142) notes Pindar's "irresistible power" and "immense resources of imagery and expression." His words seem to strain and rock with the richness of implication he has forced into them under the high pressure of his soaring visions. He has an instinct for grandeur, delighting in strong thoughts and splendor of imagery that throws glistening light on human events by the brilliant opalescence of his language.

One element of Pindar's verbal artistry is his rich play of descriptive terms. As Gildersleeve notes, "The word 'splendor' and all its synonyms seem to be made for Pindar. He drains dry the Greek vocabulary of words for light and bright, shine and shimmer, glitter and glister, ray and radience, flame and flare and flash, gleam and glow, burn and blaze" (xxxvi).

Another is bold metaphor: A people's ruler is a ship's helmsman (*P*.1.86), wealth is a shining star (*O*.2.54-56), ephemeral man is a dream of a shadow (*P*.8.95), a poem is outpoured nectar, sweet fruit of the mind (*O*.7.8-9), and so on in inexhaustible creativity.

A device which adds opulence to Pindar's language is his frequent use of compound epithets: Zeus is ἐγχεικέραυνος--using the thunderbolt like a spear (*O*.13.77); or when he is hurling gleaming lightning he is φοινικοστερόπας (*O*.9.6). Because words dominate and determine the music which interprets them in an ode, we hear of ἀναξιφόρμιγγες ὕμνοι (*O*.2.1). A three-time victor in the Games is hailed as τρισολυμπιονίκας (*O*.13.1). Many of these highly-charged descriptive adjectives are not found elsewhere and are likely Pindar's own creation. Horace admired him for this inventiveness: *nova . . . verba devolvit* (*O*.4.2.11). Further examples would be ποικιλοφόρμιγξ for a song accompanied by the lyre with varied notes (*O*.4.3) and ποικιλόγαρυς for the many-voiced lyre itself (*O*.3.8).

Pindar's language is consistently lofty, elevated, radiating power and grandeur. A splendid example is the great First Pythian ode, perhaps the peak of Pindar's achievement. I have analyzed elsewhere its structure, imagery, music, and use of words (Schoder 401-412). It is surely one of the highest achievements of poetic art: admirable, enjoyable, uplifting, inspiring. The words exert such taut explosiveness of content, the imagery sweeps along with such vibrant opulence, the thought weaves in and out of its complex symmetrical framework in so intricate a fugue formation that the reader is justifiably moved to an exclamation of bewilderment:

Pindar sings
In lofty tone far-off, majestic things--
Ah! earth-born scarce can hear, so far, so high!
(North 4)

The ode's wealth of thought and jets of imagery are matched by the rapidity and thunderous power of its language and melody. The result is naturally difficult to absorb, but worth the effort of repeated meticulous attention.

Pindar skillfully uses alliteration and internal assonance and rhyme, such as ἕλε Βελλεροφόντας (*O*.13.84) or οὔ τί που οὗτος (*P*.4.87). His masterful control of rhythm and meter is evidence of genius, a marvel of art. It is logaoedic in the Dorian choral pattern, lifting us, as Farnell says (378), and taking possession of us like melodious thunder. Whatever metrical structure Pindar establishes for his opening strophes is meticulously paralleled in the following antistrophe and in later strophe / antistrophe groups throughout the ode. The intervening epodes have their own somewhat different pattern, to eliminate monotony. Occasional substitutions in individual feet within the musical phrases (κῶλα) introduce a bit of "play," like "entasis" in a Doric column, to keep the impression of life and human touch, rather than of coldly perfect mathematical repetition, a Teutonic regularity and inflexibility which some metrical analysts falsely foist on living Greek musical structure. At the other extreme is Horace's calumny that Pindar's rhythms are capricious: *numerisque fertur / lege solutis* (*O* 4.2.11-12). Thomson (80) shows with what skill and conscious purpose Pindar could shift his metre from a falling to a rising rhythm and back again, in accordance with the shifts in the sense and feeling of the words. The subtlety of effect is one of the most beautiful aspects of Pindar's poetic art.

On a larger plane than that of individual words and their sound is Pindar's skill at clustering his images around some central key word or idea. Norwood (99) has developed this principle convincingly, showing that Pindar's method of composition is his own. It is non-logical. The poet broods on his theme emotionally until his imagination finds some sensible object around which the topics and imagery may crystallize. The resultant unity of the poem is not logical but aesthetic. The key to the imagery and diction stands outside the poem, revealed by some significant word that points to the unifying symbol. For example, in *Pythian* 1, the key is the

Golden Lyre, which stands for music, the principle of order and harmony, while the war, volcano, Typhon, and barbarians at Cumae represent disorder.

Another over-arching device in Pindaric structure is the technique of raising the individual event which occasions the victory ode into the plane of universal truths and significance. The particular achievement fades into the background as Pindar's imagination lifts the transitory event to the plane of absolute values, the eternal prevalence of good over evil, of the beautiful over the base, until the victor is transformed and sublimated into a glorious personification of life at its most glorious.[1] Such a triumph of thought and art constitute Pindar's title to ὀπιθόμβροτον αὔχημα δόξας (*P*.1.95), the boast of a glory that lives after the man himself.

It is clear that Hopkins, as a result of his study of Greek literature at Oxford under Jowett and others, knew Pindar well and greatly admired him. When teaching Greek at Stonyhurst and in Dublin, Hopkins studied Pindar and Greek drama intensely and started writing a book on their metrical art. In December of 1886 he wrote his friend Baillie: "very serious work touching Pindar and the theory of rhythm and the 'Dorian Measure' is on, but I cannot do what I would for want of mathematics" (*F* 275). He had already two months earlier told Bridges: "I have made a great and solid discovery about Pindar or rather about the Dorian and Aeolian Measures or Rhythms and hope to publish something when I have read some more" (*B* 228-9). He explained to Bridges three weeks later that his great discovery, on which he hoped to publish, was that

> The Dorian bar is originally *a march step in three-time executed in four steps to the bar.* Out of this simple combination of

---

[1] See Gildersleeve xviii, xliv; Finley 77.

> numbers, three and four, simple to state but a good deal more complicated than any rhythm we have, arose the structure of most of Pindar's odes and most of the choral odes of the drama. (*B* 233)

He continued:

> Pindar and all the poets continually pass from heavier feet . . . to lighter . . . where by the stress falling sometimes on a long or crochet, sometimes on a short or quaver, a beautiful variety is given. . . . With all this the rhythm came to have an infinite flexibility, of which the Greeks seem never to have tired. (*B* 234)

In January 1887, he wrote to Dixon from Dublin:

> I have done some part of a book on Pindar's metres and Greek metres in general and metre in general and almost on art in general and wider still, but that I shall ever get far on with it or, if I do, sail through all the rocks and shoals that lie before me I scarcely dare to hope and yet I do greatly desire, since the thoughts are well worth preserving: they are a solid foundation for criticism.
>
> (*D* 150)

In February 1887, he again mentioned this project to Baillie: "What I want if possible to get done first is a book on the Dorian Measure, one of the rhythms employed by Pindar and the other lyric poets, the most important and the least understood" (*F* 276).

In other letters, Hopkins asserts that his use of what he termed Sprung Rhythm has precedents in Greek and in early English and some later poetry:

> That piece of mine is very highly wrought. The long lines are not rhythm run to seed: everything is weighed and timed in them. Wait till they have taken hold of your ear and you will find it so.

No, but what it *is* like is the rhythm of Greek tragic choruses or of Pindar: which is pure sprung rhythm. (*B* 157)

Back in January 1881 he told Bridges that he has "set music to . . . the words ἀναξιφόρμιγγες ὕμνοι in Pindar" and gives a transcription of it. (*B* 123). Note that he carefully says the music is set to the words, in true Pindaric spirit, not the words set to music, as is the usual English expression. In 1863 his Diary notes Pindar's phrase Ὠκεανοῦ πέταλα and relates it to Plutarch's πέταλα πυρίνα for stars and neatly compares Shakespeare's "See how the floor of heaven is thick inlaid with patines of bright gold" (*J* 11). In November 1882 he urges Bridges to follow Pindar's principle of making a porch to his song that shines afar: "the frontispiece, Pindar says, χρὴ θέμεν τηλαυγές"--a citation of Olympian Ode 6.3-4 (*B* 159). He told Bridges in June, 1882, that his projected, unfinished ode on Edmund Campion is "dithyrambic or what they used to call Pindaric (which as we have Pindar now is unPindaric), I mean in variable stanzas and not antistrophic; like *Alexander's Feast* or *Lycidas*. It has some new rhythmical effects" (*B* 147). In one of his notebooks at Campion Hall is his musical scansion, made in Dublin, of Pindar's Third Isthmian, lines 7 and 15-16 (Cited in Gardner 99).

It is clear from all this that Hopkins was long and closely familiar with Pindar in Greek. How did this affect his poetic style? Not, I submit, by extensive *imitation*, but rather he drew from his knowledge of Pindar support for his own personal poetic ideals and manner of expression. Hopkins' style flowed directly from his own genius and poetic taste. But he found in Pindar and in Greek tragic choral lyric a kindred way of speech which encouraged him to maintain his own remarkable style, so different from most English usage, especially in the Victorian Age. Hopkins "inscaped" his language in the Pindaric pattern by native instinct. As

Gardner says,

> a deep knowledge and love of Greek undoubtedly helped to shape Hopkins' genius for subtle and idiosyncratic expression. . . . For Hopkins, Greek lyric poetry provided a definite criterion of perfection in matters of rhythm and texture, form and rhetoric--aspects of poetry in the fusion of which are united the *inwardness* of thought and emotion and the *outwardness* of movement and expression. (121, 131)

Bender agrees: Hopkins' principle of composition was similar to Pindar's though perhaps not consciously so. Study of Greek lyric odes may have reinforced a fundamental proclivity toward a non-logical structure in his poetry (96). Hines asserts that Hopkins' debt to Pindar goes beyond metrical devices to be, as it were, the substructure of Hopkins' entire aesthetic (294-307). Less than a year before he died, Hopkins wrote Bridges from Dublin that "The effect of studying masterpieces is to make me admire and do otherwise. So it must be on every original artist to some degree, on me to a marked degree. Perhaps then more reading would only *refine my singularity*, which is not what you want" (*B* 291).

It is notable that for all his knowledge and admiration of Greek literature in general, Hopkins did not develop a neo-classical style: urbane, limpid, polished, tightly logical (Bender 4). This shows the strength of his own inspiration. Neither is Pindar like most other Classical writers. He and Hopkins followed their own distinctive impulses and visions--which happen to be in remarkable agreement.

There are few explicit echoes of Pindaric thought or phrase. One might be in the poem on St. Alphonsus Rodriguez: "Honor is flashed off exploit, so we say" (73), which could have roots in Pindar's λάμπει δε οἱ κλέος (*O*.1.23), as perhaps also does the principle in the "Windhover" (36) that fire breaks out from valorous struggle. Hopkins' oft-used epithets "pied" and "dappled" are at least paralleled by Pindar's joyful ποικ λος which he employs time after time in itself or its cognates and compounds. Gardner thinks that Pindar's phrase φεὸς ὁ πάντα τεύχων βροτοῖς (Frag. 130) "almost certainly inspired the original opening of the *Deutschland*: 'God mastering me / Giver of breath and bread' and no less the more clearly 'instressed' final version: 'Thou mastering me, / God! giver of breath and bread'" (Gardner 122). Cotter sees Pindaric tone in the line in the "Wreck of the Deutschland" (28, st.33), "with a love glides / Lower than death and the dark"--both poets hailing their champion in the struggle against death and dark and in the race toward being and light (Cotter 155). In the vision expressed in the "Wreck" that God's impact on human life through natural causes "rides time like riding a river" (st. 6), one may see a reflection of Pindar's "the Olympian Father's glory flowing throughout time (αἐναον)" (*O*.14.12).

Beyond such verbal parallels, there are many more general similarities of design and spirit between Hopkins and Pindar. Exclamation is a technique characteristic of Pindar, often in conjunction with personification. A notable example of the same in Hopkins is "And you were a liar, O blue March day" in the "Eurydice" (41, st. 6). Both poets celebrate the wild beauty of Nature and manly strength, patience in the face of adversity and sorrow, the brevity of life; both have recourse to archaic or local meanings of words; both unify their poems around related imagery rather than by logical inter-relation of ideas.

Hopkins, like Pindar, exuberantly coins words and phrases of striking originality: "lovely-asunder starlight" (28, st. 5); "The heavenflung, heart-fleshed, maiden-furled / Miracle-in- Mary-of-flame" (28 st. 34); "worlds of wanwood leafmeal lie" (55); "skies/ Betweenpie mountains" (69); "thunder-purple seabeach" (45) and many more in glorious profusion of creativity that "fans fresh our wits with wonder" (45). Hopkins' piling up of epithets, unrivalled by any poet, may be considered super-Pindaric: "Earnest, earthless, equal, attuneable, ¹ vaulty, voluminous, . . . stupendous / Evening (61). Pindar himself would have loved and envied that!

Hopkins was acutely sensitive to the music of words. He recommended to Dixon his "Leaden Echo and Golden Echo" (59): "I never did anything more musical" (*D* 149). Mariani remarks that the music of that poem has its antecedents in Pindar's epinician odes and in plainsong (186), while Gardner says,

> Much of this musical effect was due to the influence of the complex or accumulated rhythm ($\mu\acute{\varepsilon}\tau\rho ov\ \acute{\varepsilon}\pi\iota\sigma\acute{v}\nu\varphi\varepsilon\tau ov$) of Greek melic poetry, which Hopkins himself calls 'individual metres'-- invented for the occasion: one ode, as in Pindar, or even one 'system', as in the dramatists and not repeated even by the inventor, much less others."[2]

Hopkins' poems "pour and pelt music" like a skylark (35). For example the melodious lines:

> As tumbled over rim in roundy wells
> Stones ring; like each tucked string tells, each hung bell's
> Bow swung finds tongue to fling out broad its name.
>
> (57)

The most extensively Pindaric of Hopkins' poems is the "Wreck of the Deutschland," which Cotter calls "a Pindaric song of triumph in Christ's victory over chaos and death" (152). Mariani says it is

> the one English ode to have captured the Pindaric spirit. Hopkins, like Pindar, is a metaphysical in his shaping power; for

---

[2] Gardner (101) is here quoting Hopkins' notes, kept at Campion Hall, on Bergk's *Poetae Lyrici Graeci*.

the most diverse and seemingly disparate subjects and ideas are
interwoven, or better, welded into an artistic whole. (73)

Hopkins himself points out to Bridges the parallel:

The Deutschland would be more generally interesting if there were more wreck and less discourse, I know, but still it is an ode and not primarily a narrative. There is some narrative in Pindar but the principal business is lyrical. (*B* 49)

The stanzaic pattern of strophe-antistrophe-epode, characteristic of Pindar, is however here lacking. But the effect of sprung rhythm and the logaoedic structure of the meter and repetition of metrical pattern in recurring stanzas is openly in Pindar's tradition, as is the power and opulence of language and the rhythm dominating the ear. But for all that, the style is unmistakably Hopkins' own, unique in English and of profound influence on later poets. As in a Pindaric ode, the thought of the "Wreck" is not arranged in a logical progression but rather is unified around a key word, what Hopkins called "the underthought" (*F* 252-3), here *water*, which symbolizes God's power and mercy: Hopkins is filled with grace like water in a well; the passengers experience the terrible power of God at sea; the nun is swept to a heavenly haven; God is asked to shower mercy on England; God is the "sway of the sea," "master of the tides, / Of the Yore-flood, of the gulf's sides . . . Stanching, quenching ocean of a motionable mind . . . With a mercy that outrides / The all of water, and ark / For the listener" (St. 1, 32, 33).[3] This great poem is vastly more truly Pindaric than what used to be called such in the histories of English literature.

Hopkins handled the traditional sonnet formula with bold originality, often turning it into an ode with all that form's orchestral richness and

---

[3] *Cf.* Bender 83-95.

emotional impact. McChesney remarks of "Harry Ploughman" (71) that "[t]he elements of chorus and solemn refrain in this poem make it more a Pindaric ode than a descriptive sonnet" (170). Hines cites the sonnet on St. Alphonsus Rodriguez (73) as an example of the way in which Hopkins' imagination transmuted Pindaric imagery: Hellenic praise of *aretè* becomes "Honour flashed off exploit" and the heroic struggle is transferred to "the war within" (301).

There can be no doubt that both Pindar and Hopkins are unique among their peers while remarkably similar in genius to each other. Nor is there any doubt that Pindar inspired Hopkins in specific and generic ways, and supplied him precedent and courage to carry on his poetic style, so "original, spare, strange" (37) as his brilliant highly individual mind, "Of realty the rarest-vinèd unraveller; a not / Rivalled insight" (44) impelled him to speak, sometimes unbidden and against his will, as he confessed. Pindar was a model, support, and kindred spirit. But it is Hopkins' own dynamic genius which accounts for the power and splendor of his poetry,

    the roll, the rise, the carol, the creation. (76)
    The achieve of, the mastery of the thing! (36)

Works Cited

Bender, Todd K. *Gerard Manley Hopkins: The Classical Background and Critical Reception of his Work.* Baltimore: Johns Hopkins Press, 1966.

Bowra, C. M., ed. *Pindar.* Oxford: Clarendon Press, 1964.

Cotter, James Finn. *Inscape: The Christology of Gerard Manley Hopkins.* Pittsburgh: University of Pittsburgh Press, 1972.

Farnell, Lewis R. *The Works of Pindar.* Vol. 1. London: Macmillan, 1930-32.

Finley, John H. *Pindar and Aeschylus.* Cambridge: Harvard UP, 1955.

Gardner, W.H. *Gerard Manley Hopkins: A Study of Poetic Idiosyncrasy in Relation to Poetic Tradition.* Vol. 2. New Haven: Yale UP, 1949.

Gildersleeve, Basil L. *Pindar: The Olympian and Pythian Odes.* New York: Harper, 1885.

Hines, Leo. "Pindaric Imagery in G.M. Hopkins." *The Month* 29 (May, 1963): 294-307.

Jebb, Richard C. *The Growth and Influence of Classical Greek Poetry.* 1893. New York: Gordian Press, 1970.

Mariani, Paul L. *A Commentary on the Complete Poems of Gerard Manley Hopkins.* Ithaca: Cornell UP, 1970.

McChesney, Donald. *A Hopkins Commentary.* London: University of London Press, 1968.

Merlet, Gustave. *Études litteraires sur les grands classiques Grecs.* Paris: Hachette, 1893.

North, Robert C., S.J. "An Eagle Not of Earth." *Classical Bulletin* 16 (1939): 4.

Norwood, G. *Pindar.* Berkeley: University of California Press, 1945.

Schoder, Raymond V., S.J. "The Artistry of the First Pythian Ode." *Classical Journal* 38 (1943): 401-12.

Thomson, G. *Greek Lyric Metres.* Cambridge: W. Heffer, 1929.

"Freshness Deep Down Things"
Hopkins' Dublin Notes on Homer
Warren Anderson

In his descriptive catalogue, "The Manuscripts of Gerard Manley Hopkins," under the heading "*M. Notes on the Classics*," Fr. Anthony Bischoff describes Item V as

> forty-five small pages in a folded sheet of paper headed "notes on Hom. Il. 4. 5. 6". . . . These notes on Homer's *Iliad* . . . were sent to Father Keating by Father Henry Browne, S.J., who succeeded Hopkins as professor of Greek at University College, Dublin. W.A.M. Peters, S.J., makes some use of these notes to illustrate Hopkins' approach to poetic imagery . . . ; but they merit further study. (Bischoff 576; Peters)[1]

The present essay provides a sampling of the further study that I have attempted.

There are actually sixty-five pages, measuring on the average 8.5 cm. by 11 cm., with Hopkins' notes on portions of the *Iliad*; an additional page

---

[1] A complete edition of the Homer notes is to be published in the Monograph Series of the International Hopkins Association.

is blank. He begins with a general introduction. This is followed by a commentary on passages, phrases, or single words from Books 4, 5, and 6. Three pages at the end contain notes on Book 3. The Dublin Note Book (G.II, second page) lists Books 4 and 5 under "Scholarship (Jan. '85)"; this follows lists of the readings required of candidates for the B.A. and for the M.A. All works are in Greek. The material on Homer is provided with dates at two points: "Nov. 1884" occurs early (11), with month and year only; "Feb. 12, '86" is found at the end of the commentary on Book 6 (62).[2] The manuscript is at Campion Hall, Oxford.[3]

The first page begins with a list of broad topics: "Homer-- Loose notes / Epic poetry how developed: (A) the matter, story; (B) the verse, hexameter; (C) the diction, use and variation of stock epithets etc."[4] The phrase "Loose notes" distinguishes this portion of the commentary from the notes set down on the blank pages interleaved in an edition of the *Iliad*. It may not have been available for his use until most or all of the sixty-five handwritten pages had been completed. In an entry on page 62, dated "Feb. 12, '86," he states, "After this I am going to make my notes mainly on my interleaved book." Other notes may, therefore, have existed. At any rate, none of these are known to have survived.

The division into matter, verse, and diction is abandoned once the first of these topics has been treated in some detail. The second enters

---

[2] Page numbers are mine; Hopkins used no numbering.

[3] The material is used by permission of the English Provincial of the Society of Jesus. I wish to thank the Master of Campion Hall for his helpfulness in this matter. Fr. Peter Levi, S.J., and others at Campion Hall were cordial and helpful while I was studying the remarkable collection of Hopkins manuscripts housed there.

[4] Individual entries do not end with a period, though it is used within an entry.

only as portions of lines that display metrical irregularity. Although these appear frequently, the topic with which the "Loose notes" show an overwhelming concern is the third: diction in general but above all, and to an astonishing extent, the "use and variation of stock epithets." For Hopkins, "stock" meant "in common use"; it did not have the present-day connotations of triteness and lack of variety, as his choice of "variation" indicates. His attitude becomes clear on every page, once he has begun to comment on the text.

He goes on to refer to "*Myths*, that is tales," surely an example of classroom strategy. Probably his students would have needed a reminder that *muthos* always meant "story," true or fictitious, and that in itself it never denoted a story specifically concerned with gods. Nevertheless, this makes for a shaky beginning. As a point of departure for his argument, Hopkins takes reference to household tasks from a chorus of Euripides' *Ion* (196-97). No doubt he intended the allusion to be useful, since this play had been on the "Scholarship" list of required readings along with *Iliad* 4 and 5. Unfortunately, his citation from Euripides could not move his argument along toward its desired end. Storytelling that helped a maidservant to get through her weaving does little to bring one near the male world of epic, with its predominantly male audience. Needing a giant step, Hopkins attempted to take it by suggesting that such storytelling was undertaken *kata rhabdon*, which he translated "by turns." Such, he notes, was the case with professional performances of Homer by teams of rhapsodes and the after-dinner singing of *skolia*, short traditional poems which the guests, one after another, performed to the lyre.

The attempt failed completely. "By turns" cannot render *kata rhabdon*. The phrase comes from Pindar's Isthmian victory odes (4.42); it is used when the poet is considering the fortunes of Ajax. From the tragedy by Sophocles that bears his name, we know that the hero suffered humiliation in the sight of his fellow Greeks before Troy. Homer vindicated him, according to Pindar, by honoring his greatness *kata rhabdon . . . thespesiōn epeōn* (42-43), "according to the measure of his marvellous verses."[5] For the proper meaning of this passage, see Liddell-Scott-Jones, *A Greek-English Lexicon* (s.v. *rhabdos* I.6). It had been available ever since 1843, when the first edition appeared. The one available to Hopkins was perhaps the sixth (1869) or the seventh, published in 1882 and reprinted in 1885. On the point in question, any of them would have given him the information that he needed. Obviously he had not consulted the entry, driven as he was by excessive conscientiousness about daily tasks and diminished increasingly in bodily well-being.

With scattered exceptions, the whole of the introductory essay is a fantasy of wishful thinking. For its sources, one must look to the preconceptions that had power during the later decades of the nineteenth century. These are much more evident than the contributions of the individual who is commenting; his individuality will not become apparent until the commentary proper is under way. The Victorian stance made it possible, even seemingly reasonable, to speak of securing "the story" from change and pegging down the local village tales.

Hopkins passes to another claim: "The fertile singer, poet, wd. be ready to treat the story anywhere, take it up at any point. So *Odyssey* beginning/*/hamothen*" (2). But the correct meaning of *Od.* 1. 10 *hamothen* is "at some point," and the poet gives it a diffident tone by his addition of the qualifying particle *ge*, "at least," or "at any rate." Although Hopkins had

---

[5] The story is not found in the *Iliad*; the *Odyssey* gives only a brief account (11. 543-67).

in most respects a superb command of Greek, it did not include a knowledge of the particles. So far as can be judged from the notes he took at Highgate and Oxford, his teachers had no interest in them. This was not true of Benjamin Jowett, a masterful translator of Plato, and Hopkins did attend Jowett's lectures. He does not seem to have gotten much out of them, however. His notes contain some evidence that he disliked the Master of Balliol; certainly he showed no great reverence for the high seriousness of the lectures and the lecturer.[6] From 1870 on, he might have profited from the rendering in William Walter Merry's widely used edition: "Of these things (from some point of them at least), tell us too."

He now takes further his notion of the nature and development of epic:

Verse pieces in a prose whole - Cp. the snatches in the Eddas.

. . . .

(Phemius and the Suitors. Penelope coming to listen)

The next step was to have versified every part of the story, versified the whole story: this was an epic. Then came some Homer and conceived of epic as a *kind*, with its own unity. Homer had done this: he chooses a hero, Achilles, Ulysses and an action or motive, Achilles' anger, Ulysses' return and revenge. Both are comedies (in Dante's sense) in issue, tragedies in feeling.
(3)

Poetic insertions had been an accepted part of prose narrative in English literature throughout the eighteenth century and sometimes beyond it. Hopkins now mentions for a second time the fact of their occurrence. Appealing to the Eddas does not help his case. The "Edda" ascribed to

---

[6] By contrast, he admired Riddell and apparently enjoyed his lectures on the *Odyssey*.

Snorri Sturlason is a dialogue on the art of the skald, embellished with poetic examples. In the "Poetic Edda" (to which the title of Snorri's work has been transferred), as in the companion material discovered later, prose appears only rarely; it provides commentary or prologue or "bridging" passages before or after a lay. This constitutes the opposite of what Hopkins is imagining. His untenable proposal reflects only the reluctance of Victorians, even as late as the 1880's, to acknowledge the early primacy of poetry over prose and its independence from the prose language-world.

From this *Ur*-epic he sees a development to a second stage, in which poetry has wholly taken over the function of storytelling. Now epic emerges as a formal whole. In a third and final stage, a master poet appears. His achievement is to endow epic with unity, treating it as an individual genre. When Hopkins speaks of the master poet who "chooses a hero . . . and an action or motive," both the words and the attitude that underlies them are consonant with the approach taken by German Homerists of the time. His inclusion of the generic aspect, however, shows that he has turned to acknowledge the real or supposed claims of Aristotle's *Poetics*. In England, scholars and more particularly men of letters assumed the existence of a single poet, magnificently gifted. Homer, so they thought, took the mass of versified sagas or myths or *Märchen* and organized this material around a central heroic figure and a central theme. The belief is not to be smiled at: many classical scholars today maintain a somewhat similar view, elaborately modified. One difference lies in our realization of what a few scholars in Germany had seen a century and more before our time. This is the realization that the *Iliad* and *Odyssey* stand at the end of a long process by which epic was developed and refined. Thus whatever supreme redactor the name "Homer" describes was aided by earlier poets, men who had worked out the basic features of the two poems.

As the introductory portion of the notes continues, the question of genre reappears. The two epics are said to be comedies in that they end happily, a criterion taken from the famous letter written by Dante to Can Grande. Yet they have a tragic "feeling," and here Hopkins deliberately goes outside the conceptions employed by Dante--change between happiness and unhappiness, high or low style. On the strength of those misconceived criteria, the medieval poet could classify Vergil's epic as tragedy and his own as *commedia*. His Victorian successor, substituting feeling for style, has a pair of standards that might serve for viewing "The Wreck of the Deutschland." Whether they can prove useful for an analysis of portions of the *Iliad* is another matter.

Hopkins goes on to theorize about the origin of the phrase *rhaptein aoidēn*, "to stitch song" or sew it together. Probably, he believes, it was "suggested by singing before women sewing or shoemakers stitching shoes and the stitching is that of verse to verse, not of fit to fit. The feet or syllables are stitches, the verses seams" (5). He has already rejected the probable derivation of *rhapsōidos*, "rhapsode," from *rhaptein*, despite its endorsement by Liddell and Scott and by Monro. Here and elsewhere, he concerns himself with his own vision of what might have happened; and he regularly presents possibility as probability. He will draw upon the statements of the lexicon when they support his case, or when he can rebut them to his own satisfaction. One thing alone mattered to him, and it is what truly matters to us: the succession of images that his encounter with Homeric epic brought to mind. Such an idea is that of singing before needlewomen or cobblers. The idea of work-songs brings him back to his original citation from Euripides about songs heard at the loom. Beyond question, this type of singing has universal importance. Whether the explanation of *rhaptein aoidēn* that Hopkins puts forward should be thought convincing none can say; yet his vignette charms at least through its vividness. For a moment, we glimpse a world almost untouched by the poems. Neither "stitch" nor "seam" can be found in them, and "sew" appears but once ("Margaret Clitheroe" 145).[7]

When he speaks of the "rhapsodists," the professional reciters of Homer, Hopkins maintains that Greek drama "was not so dramatic as this rhapsodising, not so impassioned" (6). In a parenthesis he adds, "For its effect see the *Ion*," Plato's dialogue in which a master rhapsode discusses his art with Socrates. He goes on to argue that while epic was still in the formative stage, bards were singers to the lyre, but once actual epic poems had been fashioned, those who performed them were rhapsodes.

Two points may be noted here. First, the *Ion* displays a marked characteristic that Hopkins, for some reason, does not mention. The celebrated rhapsode has an additional role: he serves as a commentator on the Homeric poems, an "interpreter" in the academic sense, and takes inordinate pride in his ability to do so. Plato makes this aspect entirely clear. Hopkins either is unaware of it or ignores its presence; he himself is now interpreting Homer for an audience. There is also the fact, or report, that he was capable of doing so with a startling degree of physical action, reenacting in the classroom the dragging of Hector's body around Troy.[8]

Moreover, the shift from lyre-singer to rhapsode, as it is presented in these Dublin notes, is an imaginative, highly idiosyncratic telescoping of

---

[7] The poems are cited according to item number and line number in Gardner and MacKenzie. This is the text on which Dilligan and Bender's *Concordance* is based. My comments on words used in the poetry rely on Dilligan and Bender's presentation of the evidence.

[8] The story seems to have become known initially through an article in the *Downside Review* for 1933 by Dom Wulstan Phillipson. It reappeared in 1940 in an article by Heywood (19), and Gardner and others have given it wide currency.

a development known to have been far more complex. Monro marshals and ably assesses the facts that go to make up its complexity. To this painstaking presentation Hopkins paid no attention whatsoever, so far as one can judge from the notes. He has gone voyaging alone; if this meant gainsaying Plato and the Greeks generally on the status of Phemius, so be it. Though he is too well-trained, too intelligent not to keep the coastline of reality in sight, nothing had real consequence for him except holding to the eccentric pattern of his own course. It is true that, unlike many German classicists of the time, he had no consciously predetermined position which he was concerned to defend. Nevertheless, he is not a scholar here. At some points the supposed historical development, possesses a basis in fact; as a whole, it has been created by Hopkins. Like the rest of his commentary, it is a palimpsest. Underneath his charting of early Greek epic, we see the map of his own mind.

Predictably, he does not overlook the role of the gods. The outlines of a theodicy begin to take shape:

> Divine providence: Zeus does not directly act . . . , Athene and Apollo act under him. . . . In the Iliad Athene and Apollo act on opposite sides like right and left hands of providence. Apollo begins, for the Trojans, and sets the ball rolling; Athene in the scene in the council checks the action, in behalf of the Greeks. (7)

The phrase "divine providence" has such strong associations with Christianity that its usefulness here may be endangered. Possibly it gave the students a familiar peg on which they could hang unfamiliar ideas; and of these there would be an astonishing abundance. If the tradition that his listeners proved inattentive to Hopkins on Homer has any truth, it was not because he failed to challenge their imagination or to use language free from academic pompousness. As for the facts, Zeus does act through the other Olympians or through lesser, personified forces. Moreover, his daughter and son take opposite sides in the struggle for Troy, like Zeus and his consort Hera. It is understandable that Hopkins should have omitted the larger purpose behind these discords: *Dios d' eteleieto boulē,* "and the plan of Zeus was being fulfilled" (*Iliad* 1.5). Nonetheless, not far below the surface of his thought we see this purpose, transmuted into the master concept--the mastering concept--of the will of God. The sudden, puzzling return to "providence" suggests, at the very least, the likelihood that the connection is not arbitrary or merely imaginary. Athena and Apollo are its "right and left hands," for all their seemingly opposite purposes.

Hopkins uses the word "providence" only twice in his poetry.[9] The lesser of these instances comes from "The Blessed Virgin compared to the Air we Breathe," written not long before the notes on Homer, in May of 1883: "God has let dispense / Her prayers his providence" (60, 40-41). That is, God has allowed the intercessory prayers of the Virgin to be "God's glory, justice, and grace." A more arresting use comes from "The Wreck of the Deutschland." It too exemplifies the poet's Marian thought. As narrator, he speaks of "the / Comfortless unconfessed" among those who died, then at once corrects himself: "No not uncomforted: lovely-felicitous Providence / . . . . / . . . could obey so" and make of the "shipwrack" a harvest (28, st. 31). As the preceding stanza shows, the nun who had called out "'O Christ, Christ, come quickly'" (st. 24) is identified with Mary in re-conceiving Christ (st. 30). Thereby she re-presents Christ, the "Providence" that brings *felicitas.*

All this may seem remote from a statement that Apollo and Athena "act on opposite sides like right and left hands of providence." To deny a

---

[9] Contrast "grace": 28 occurrences.

connection, however, we must suppose Hopkins capable of conceiving divine providence as a reality without giving it a mental context of God's grace. Surely the idea could have had no meaning for him in terms of a fallen world. The term of comparison, "like," is not an option, not a sign of chance preference here for simile over metaphor; it marks the boundary between separate realms. He never uses this image of right and left hand sacramentally in his poetry. What the poems do give us, with overwhelming variety, is the multitude of aspects whereby God's chastening and his love are seen to be one. Nowhere has this theme been made more nearly central than in "The Wreck"; nor are any of its lines more eloquent than those that tell of the passengers and seamen whose "doom" was "to be drowned; / Yet did the dark side of the bay of thy blessing / Not vault them . . . in?" (12). The echo of stanza 9, "[God who] Hast thy dark descending and most art merciful then," sounds clearly, but the earlier stanza deals only with a single dimension. "Bay" goes beyond this, suggesting a many-dimensioned inner world; it is out of this world that Hopkins writes twenty years later, when he characterizes the gods of Homer.

What he writes can surprise. Even when we bear in mind the inveterate bloody-mindedness of undergraduates, it does seem that some listeners may not have expected to hear the calling down of plague upon the Greek host spoken of as setting the ball rolling (*Iliad* 1. 50-51).[10] Of course, it may have been good teaching for that very reason; what follows is crisp and straightforward. The information, however, lacks accuracy. Evidently Hopkins had not consulted any of the standard sources, not even his own class text.

---

[10] First against the mules and dogs; then against the men.

If the professional competence displayed in the Dublin notes does not come off with a great deal of credit, their author should not be judged harshly for it. Neither Highgate nor Oxford had trained him adequately in the study of Homer; his notes on James Riddell's lectures at Oxford exist to back up this assessment. The fact is that English classicists had lagged far behind the Germans as Homerists. In 1885, George Wilkins brought out in Dublin and London *The Growth of the Homeric Poems*. The theme of Chapter 14, "The English School of Homeric Criticism," is stated at the outset: "what has been done, or rather left undone, in Homeric criticism by the English classical school" (173). Harsh words, but deserved. Throughout most of the nineteenth century, until the middle and late 1880's, scholars in England produced no edition of Homer designed for readers more advanced than schoolboys. At mid-point in the eighties, a change occurred. The class text that Hopkins had adopted (if the choice was his) as the most modern one available in English, Monro's first edition of 1884, perpetuated the tradition of Thomas Kerchever Arnold, Paley, and, for the *Odyssey*, Merry and Riddell--that same Riddell whose Oxford lectures on this work Hopkins had attended. In 1886, however, Walter Leaf published the two massive volumes of *The Iliad*, each more than 600 pages. It is not a matter of *quantum* merely--Arnold and Paley both produced long books-- but of *quale*: in his preparation of the critical apparatus and the extremely full notes, Leaf set editorial standards such that his edition is still consulted. A new tradition had gotten under way, one which was to produce achievements in editing and annotation like Jebb's Sophocles and Gow's Theocritus. It gathered force during the remaining years of the century. At the end of 1899, when Leaf wrote the Preface to the second edition of his *Iliad*, he was able to say, "I have satisfaction in thinking that the proportion of valuable contributions from English scholars has largely increased of late years" (v-vi).

Although Hopkins lived to see the beginning of this new order of things, he did not profit from it. Every circumstance seemed to be against him. Increasingly weakening illnesses, the hair shirt of an excessive scrupulousness concerning his duties, and a lack of confidence in what he had accomplished, whether as priest or as classicist and teacher: all of these things plagued him. Readers of the Dublin notes must not expect contributions to the study of Homer. What they find in these pages will, it is hoped, be something quite different: evidence that even the unassuming, uncertain effort represented there can prove to be "the precious life-blood of a master spirit."

When he speaks later of a relay of rhapsodes, "a walking Iliad," Hopkins sees in them a significant advantage:

> Such a body . . . , as someone (Gladstone?) has suggested, serves instead of a book and writing; it is a living monument or record, walking book, and the poet need not himself know more by heart at a time than the piece he teaches each. . . . They are to him a worktable, a carpenter's bench, his *bench*, holding his work for him as he works, his reel to wind it off on. (9)

That final statement did not come from Gladstone, or from any classicist. Suddenly we are hearing the voice of Hopkins the poet. To what end this gear and tackle and trim have so unexpectedly been set before us is not easy to determine. The images change as one phrase succeeds another: "worktable" can suggest no more than the surface, with materials placed on it; the workman must be brought in too, and given a central place. "Carpenter's bench" accomplishes this. Why, then, repeat "bench" and underline it? As early as Chaucer, the substantive denoted "the rough strong table at which carpenters and other mechanics work" (*OED* s.v. 4.b). Yet something else seems to be struggling for clearer utterance; we cannot tell what it is.

When the image changes again, radically this time, the reader comes upon one of the most memorable rewards provided by the Homer notes. Here, at precisely the right juncture in Hopkins' life, is the first appearance of a metaphor that will become famous in "Spelt from Sibyl's Leaves" (61): "Let life, waned, ah let life wind / Off her once skeined stained veined variety upon, all on two spools. . . ."[11] Of this poem, Professor MacKenzie says:

> The first half is to be found drafted out in the rough Dublin Notebook on a page which we can date October 1884; another page, worked upon two months later, carries the sonnet through successive revisions up to the middle of l. 10: "O this is our tale too!". Here he seems to have stuck. . . . Not until two years later did he finish the poem. Yet the whole sonnet issues out of that soul-dark winter of 1884-85 revealed in his intimate meditation notes, which show the continual action of his elective will seeking to rise above his own misery. (*P* xlii)

The whole of the poem does come out of that black winter; and "his reel to wind it off on" prefigures the final shape of its tenth line, the point past which he could not manage to advance in December 1884.

Having attempted to provide his students with an introduction to the *Iliad*, Hopkins sets at the top of his first page of commentary the month, year, and place: "(Nov. 1884 Dublin)" (11). The time of his greatest despair has now begun. What he says about the *Iliad* in these notes, however, shows him free for the moment from other constraints, notably the grading of examinations during the testing periods and the day-to-day chore of assigning marks for classroom work. It afforded a release, moreover, for

---

[11] Compare the "rein" of the windhover (36).

certain kinds of intellectual and emotional energy. These were forces otherwise suppressed or dissipated by the circumstances imposed on him, or self-imposed, during the desolate time that began with the onset of winter in 1884.

Out of hundreds of examples, a few must suffice. Those immediately following come from *Iliad* 4. "387 *hippēlata*: dash, courage." Literally "horse-driver," the term describes one who fights from a chariot. It marks class distinctions in war, but Hopkins ignores this. For him, it marks the outward and inward manifestations of an individual's *haecceitas*. He does not translate; he cites the qualities that the term evokes in him. "394, 395 pointed epithets," he writes. Although the rest of the note is in part arbitrary and blundering, taken as a whole it serves to bring out more clearly what had first appeared in the comment on *hippēlata*, his belief that "stock epithets" have their meaning within the given context. In a word, they are "pointed." A particular phrase or line--most often a single word--would set off his imagination, whether in this or in some other direction; he seldom concerned himself with the larger view. On 414 he comments, "In the breaker-image that follows the 'combing' answers to the Gks. arming...." The rest of the note is in the same vein, a mistaken attempt to find correspondences for all of the main elements of the simile. This can be done with the Miltonic simile but not with the Homeric. More important is what "combing" suggests: that a connection hardly hinted at before has begun to emerge. It is the link between the struggle and death that are constants of the epic called by Simone Weil "the poem of force" and "The Wreck of the Deutschland," seen both as violence and theodicy.

The comment on some of the fighting is in another vein: "457.... Remark in the fights wh[ich] follow the partiality: the Gks. strike fair blows but are struck unawares." This does not describe Homer's world; it distorts the realities of that world to fit the preconceptions of middle- and upper-class Victorian morality, epitomized in the public school cry "Play the game!" To return to the "stock" adjective: *megathumos*, defined in the 1873 Liddell and Scott as "high minded" or "great-hearted," receives astonishingly varied treatment. For two occurrences coming in close succession (464, 467) Hopkins says, "one as bold as the other; the first presuming, the second indignant at his presumption," and for a later instance (479) "ruthless consciousness of his strength." Granted, one should be aware of context when dealing with Homer's formulaic adjectives. W.B. Stanford, that ornament of Dublin scholarship, makes this clear in his edition of the *Odyssey*; so does Robert Fitzgerald in his verse translation. Hopkins, however, comes very close to being wholly subjective.

The notes on *Iliad* 5 (which must be our limit) confirm the presence of tendencies already evident. In the declaration "Pallas Athena will not let me take flight in terror" (256), the commentator sees a possible suggestion of *pallein*, a verb which can mean "quake with fear." This reminds him of Heracles' tortured cry "O Pallas, Pallas!" in Sophocles' tragedy *The Women of Trachis* (1031). The hero calls on Athena, he maintains, "for no other reason of inscape . . . but this." There is another reason, and an excellent one. As Jebb was to point out in his 1892 edition, "Athena was always a guardian goddess to her half-brother, Heracles" (151), a claim that he goes on to substantiate with his usual thoroughness and mastery of Greek. He was the scholar that Hopkins could never be. In 432, Diomedes has the standard phrase *boēn agathos*, "good at the war-cry": We find the rendering "here swift to seize his prey." It would be wrong to suppose that Hopkins felt free to tailor any adjective or phrase to fit its immediate context. After a note on 479, he writes, "Epithets plain till / 499"--and straightway launches upon a series of startling renderings for terms in 499 and later.

We have seen what play he makes with *megathumos*. Once (547) Homer almost defeats his ingenuity, when Diocles is thus described in the midst of a genealogy. "As nearly idle as an epithet can ever be," Hopkins protests. His own are never idle in the poetry, and he sees every epithet as having a job to do. Thus he rallies quickly with the words "but we may suppose him the father of gallant sons," drawing as usual upon the context (548-49). It is therefore strange to find him stating, only a few entries earlier, that in 522-26 "the simile of the clouds on mountaintops is curious in this, that in making the Gks. the clouds it suggests the Trojans are the winds and will scatter them, but they do not. It is therefore pure unreflecting imagination." In our own day, M.M. Willcock too finds it curious (n. *ad loc.*), but he understands its purpose:

> An extraordinary simile: the Greeks stood their ground like clouds in a windless sky. As a description this does not help very much, but the picture of peaceful nature has a definite effect, of distracting the audience momentarily from the deadly fighting on the plain.

As C.M. Bowra says, in *Iliad* 5 "there is hardly anything but fighting" (123). Where the simile is concerned a great many classicists, at least in the English-speaking countries, have gone to school with Bowra; Willcock seems to have learned his lesson well. One might wonder whether Hopkins, speaking as he does here, has wholly shaken off the influence of Romanticism so apparent at times in his youthful poetry.

The remaining notes on Book 5 contain much to provoke disagreement and admiration, sometimes in the same breath. When Athena mounts a war-chariot (750 *ochea*), Hopkins imagines "the floor buckling under her tread." The turn of speech has some interest coming from the author of "The Windhover." He is thinking, quite correctly, of the leather *himantes*; Leaf (n. on 727 *diphros*) aptly describes these as "straps strained tight and interwoven, which formed a springy surface" on which the charioteer stood. In the same line, Hopkins misinterprets *phlogea*, "[the chariot] blazing like fire," as referring to them. He finds near-allegory (751) or allegorical elements (765-66) where nothing of the sort exists. The mention of a pair of "running rivers, where Simoeis and Skamandros dash their waters together" (773-74 tr. Lattimore) moves him to speak of them as "silvering in the map of the *landscape*" through the effect of being described by name. This singularly attractive phrase, which he never used in poetry (though Bridges did), corresponds to nothing in the text. It might conceivably be traced to the use in 770 of *ēeroeides*, literally "mistily," of viewing a distant prospect; but plainly it is Hopkins' own to an overwhelming degree.

This last example fittingly rounds off our sampling, for it illustrates once more that almost total subjectivity which has already been remarked. As classical scholarship the Dublin notes show acquired techniques, but they embody no real advance over those taken at Oxford or indeed at Highgate. The dazzling future augured by a double first in Greats never became a reality. Hopkins lacked an overview of Homer, and he lacked the physical and mental energy requisite for its attainment. He could picture the immediate moment of the narrative with his customary fresh, imaginative mode of insight, untroubled by considerations of objective correctness; beyond that momentary vision he could not or would not go. It was a loss for his students, and his teaching must have suffered accordingly.

Besides the kingfisher flashes of beauty or oddness that "silver in" the landscape of a poet's sensibilities, what can be placed on the credit side has nothing to do with the classroom, but comes from a larger calculus. It is the impression, increasingly strong as one reads these notes, that the *Iliad* could reach Hopkins during a time when even his unwavering Catholic faith could not bring sure comfort. This was the time of "No worst, there is none," a cry of anguish hardly to be matched. Yet in happier times he had written, "nature is never spent; / There lives the dearest freshness deep down things" (31. 9-10). Something of that freshness came to him through Homer, to be set against the note of doom and sorrow. Throughout the period when he set down his comments on the *Iliad*, such mercies were few; let us rejoice and be glad in them.

Works Cited

Bischoff, D. Anthony, S.J. "The Manuscripts of Gerard Manley Hopkins." *Thought* 26 (Winter, 1951-1952): 551-80.

Bowra, C.M. *Tradition and Design in the Iliad*. Oxford: Clarendon Press, 1930.

Dilligan, Robert J., and Todd K. Bender. *A Concordance to the English Poetry of Gerard Manley Hopkins*. Madison: University of Wisconsin Press, 1970.

Heywood, Terence. "Gerard Manley Hopkins--His Literary Ancestry." *English* 3 (Spring 1940): 16-24.

Jebb, R.C. *Sophocles: The Plays and Fragments. Part V. The Trachiniae*. Cambridge: Cambridge UP, 1892.

Lattimore, Richmond A., tr. *The Iliad of Homer*. Chicago: Chicago UP, 1959.

Leaf, Walter, ed. *The Iliad*. London: Macmillan, 1886.

---, ed. *The Iliad*. 2nd ed. London: Macmillan, 1900.

Liddell, Henry George, Robert Scott, and Henry Stuart Jones. *A Greek-English Lexicon*. 9th ed. Oxford: Clarendon Press, 1940.

Peters, W.A.M., S.J. *Gerard Manley Hopkins: A Critical Essay towards the Understanding of his Poetry*. 2nd ed. London: Oxford UP, 1970.

Phillipson, Dom Wulstan. "Gerard Manley Hopkins." *Downside Review* 51 (April 1933): 326-48.

Wilkins, George. *The Growth of the Homeric Poems*. Dublin: Hodges, Figgis; London: Longmans, Green, 1885.

Willcock, M.M. *A Commentary on Homer's Iliad, Books I-VI*. London: Macmillan, 1970.

Sounding Alpha and Omega in Dante, Milton, and Hopkins

James Finn Cotter

In Canto XXVI of the *Paradiso*, Dante concludes his treatment of the three theological virtues with St. John's examination of the pilgrim on the nature of love. So dazzled is Dante by the sight of the Apostle that he has been struck blind, and he remains sightless until the midpoint of the canto when, after responding to St. John's questions, he regains his vision by gazing on Beatrice--who here plays Ananias to Dante's Paul, reversing the "io non Paulo" of *Inferno* II, 32. Ideally, the reader should read (if it were possible!) with eyes shut, listening to the words. When the discussion with Adam begins, Dante persists in being chiefly concerned with speech.[1]

---

[1] Helpful *lectures* on this canto include Cremona, Foster and Boyde, and Getto. See also Mengaldo.

"Until you can regain / The sight you lost in seeing me," St. John suggests, "You well would compensate for it by speaking [*ragionando*]."[2] The word implies rational discourse and exactly describes the style of the examination. Some critics have found the language about love too cold and unfeeling, but the poet, by bringing reason and love together, as Shakespeare's Bottom would have it, unites Virgil and Beatrice in their roles as his guides. Far from being remotely intellectual, the music of the poetry is full of surprising echoes and resonances.

"Begin then, and tell at what mark your soul / Is aimed," St. John leads the pilgrim into the discussion; he answers:

"Lo ben che fa contenta questa corte,
 Alfa e O è di quanta scrittura
 mi legge Amore o lievemente o forte."
   (16-18)
("The Good which brings contentment to the court
Is Alpha and Omega of all the Scriptures
Love reads to me with soft or louder tones.")

Dante refers to St. John's own Apocalypse as expressing the aim (the Good or God) of all the Scripture, for as the last book of the revealed word it was thought to be its all-inclusive summary. To indicate this, Dante cites the verse: "'I am the Alpha and the Omega, the beginning and the end,' says the Lord God" (1:8). The phrase is repeated in 21:6 and 22:13, where it clearly applies to Christ. Commentators usually referred all three passages to the incarnate Son, citing the Prologue to St. John's Gospel: Alpha denotes the Word "in the beginning" and Omega denotes "the Word become

---

[2] The English version is from my translation of the *Divine Comedy*. The Italian text is that edited by Giorgio Petrocchi in Singleton. Where reliable English versions of other works cited are available, I have used them; otherwise the original and my translation are quoted.

flesh": "Principium, quia in principio erat Verbum; finis, quia Verbum caro factum est" (Haimo of Auxerre (ps.-Haimo of Halberstadt) 117, col. 948).[3] Later in his analysis of love, the poet explicitly refers to the incarnation as one of the cords that draws him to God: "The death that he endured that I might live" (59).

For Dante, Christ embodies the fullness of love and the goal of his journey. The same commentators who identify Alpha and Omega with the incarnate Word also gloss this verse (1:8) to show how all things are summed up in him from creation to parousia. Eloquently typical in glossing this verse, Bruno of Asti writes:

> Est ergo Christus alpha et omega, primus et novissimus, initium et finis, primus ante omnia, finis post omnia, a quo cuncta procedunt, ad quem cuncta redeunt; intra quem omnia, extra quem nihil; ad quem qui pervenerit, ultra non habet, quo vadat. Et ipse quidem revera est, quoniam semper est. Ipse est qui erat, quoniam in principio erat, ipse etiam venturus est. (Haimo 165, cols. 610-11)[4]
>
> (Christ then is Alpha and Omega, first and last, beginning and end, first before all, end after all, from whom everything proceeds, to whom everything returns; within whom are all things, outside of whom is nothing; to whom whoever comes, there is no one else to whom to go. And he really is, because he is forever. He is who was, because he was in the beginning and he is the same who will come again.)

---

[3] See also Primasius 68, cols. 799, 922, 932; Ven. Bede 93, col. 205; and Alcuin 100, col. 1095.

[4] See also Haimo 117, cols. 1195, 1217, and Honorius Augustodunensis 172, cols. 1167-89.

Dante, by alluding to "Alfa e O" in the form in which the words usually appeared in St. John's text, recalls the rich exegetical tradition that developed around the passage.

All Scripture ("quanta scrittura") is epitomized in the Word made flesh. Hugh of St. Cher expresses the accepted teaching: "For the whole Divine Scripture is one book, and that one Book is Christ, for the whole Divine Scripture speaks of Christ and is fulfilled in Christ" (*Noah's Ark* 86).[5]
Love reads the Scripture to Dante, in the form of an auditory experience, "forte," as a listener hears the Scripture read in church, or "lievemente," as a person privately reading Scripture listens meditatively to the written words. Throughout the examination, St. John is identified as "un spiro" ("a breath") and "medesma voce" ("the same voice") in lines 3 and 19. When the Apostle speaks in lines 46-51, Dante simply says "E io udi" ("And I heard") to emphasize his own total dependence on hearing words and the Word.

The Word incarnate is Alpha-Omega, and the poet's words are intended to voice the iconographic heritage. The symbols were still current in Dante's day both in their Greek form A-Ω or ω and Latin equivalent, *A-O*. In the ninth century, Raban Maur in his *Liber de laudibus Sanctae Crucis*, which features *carmina figurata* with sets of letters enclosed in the contours of figures or patterns, created an image of the crucified Christ whose cruciform nimbus contains *A* in the left arm, *M* in the upper center, and Ω on the left (Migne 107, cols. 149-50). The three letters are said to represent "every beginning, middle (*Medium*), and end comprehended by

---

[5] See also the original, *De Arca Noe Morali* 176, col. 642. See also Honorius 172, cols. 1167-68. and Lubac 318-28.

Christ."[6] The three letters also spell out the verb *AMO* ("I love"). In *Paradise* 18, 94-99, Dante draws attention to the letter *M* when it is written in the sky and which then forms the eagle of justice. In *Purgatory* 23, 32, Dante says the letters *OMO* can be read as configuring the face of man in outline from. Raban Maur employs the letters *ORO* ("I pray") to form the eyes of Christ with the two *O*'s, so that the single line across Christ's vision is: *A O O Ω*. In the thirteenth century, Joachim of Fiore in his *Liber Figurarum* and *Expositio in Apocalypsim* symbolizes the Trinity as three interlinking circles preceded by an Alpha above and an Omega below them. Written through the center of the circles are the letters of the tetragrammaton as Joachim interpreted it: *I E U E* (Reeves 192-93 and pl. 26).[7] Here the *I* stands for the Father, the *U* for the Son, and the *E* for the Holy Spirit. In the *Liber Figurarum* the design features the name *Adam* on the left side and the words *Finis Mundi* on the right. According to Joachim, since the *A* is made up of three lines, it symbolizes the three Persons of the Trinity and "sounds nothing other than *Sanctus, Sanctus, Sanctus*," while the rotundity of the *O* represents the unity of the Trinity and "resonates nothing other than *Dominus Deus Omnipotens*."[8] Against the background of such figurative learning, Dante interprets "Alpha e O" and the Divine Name.

---

[6] See also figure 2, where *O* appears at the extremities and middle of a lettered cross and square (cols. 155, 158). For a helpful survey, see Chatillon. A facsimile of the Vienna manuscript appears in the series *Codices Selecti*, vol. 33; see Works Cited for complete bibliographical information..

[7] For a facsimile of the *Figurae* (Oxford, Corpus Christi College Ms. 255A) see Tondelli 2, pl. 11a-b. For the *Expositio in Apocalypsim* manuscript (Paris, Bibl. Nat. Lat. 417, fol 87r), see also Reeves 39-40 and pl. 3.

[8] Reeves (51), quoting Joachim's *Psalterium decem chordarum*. See also the chapter, "Joachim's *Figurae* and Dante's Symbolism" (317-29).

Christ embodies beginning, middle, and end, and Dante's poetry is meant to incarnate the same texts and lessons (other meanings of "scrittura") in his own speech. Dante's text sounds the meaning he has learned by vocalizing Alpha and Omega. First the word "amor" or "amore," repeated seven times up to line 66 where the examination ends, is "*AmOr*," the central word of the poem--literally, since it represents the final goal of the journey: "l'amor que move il sole e l'altre stella" (XXXIII, 143). At the end of the discourse with St. John, the heavens resound with the song, "S*a*nt*o*, s*a*nt*o*, s*a*nt*o*," again an *A-O* word which repeats the cry of Apocalypse 4:8. In Dante's heaven the blessed sing in Italian rather than Latin because "s*A*nt*O*" sounds the lesson the poet has heard and learned. Like Joachim, Dante sounds the Trinity in Alpha-Omega.

Once the discussion develops, the *A-O* assonance dominates: lines 58-70 are all *A-O* rhymes and deliberately ring the vowels: "tr*a*tt*o* m'h*a*nn*o* del m*a*r de l'*a*mor t*o*rt*o*" ("Have hauled me from the sea of wrongful love") (62)).[9] The climax comes with Dante's conclusion and his audience's response:

>"Le fr*o*nde *o*nde s'infr*o*nd*a* tutt*o* l'*o*rt*o*
>de l'*o*rt*o*l*a*no ettern*o*, *a*m' i*o* c*o*t*a*nt*o*
>qu*a*nt*o* d*a* lui *a* l*o*r di bene e p*o*rt*o*."
>Si c*o*m' i*o* t*a*cqui, un d*o*lcissimo c*a*nt*o*
>ris*o*n*o* per l*o* ciel*o*, e l*a* mi*a* d*o*nn*a*
>dice*a* c*o*n li *a*ltri: "S*a*nt*o*, s*a*nt*o*, s*a*nt*o*!"
>
>(64-69)

("As for the leaves that leaf out the whole garden

---

[9] Between lines 58 and 106 of *Paradiso* XXVI, *A* and *O* rhymes occur in 13 of 16 tercets for an average of 81.3 percent. Based on a survey of *A-O* rhymes in 16 cantos chosen at random, this percentage contrasts with an average of 55.9 percent for such rhymes.

> Of the eternal gardener, I love each one
> In measure as it grows in goodness from him."
> As soon as I grew still a most sweet song
> Resounded through the heavens, and my lady
> Sang with the others, "Holy, Holy, Holy!")

Here the medium imparts the poet's message. Dante is not only a hearer of the Word but a doer who transmits it. Like St. Paul, he preaches what he practices, not as "sounding brass or tinkling cymbal," but as a man possessed by love (I Cor. 13:1).

A remarkable bonding of words together occurs in lines 64-65: "fronde onde s'infronda" and "l'orto / l'ortolano." The repetition echoes Dante's observation about the binding of the vowels in *Il Convivio* IV, 6.3-5. There Dante probes the root of the word "autore" to demonstrate that an author is by definition a "word-binder" ("legare parole, cioe auieo") (Dante, *Il Convivio I* II, 59).[10] The passage is important for the light it sheds on the poet's use of *A* and *O*:

> We must know, then, that authority is nothing else than an act of an author. This word may have two origins: one from a verb quite fallen into disuse in grammar which means to bind words together, namely AUIEO. And anyone who considers it in its first person present will plainly see that it demonstrates its own meaning, that it is made entirely of the binding of words, that is of the five vowels alone which are the soul and connecting bonds of every word; and is composed of them in a way that may be transposed to represent the image of a bond (che solo di legame di parole è fatto, cioè di sole cinque vocali, che sono anima

---

[10] See the article on "autore" in *Enciclopedia dantesca*, I, 454-56.

elegame d'ogni parole, e composo d'esse per modo volubile, a figurare imagine di legame).[11]

Dante explains this binding by showing how the regular order of AEIOU can be rotated to create the word AUIEO ("I bind"). His explanation has a few twists and turns of its own:

Because beginning with A we then turn back ("quindi si rivolve") into U and come directly by I into E, whence we turn back again to the O; so that this figure of a bond really represents the vowels AEIOU. And how far "author" comes from this verb we learn only from the poets, who have bound their words together with musical art ("che con l'arte musaica le loro parole hanno legate") (Hillard 253; Busnelli 60).[12]

The verb "auieo" is the Ur-word created by looping the basic vowels together by a tie that brings them back to their pristine order. The process is as follows:

$$\widehat{A} \; E \; I \; O \; \widehat{U} \; \rightarrow \; \widehat{A} \; \widehat{E \; I \; O} \; \widehat{U} \; \rightarrow \; \widehat{A} \; \widehat{E} \; \widehat{I} \; \widehat{O} \; \widehat{U}$$

Or, more simply, A E I O U.

The poet, whose name "vates" derives from the same root "uiere" ("uincire") according to Isidore's *Etymologiae* VIII, 7.3, binds words into an intelligible construction ("coniugatio") by an art learned from the muses. This musical

---

[11] The translation here, slightly adapted, is from Hillard 252-53. The Italian text is Busnelli 59. See Dante's discussion of "coniugatio" in *De Vulgari Eloquentia* II, 6.2.

[12] Book and author are also connected by "legato" in *Paradiso* XXXIII, 86. See Ahern.

art is exactly embodied in Dante's own writing in Canto XXVI.

The verb "AUIEO" begins with *A* and ends with *O*. The rotating of *A* and *O* goes back to Tertullian in a passage from *De Monogamia* V, repeated almost verbatim (but much abbreviated) in Isidore's *Etymologiae* I, 3.9 (82, cols. 76-77) where Dante certainly read it:

> So, too, the two letters of Greece, the first and the last, the Lord assumes to Himself, as figures of the beginning and end which concur in Himself: so that, just as Alpha rolls on ["volvitur"] till it reaches Omega, and again Omega rolls back till it reaches Alpha, in the same way He might show that in Himself is both the downward course of the beginning on to the end, and the backward course of the end up to the beginning; so that every economy, ending in Him through whom it began,--through the Word of God, that is, who was made flesh,--may have an end correspondent to its beginning. And so truly in Christ are all things recalled to "the beginning."[13]

Tertullian proceeds to trace this "economia" back to the first man in Paradise, Adam. But the "second man," from above, bears a new likeness, that of the firstborn from the dead, the new Adam:

> But again: if the beginning passes on to the end (as Alpha to Omega), and as the end passes back to the beginning (as Omega to Alpha), thus the origin is transferred to Christ, the physical to the spiritual--inasmuch as 'it is not the spiritual that comes first, but the physical, and then the spiritual.'" (I Cor. 15:46; Roberts IV 62)[14]

---

[13] In Roberts 62. For the original text, see *Opus Tertulliani* II in *Corpus Christianorum: Series Latina*, II 1234-35.

[14] In early Christian art, A-Ω and Ω-A are often interchangeable.

The second half of Canto XXVI involves the pilgrim's meeting with Adam who answers his unvoiced question (in reverse order!) about the origin of language. Adam, the first man, is the last person Dante interviews (St. Bernard is a guide) on his way to the final encounter with the God-Man in the vision that concludes the *Commedia*. The discussion with Adam also continues the *A* and *O* assonance: Lines 85-104 are all *A* or *O* rhymes. Indeed, all the rhyming words from lines 40 to 109 contain one of the two vowels. *A*d*a*m's own name suggests Alpha, the beginning, as does the poet's description of him as "l'*a*nim*a* prim*a*i*a*." Adam's sin is termed "tr*a*p*a*ss*a*r." The first address to Adam chimes with assonance: "*O* p*o*m*o* che m*a*tur*o* / s*o*l*o* pr*o*d*o*tt*o* f*o*sti, *o* p*a*dre *a*ntic*o*" ("O fruit, the only one / Produced already ripe, O ancient father" (91-92)). The momentum of the sonorous effect flows through the canto and reaches its crescendo in the opening nine lines of the next canto with its assonance and series of interjections (four "Oh's" in lines 7 to 9). Its first line begins with Alpha ("Al Padre") and ends with Omega ("lo Spirito Santo").

As applied to the poet, the verb "auieo" by its origin binds him to God who is called the "verace autore" ("true Author") in line 40. The only other time "autore" is used in the *Commedia* occurs when Dante greets Virgil as "'l mio autore" in *Inferno* I, 85. For Dante, poetic authorship comes from the incarnate Word, the Book of LIfe, who is the source and synopsis of all other lives. In what the church fathers regarded as a Christic theophany, the God-Man prophesied his own incarnation in a passage Dante paraphrases from Exodus 33:19. The Lord promised Moses to show him His glory: "Io ti farò vedere ogne valore" (46). Dante insists on the self-revelatory nature of this wording of the Word by adding, "di sé parlando." In Exodus 3:14, God revealed his sacred Name to Moses as "I am who am." The tetragrammaton, written entirely of consonants in

Hebrew as JHVH, was often adopted into Greek as the trigrammaton of vowels IAO. This version was widely known and is cited by Origen, Jerome, Macrobius, and others.[15] St. John himself probably knew of it, as Austin Farrer observes: "That he was thinking of them [God and Christ] under the Name JHVH is quite certain; and that he used the Greek equivalent IAΩ is probable in itself, and strongly confirmed by what we can see him to have done" (264). Farrer believes that John did not use the trigrammaton itself in the Apocalypse because of his Jewish reservations, but that he hints at it in riddles (264-65). IAO is composed of the middle, the first and the last of the Greek vowels, and St. John, by employing two of the three, implies the presence of the third in "I am." The Johannine theme of "I am" as Christ's self-declaration is well established in the Gospel of John (8:58, 88).[16] "I am A and O" is John's IAO.

Adam tells Dante that God's original name in the Garden of Eden was simply "*I*": "*I s'appellava in terra il sommo bene / onde vien la letizia che mi fascia*" ("The highest Good from whom comes all the joy / That clothes me was called 'I' upon the earth," (134-35)). After the fall, God was called *El*: "*e El si chiamò poi*" (136). The poet carefully places the *I* first in its line and the *El* second. Dante has changed his mind since he wrote about the subject in the *De Vulgari Eloquentia* I, 4, where he stated that *El* was the first word pronounced by Adam. Perhaps the change arose from his further reflections on the origin of language and "Author" as the key to creation. The unbound form of the vowels AEIOU and the root of "autore"

---

[15] For patristic references to IAO, see *Dictionnaire de théologie catholique* IV, pt. 1, col. 955.

[16] See Brown 533-38. Dante's use of "Io" and "Io sono" deserves a study in itself.

in AUIEO preserve the syllable *I* in the middle during the process of their rotation. The Word, as the original bond of the universe and maker of language holds a central place while people's dialects change after the fall from Eden and the confusion caused by the tower of Babel. From beginning to end, the creating Word is the redeeming Word. Christ redeems language by restoring it to its original innocence so that every letter counts. Dante insists in the *De Vulgari* (II, 7.6) that monosyllable words like *a, e, i, o, u* and interjections remain essential to poetic communication. An individual sound can be a basic instrument of meaning. For the "true Author," a single syllable can contain the whole of Being.

In his discussion of time in the *Confessions* (XI, 28), St. Augustine states that, when one is reciting a psalm from memory, the mind's attention passes from syllable to syllable while focusing on each. A syllable is anticipated in the future, sounded in the present, and recedes into the past. The process is a microcosm of all passing time containing within its present the macrocosm of reality:

> What is true of the whole psalm is also true of all its parts and of each syllable. It is true of any longer action in which I may be engaged and of which the recitation of the psalm may only be a small part. It is true of a man's whole life, of which all his actions are parts. It is true of the whole history of mankind, of which each man's life is a part. (278)

Because time passes, it is redeemable, and the process of redemption resembles the recitation of the psalm: the Word becomes a syllable in time. In the *De Trinitate* (XV, 11), Augustine compares the word manifested by articulated sound to the Word manifested by sensible flesh (*Trinity* III 209). St. Thomas Aquinas explains the Incarnation in similar terms:

> When the Word was in the Father's bosom he was known only by the Father, but when he became a spoken and embodied word

of mouth then was he made manifest to us: "He was seen upon earth, and conversed with men." A word uttered is heard by ear, but is not read until set down in letters. The Word of God could be both seen and felt, being written in our flesh. (276)[17]

Dante set down in letters the Word to be manifested to the ear, and through the eye and ear revealed to the mind and heart. He created "visible speech" ("visible parlare," *Purg.* 10, 95) to embody in imagery and word-of-mouth the Lord seen and heard by men.

Dante's use of letters for spelling out the incarnate Word can also be seen in his reference to *DXV* in *Purgatorio* XXXII, 43. As Robert Kaske has demonstrated, the initials refer to the Christic monogram D(eus) X V(ir), the God-Man (122-29).[18] Dante is guided by *Virgil*, the man who embodies all the ideal qualities of humanity and the poet who leads the pilgrim to his natural perfection on the height of Purgatory mountain. Virgil represents the human side of Dante's transformation into Christ the perfect Man. The first words of the first psalm, "Beatus vir," were often taken to allude to Christ, the only truly Blessed Man without sin who walked the path of righteousness. "*Beatus Vir*" also echoes the names of *Beat*rice and *Vir*gil as the divine and human natures that unite to make Dante an alter-Christus. For Dante, born under the sign of the Gemini twins, the *Commedia* incompasses a journey into wholeness from beginning to end.

To define his own identity as an "autore" and to tie "the universal form of this knot" (*La forma universal di questa nodo*," XXXIII, 91), Dante may have weighted E and I within the verb AUIEO as divine names, just as he has done for A representing the humanity and O the divinity of Christ

---

[17] Aquinas quotes Baruch 3:38. See also 1 John 1:1 and 2 Corinthians 3:3.

[18] A-Ω also were often separated by a *chi* (X) and *rho* (P).

(or the reverse according to some patristic commentators on Apocalypse 1:8). In addition, the poet had already drawn attention to the initial *U* of "*U*omo" ("Man") by the acrostic in *Purgatorio* XII which spells out *UOM* through lines 25-63. If *U* represents humanity, each of the vowels has been accounted for. *E*(l) and *U*(ir) or *U*(omo) also indicate and announce the God-Man in the AUIEO constellation, giving all the letters a spiritual equivalence to their physical reality. The rotation of the vowels around the central *I* presents another striking image of the cycling motion that marks the whole of Dante's paradise. The binding of the vowels also undoes the damage of Babel: Edenic (*I*), Hebrew (*E*), Greek (*A-O*), and Latin-Italo (*U*) languages all unite to tie the knot in the one true Author.

No sustained passage of *A* and *O* assonance, such as is found in Dante's *Paradiso* XXVI, occurs in John Milton's *Paradise Lost*, but there are some lines worth noting. The epic opens with *A* and *O* in reverse, an appropriate symbol of the fall's reversal: "*O*f M*a*ns First Dis*o*bedience," and ends with the same reversed order: "thir s*o*lit*a*rie w*a*y."[19] The poet appears to consciously echo the Alpha-Omega convention of letters, if not sounds, in the Father's address to the Son in Book III:

    O S*o*n, in wh*o*m my S*o*ul h*a*th chief delight,
    S*o*n *o*f my b*o*s*o*m, S*o*n wh*o a*rt *a*lone
    My W*o*rd, my wisd*o*m, *a*nd effectu*a*l might,
    *A*ll h*a*st thou spok'n *a*s my thoughts *a*re, *a*ll
    *A*s my Etern*a*l purp*o*se h*a*th decreed:

---

[19] I have used Helen Darbishire's edition of Milton because it retains the earlier spelling. Because of the the Great Vowel Shift and other changes, English orthography and phonology tended in different directions. I have marked all *A* and *O* vowels, even for dipthongs, when they appear in the text since, regardless of pronunciation, their presence warrants attention. When *A-O* assonance occurs, I discuss it or rely on the reader to sound it out.

Man shall not quite be lost, but sav'd who will. . . .
                              (168-173)
Note the chiasmus in the line, "All hast thou . . . thoughts are, all." And further in the same speech:
> By mee upheld, that he may know how frail
> His fall'n condition is, and to me ow
> All his deliv'rance, and to none but mee.
>   (180-82)

The emphasis effected by the enjambment rolling over "ow" to the next line beginning "All," seems intended and cogent, especially following the personal pronoun "mee." Man does "ow / All" to Alpha-Omega. For Milton, One alone atones for the fall: the incarnate "God and Man, Son both of God and Man" (316).

The tradition of Alpha and Omega involves visual as well as auditory configurations. Often the Word, identified by his cruciform nimbus, is shown in Christian art as the architect of the universe described in Genesis. He, the Logos-Son, can be also identified by the symbols of his profession: the compass and circle. In the famous frontispiece of the *Bible Moralisèe* in the National Library at Vienna (Vindob. 2554), for example, Christ the Creator is seen with an Alpha-compass shaping the Omega-cosmos. The illumination provides a powerful reminder of an iconography all but unrecognized today. In Book VII of *Paradise Lost*, Milton pictures the "Omnific Word" as the architect who designs and orders creation, the "great Work-Maister" or "Artifex Verbum" of the fathers:

> He took the gold'n Compasses, prepar'd
> In Gods Eternal store, to circumscribe
> This Universe, and all created things:
> One foot he centerd, and the other turnd
> Round through the vast profunditie obscure,

And said, Thus farr extend, thus farr thy bounds,
This be thy just Circumference, O World.

(225-31)

The twin compass of "the sovran Architect," an emblem and homograph of Alpha, draws the "just" circle Omega to circumscribe *"Chaos." Chaos* receives its true meaning from the Word, Alpha-Omega, Christ: chAOs, CHaoS. "For *Chaos* heard his voice. . . ." (221).[20]

That Milton was aware of the mythopoeic usage of voicing *A* and *O* is evident in his Sonnet 18, "On the late Massacher in Piemont," which also contains a number of allusions to the Apocalypse. The poem begins and closes with *A* and *O* vowels and reverberates with their assonance, rolling from line to line until it comes to rest on a final syllable of pure lament. To mark the *a* and *o* vowels is unnecessary since they ring out on their own:

    Avenge O Lord thy slaughter'd Saints, whose bones
      Lie scatter'd on the Alpine mountains cold,
      Ev'n them who kept thy truth so pure of old
      When all our Fathers worship't Stocks and Stones,
    Forget not: in thy book record their groanes
      Who were thy Sheep and in their antient Fold
      Slayn by the bloody *Piemontese* that roll'd
      Mother with Infant down the Rocks. Their moans
    The Vale redoubl'd to the Hills, and they
      To Heav'n. Their martyr'd blood and ashes sow
      O're all th'*Italian* fields where still doth sway
    The triple Tyrant: that from these may grow

---

[20] The compass image in creation is found in Proverbs 8:27-29. Dante also used the image in *Paradiso* XIX 40-46 (all *O* rhymes). For some studies on Dante's influence on Milton, see Samuel and Swain.

> A hunderd-fold, who having learnt thy way
> Early may fly the *Babylonian* wo.

All the rhymes of the sonnet consist of *A* and *O* assonance, with the long *O*'s carrying the burden of lamentation to the end where it becomes the last lingering sound. The poem resounds with the "woe, woe, woe" of Apocalypse 8:13.[21]

A mosaic of allusions to the Old Testament prophets has been found in the poem, together with traces of Exodus and the Psalms (Goldstein). Tertullian's famous apothegm has often been quoted: "The blood of the martyrs is the seed of the Church" (*Apologeticus* 50, *Corpus Christianorum* I, 171).[22] The Apocalypse, however, sounds the dominant note. The opening recalls the cry of the martyrs in Chapter 6: "How long, O Lord, holy and true, dost thou not judge and avenge our blood on them that dwell on the earth?" (6:10). There are further allusions to "Sheep" and "antient fold" (4:4), "Mother with Infant" (12:1-17), "martyr'd blood" (17:6), "triple Tyrant" (the Pope as Antichrist), and "Babylonian wo" (the fall of Babylon described in Chapter 18). The sequence of allusions suggests that Milton may have intended his sonnet to be a mini-Apocalypse, following a similar chronology--if one can employ such a word in describing the events of the Apocalypse--as is found in the original book.

Milton's use of the word "hunderd-fold" is significant; it is not only the hundredth word in the sonnet, with echoes of the sower whose seed "brought forth, some an hundredfold," but it suggests the Apocalyptic fold

---

[21] The assonance, without reference to Alpha-Omega, has been noted by Kester Svendsen and Mark Van Doren (121-25).

[22] See Jones. On the poem as a ritual "collect in verse" (Thomas Macaulay's phrase), see Miller.

164 G. M. Hopkins: New Essays

of saints and martyrs in the hundreds of thousands who will sing before the throne of the Lamb. While the sonnet begins with an appeal for vengeance, it closes on a meditative and prayerful cry of pain accepted and made fruitful, from the anger of *Avenge* to the requiem of *woe*. The rhyming of "wo" with "sow" and "grow," together with the emphasis on "thy way" in the *A*-rhyme of the sestet, voices a note of reconciliation, a transformation of grief into hope.

Sonnet 18 takes the form of a public protest against the murder of the Vaudois, descendants of the Waldenses, who believed the Bible to be the sole guide to salvation and who were attacked by the Duke of Savoy's soldiers on April 24, 1655. The poet's petition: "Forget not: in thy book record . . ." recalls not only the book of life, where all such deeds and sufferings are recorded (20:12), but the book in which John writes his visions, as well as Milton's own writing as an author. By echoing the assonance of Alpha and Omega, by employing the style and tone of the Apocalypse, and by alluding to its events, Milton brings the past and future dimensions of that book into present focus for his time and audience. He becomes another John bearing witness to God's Word.

Gerard Manley Hopkins made extensive use of the Alpha-Omega tradition in his poetry.[23] In his observations of nature, Hopkins directly connects Omega as a shape in its capital form with the perception of beauty in his Oxford dialogue "On the Origin of Beauty." An inner law is at work in the shaping of the leaves of a chestnut fan, a symmetry emerging as the leaves diminish in size on the stalk:

---

[23] See my *Inscape: The Christology and Poetry of Gerard Manley Hopkins* 276-95. For Dante and Hopkins, see *Inscape* 17, 137, 218, 270-71, 280, 285-86; for Milton and Hopkins, see 35, 36, 76, 105, 163, 227, 237, as well as the notes referred to on those pages. See also Bump and Healy.

> Although from their diminishing they do not form part of that most regular of figures the circle, yet in their diminishing they shape out another figure, do they not? partly regular, though containing variety; I mean that of a Greek Omega. (*J* 92)

Visually, this figure is the in-shape of inscape.

This visual pattern Hopkins translates into phonetic experience, using the exclamation *O* to inscape the presence of Christ-Omega in nature. In "The Wreck of the Deutschland," the poet's confession: "O Christ, O God" (28 st. 2) and the nun's crucial call: "O Christ, Christ, come quickly" (st. 24) express the Christian's act of faith and echo the last words of the Apocalypse and closing verse of the whole Bible. Jesus is invoked as "O maid's child" in "Spring" (33), "O Hero savest" in "The Loss of the Eurydice" (41), "O Christ-done deed" in "The Soldier" (63), and "O thou lord of life" in "Thou art indeed just" (74).

"Ah, Nature, framed in fault," from "Brothers" (54), reminds us of the association of Alpha with the beginning in Adam and the fall, while the "ah!" before the "bright wings" in the final line of "God's Grandeur" (31) recalls the redemption through the Holy Spirit sent as a Paraclete by Christ. In "Spring and Fall" (55), the poet addresses a young girl and reflects on the changes in the seasons and life:

> Ah! as the heart grows older
> It will come to such sights colder
> By and by, nor spare a sigh
> Though worlds of wanwood leafmeal lie.

The coined word "wanwood" conveys an inner meaning in its *A* and *O* structure, and "Ah"--"older" sounds it out as well.

In "Carrion Comfort" (64), Hopkins apostrophizes Christ as both Alpha and Omega: "But ah, but O thou terrible." If the *O* interjection calls on Christ in the wonder and dread of the recognition of inscape, the *A* sounds the responsive cry of the heart in instress. "Ah! as the heart grows older," in "Spring and Fall" catches the sigh of sorrow at finding out that the "fresh thoughts" of childhood do not endure to the end. Responding to the nun's inscaping of Christ in the "Deutschland," the poet exclaims: "Ah! there was a heart right!" (st. 29) and, speaking to himself, remarks: "Ah, touched in your bower of bone / Are you!" (st. 18). For Hopkins, such expressions of instress go directly to Christ-Omega as they rise from the Alpha of his love, heart speaking to heart: "Cor ad cor loquitur."

"I wake and feel the fell of dark" (67) dramatizes the poet's sense of total estrangement from his Lord. The use of "fell," the past tense of "fall," connotes both the reality of original sin and the promise of atonement. Human nature fell, but it has also been redeemed: the fall is past and ever present. "With witness I speak this," Hopkins adds, offering his own testimony to both experiences of sin and grace. The voicing of his witness, however, gives him small comfort, for his cries fall on deaf ears:

> And my lament
> Is cries countless, cries like dead letters sent
> To dearest him that lives alas! away.

Hopkins here puns on "dead letters" both as lost correspondence but also, and more tellingly, as the lifeless syllables his prayers now form to Christ. *A* and *O* are the dead letters sent to his beloved Master who lives "alas! away." The Alpha of his cry remains, but no Omega sounds in these words.

"Felix Randal" (53) opens with an exclamation of surprise: "Felix Randal the farrier, O is he dead then?" The *O*, perfectly natural in its context, is pregnant with meaning, for the blacksmith's death is his end and encounter with Christ. The *O* foreshadows the closing image of the "bright and battering sandal," the Omega-shaped horseshoe, still a popular symbol of good luck and a form that takes such a hold on the mind that, as

Hopkins notes, it seems to have an absolute existence. At the close of the octave the poet concludes: "Ah well, God rest him all road ever he offended!" Here the *A* echoes the comfort of instress, which is the heart's own wellbeing in the possession of its first and last resting place. The homely use of "*all road*" is particularly apt in transforming, as the horseshoe is to be re-cast, the Lancashire equivalent of "every way" into an *A-O* verbal icon.

Parallels of Alpha-instress and Omega-inscape help explain a phrase in "The Windhover" (36) that has been variously interpreted. After calling on Christ inscaped in the falcon as "O my chevalier," Hopkins turns to address Christ instressed in his own heart as "ah my dear." From the outward encounter of the falcon in its curving flight and plunging fall, the poet turns inward to reflect on his own struggle to identify with Christ-Omega. With the colors of a page from an illuminated book, the round "blue-bleak embers" burst open in the fire of love: "F*a*ll, g*a*ll themselves, and g*a*sh g*o*ld-vermili*o*n." The *A* of the "fall" and "gall" of crucifixion is alchemized and transfigured into the *O* of "gold."

Like many other critics, Marylou Motto has perceptively noted the presence of such interjections and their importance in Hopkins' poetry, but unfortunately finds them meaningless; she writes:

> The "ahs" and "ohs" stand apart from their argumentative, narrative, or descriptive contexts. Although the reader is surely meant to penetrate their surface, to feel the emotion of the speaker, and the fact that what is about to emerge has great importance, the exclamations themselves are without denotative referential meaning. (98)

The examples already given, and the tradition from which they come, should dispel any doubts about the simplicity of Hopkins' intentions and the complexities of his devices. One further example, an astonishing poem in itself, should settle the question for good.

"That Nature is a Heraclitean Fire and of the comfort of the Resurrection" (72) is Hopkins' most overtly Apocalyptic poem.[24] All the rhymes have *A* and *O* assonance, with *A* sounds in the octave and both *A* and *O* used in the sestet and three codas. The *A* assonance runs throughout the lines of the octave, as in "l*a*shes l*a*ce, l*a*nce, and p*a*ir." The device is particularly appropriate in depicting man's loss of innocence and his deathbound path to oblivion as his "m*a*sks and m*a*nm*a*rks" disappear: "M*a*nshape, th*a*t shone / Sheer off, disseve*a*l, *a* star, | death blots black out." But the *O* assonance, present from the start, surfaces at last in the final lines that affirm the resurrection:

In *a* flash, *a*t *a* trumpet cr*a*sh,
I *a*m *a*ll *a*t once wh*a*t Christ is, | since he w*a*s what I *a*m, and
This Jack, j*o*ke, p*oo*r p*o*tsherd, | p*a*tch, m*a*tchw*oo*d, imm*o*rt*a*l di*a*m*o*nd,
Is imm*o*rt*a*l di*a*m*o*nd.

"Jack" is actually another "John," witnessing to new life as *A* turns back to *O*. The trigrammaton IAO, where *I* is the Divine Name, also rises from these lines in the chiasmus, "*I* am . . . what Chr*i*st *i*s, s*i*nce he was what *I* am," and "*i*mmortal d*i*amond." Indeed, "immortal" contains the three letters: "*I*mm*O*rt*A*l." More striking still, the word "diamond" is "AMO," imbeds the Name itself: "d*I*Am*O*nd" and even spells out "*I* am A O."

Hopkins has discovered the secret name written on the white stone of the apocalypse: "He that hath an ear to hear, let him hear what the Spirit saith unto the churches; to him that overcometh will I give to eat of

---

[24] For more on Apocalyptic allusion in the sonnet, see Cotter, "Apocalyptic."

the hidden manna, and will give him a white stone, and in the stone a new name written, which no man knoweth saving he that receiveth it" (2:17). For Hopkins, the white stone recalls Christ himself who was traditionally seen as the inscribed stone of this passage. "The Word incarnate," writes Alcuin in his gloss, "is he who appeared shining among men without any impurity of sin and illuminated the darkness of our mortality with the light of his divinity" (100, col. 1106; Haimo 119, col. 975). For Hopkins, too, the Latin root of "diamond," "adamas" recalls the old and new Adam, the immortality lost and returned through the resurrection. "Adamas" was also glossed as

> the Lord and Savior who being in the form of God, thought it not robbery to be equal with God, but emptied himself, taking the form of a servant, being made in the likeness of men and in habit found as man. He humbled himself, and became obedient unto death, even death on a cross. For which cause God hath exalted him and hath given him a name which is above every name. (Phil. 2:5-9)[25]

This passage, thrice commented on by Hopkins, forms the basis of his whole idea of the Great Sacrifice by which Alpha descended into the world and rolled back to ascend as Omega.

These three poets employed *A* and *O* assonance and exclamations that can be traced back to the Early Church. The many inscriptions, monuments, and mosaics that display the Alpha-Omega monogram provide iconographic evidence of an oral-aural experience, seen in the Orans figures,

---

[25] See Lauretus 54. This standard collection of "distinctiones," first published in Cologne in 1681, has been reprinted many times, most recently in Munich in 1971.

and touched on in the ancient texts.[26] In the second century, Irenaeus warned the Gnostic Marcus about mythologizing Omega "which sounds out the glory of Him who produced" the universe, the Word to whom "the glory of that sound is transmitted upwards" (*Adversus* I, 14.7 in Roberts I 338). Nevertheless, later Christian writers, like Primasius in the sixth century, would re-baptize these Gnostic teachings in their own expositions of Alpha and Omega (*Commentaria* 22:8 in Migne 68 cols. 932-33). Paulinus of Nola and other poets refer to Alpha and Omega and carried the tradition to poetry. In his *Cathemerinon* (IX, 10-12, Migne 59 col. 863), Prudentius recalls the Apocalypse and Prologue of St. John:

> Corde natus ex parentis ante mundi exordium
> alpha et Ω cognominatus: ipse fons et clausula
> omnium quae sunt, fuerunt, quaeque post futura sunt.
>   (*Poema*, Migne 59 col. 863)
> (Born from the Father's love before the world's beginning,
> Alpha and Omega named, the fountain and the ending
> Of all that is and was and will hereafter be.)

In the twelfth century, Hildebert of Lavardin begins his hymn "De Sancta Trinitate" with "Alpha et Ω, magne Deus," and employs pervasive assonance of *A-O* throughout the 250 lines of his poem (46-53).[27] His contemporary, Pietro da Eboli calls on God as "author" in his epic poem, *De rebus Siculis*

---

[26] For a review of the artistic heritage, see the entry for "A et ω" in *Dictionnaire d'archéologie chrétienne et de liturgie* I cols. 1-25. An interesting variation on the *A-O* image is the pentalpha, created by a circle containing five alphas that make up a star or diamond-shaped pentacle. Piero Valeriano writes that "the five wounds of Christ . . . appropriately constitute a pentalpha" (351). The *Gawain* poet says that the pentangle "Overal" England is called þe endeles knot" (18, l. 630). Dante uses the pentagon to illustrate man's natural perfection (*Convivio* IV, 7). See also Cornelius à Lapide on Apocalypse 1:8 with an illustration of the pentalpha.

[27] See also Lütolf 74 items 1616-21.

carmen (XXII): "Alfa deus, deus O, mundi moderator et auctor."[28] Finally, in the liturgy the *A* syllable received melodious ornamentation and repetition; in the "Amen" at the conclusion of hymns, while the "jubilus" led to prolongation of the two *A*'s in "Alleluia" ("Praise IA"). Both developments date back to the Old Roman repertory and Mozarabic, Ambrosian, and Gregorian chants.[29] The "Great O" Antiphons celebrate the coming savior in Advent; the seven antiphons are still sung at the Magnificat for vespers during the week before the Christmas vigil.[30] Outside the liturgy, the "XV O's," a collection of prayers devoted to the Passion, remained popular in England until the seventeenth century.[31]

Dante, Milton, and Hopkins advanced, as we all do, from sound to alphabet and back to sound to communicate their meaning and the mystery beyond meaning. Wording the Word through whom all things were made, they heralded the Lord to whom all things are tending. "Principium a quo omnia sunt et causantur, et finis ad quam omnia tendunt et ordinatur" (Nicholas of Gorran 184a). In their poetry, the Word made flesh has become "visible speech" and audible writing. Letters incarnate spoken words and images, while imagery incarnates words and letters. For, as St. Augustine states in his *De Trinitate* (XV, 10): "Sight and hearing are two things mutually distinct in the bodily senses, but to see and to hear are the

---

[28] Cited by Nardi 319. On "Alfa ed O," see 317-20.

[29] See "Jubilus" in *Dictionnaire d'archéologie* VLII col. 1770.

[30] See "O (Antiennes)" in *Dictionnaire d'archéologie* XII, cols. 1817-19. The Cynewulf poet employs some dozen "O Antiphons" in the first part of *The Christ*. See Cook 71-72.

[31] For the text of the "XV OOs" or "XV OIS," see Bennett 170-81. The Latin prayers were often attributed to St. Bridget (vii).

same thing in the mind" (*Of the Trinity* III 209). The incarnation-event is this seeing, hearing, and reading. St. Paul quotes the word of God to confirm his call as a preacher of that word: "Scripture tells us: 'The word is near at hand, it is on thy lips and in thy heart,' that is, the word of faith, which we preach" (Rom. 10:8). The Son, according to Milton's *Paradise Lost*, restored mankind "by coming in the Flesh" and "Proclaiming Life to all who shall believe / In his redemption" (XII, 405, 407-08). Those who received his word then preached to the world "the tidings brought from Heav'n" and "Thir doctrine and thir story writt'n left" (504, 506). Spoken and written words reveal the Logos to the mind and heart. "Heaven and earth have set their hand" to Dante's "sacred poem" (*Par.* XXV, 1-2) to re-echo the incarnation.

Humanity is the alphabet that Alpha-Omega begins and ends by being man. "Christ the Son of God," writes St. Bonaventure in his *Itinerarium Mentis ad Deum* (VII, 7), speaking for the authors before and after him, is "in one Being the first and the last, the highest and the lowest, the circumference and the center, the Alpha and the Omega, the caused and the cause, the creator and the creature, the book written within and without" (42, 37-38).[32] What they had heard, what they had seen and handled, Dante, Milton, and Hopkins set down in letters of the Word of Life so that the book within has become the book without: "Word, that heard and kept thee and uttered thee outright" (28 st. 30).

---

[32] "The book within and without" is from Apocalypse 5:1.

Works Cited

Ahern, John. "Binding the Book: Hermeneutics and Manuscript Production in *Paradiso* 33." *PMLA* 97 (1982): 800-09.

Alcuin. *Commentarius*. Migne. Vol. 100.

Alighieri, Dante. *De Vulgari Eloquentia*. Ravenna: Longo, 1981.

---. *Il Convivio*. Ed. G. Busnelli and G. Vandelli. 2nd ed., ed. A.E. Quaglio. Florence: Le Monnier, 1964.

Aquinas, Thomas. *Commentary on the Apostles' Creed*. *St. Thomas Aquinas: Theological Texts*. Ed. and Trans. Thomas Gilby. Oxford: Oxford UP, 1955.

Augustine. *Confessions*. Trans. R.S. Pine-Coffin. Baltimore, Md.: Penguin, 1961.

---. *On the Trinity*. *Nicene and Post-Nicene Fathers*. Ed. Philip Schaff. Buffalo: Christian Literature Co., 1887.

Augustodunensis, Honorius. *Elucidarium*. Migne. Vol. 172.

Bede, Venerable. *Explanatio Apocalysis*. Migne. Vol. 93.

Bennett, J.A.W., ed. *Devotional Pieces in Verse and Prose*. The Scottish Text Society, 3rd Series, 23. Edinburgh: G. Blackwood, 1955.

Bonaventure. *The Mind's Road to God*. Trans. George Boas. The Library of Liberal Arts. New York: Liberal Arts Press, 1953.

Brown, Raymond S., S.S., ed. *The Gospel According to John (X-XIII)*. Vol. 24. *The Anchor Bible*. Garden City: Doubleday, 1966.

Bump, Jerome. "Influence and Intertextuality: Hopkins and the School of Dante." *JEGP* 83 (1984): 355-79.

Busnelli, G., and G. Vandelli, eds. *Il Convivio*. By Dante Alighieri. 2nd ed., ed. A.E. Quaglio. Florence: Le Monnier, 1964.

Chatillon, François. "*Arbiter Omnipotens* et le symbolisme de l'Alpha et de l'Omega." *Revue du Moyen Age Latin* 11 (1955): 5-50.

Cook, Albert S., ed. *The Christ of Cynewulf*. 1900. Hamden, Conn.: Archon Books, 1964.

Cotter, James Finn. "Apocalyptic Imagery in 'That Nature is a Heraclitean Fire.'" *VP* 24 (1986): 261-73.

---, trans. *Divine Comedy*. By Dante Alighieri. Warwick, N.Y.: Amity House, 1988.

---. *Inscape: The Christology and Poetry of Gerard Manley Hopkins*. Pittsburgh: University of Pittsburgh Press, 1972.

Cremona, Joseph. "Paradiso XXVI." *Cambridge Readings in Dante's Comedy*. Ed. Kenelm Foster and Patrick Boyde. Cambridge: Cambridge UP, 1981. 174-90.

Dictionnaire d'archéologie chrétienne et de liturgie. Paris: Letouzey et Ané, 1907.

Dictionnaire de théologie catholique. Paris: Letouzey et Ané, 1911.

Donadoni, Eugenio. "Canto XXVI." *Letture dantesche: Paradiso*. Ed. Giovanni Getto. Florence: Sansoni, 1961. 527-48.

Enciclopedia dantesca. Rome: Instituto della Enciclopedia Italiana, 1971.

Farrer, Austin. *A Rebirth of Images: The Making of St. John's Apocalypse*. London: Dacre Press, 1949.

Getto, Giovanni. "Canto XXVI." *Lectura Dante Scaligera: Paradiso*. Florence: Le Monnier, 1968. 931-55.

Goldstein, Charles E. "The Hebrew Element in Milton's Sonnet XVIII." *Milton Quarterly* 9 (1975): 111-14.

Haimo of Auxerre (ps.-Haimo of Halberstadt). *Expositio in Apocalypsim*. Migne. Vol. 117.

Healy, Sr. M. Aquinas. "Milton and Hopkins." *University of Toronto Quarterly* 22 (1952): 18-25.

Hildebert of Lavardin. *Hildeberti Canomannensis Episcopi Carmina Minora.* Ed. H. Brian Scott. Leipzig: Teubner, 1969.

Hillard, Katharine, trans. *The Banquet.* By Dante Alighieri. London: Keegan Paul, Trench & Co., 1889.

Hugh of St. Cher. *De Arca Noe Morali.* Migne. Vol. 176.

---. *Noah's Ark. Hugh of Saint-Victor: Selected Spiritual Writings.* Trans. a religious of C.S.M.V. New York: Harper & Row, 1962.

Irenaeus. *Adversus Haereses.* Roberts Vol. 1.

Isidore. *Etymologiae.* Migne. Vol. 82.

Jones, Nicholas R. "The Education of the Faithful in Milton's Piedmontese Sonnet." *Milton Studies* 10 (1977): 167-76.

Kaske, Robert. "Dante's *DXV.*" *Dante: A Collection of Critical Essays.* Ed. John Freccero. Englewood Cliffs, N.J.: Prentice-Hall, 1965.

Lubac, Henri de. *Exégèse Médiévale.* Paris: Aubier, 1959.

Lapide, Cornelius à. *Commentaria in Sacram Scripturam.* Paris: L. Vivés, 1868.

Lauretus, Hieronymous. *Silva Allegoriarum Totius Sacrae Scripturae.* 1681. Munich: W. Fink, 1971.

Lütolf, Max, ed. *Analecta hymnica Medii Aevi: Register* I. Bern: Francke, 1978.

Maurus, Rabanus (Raban Maur). *Hrabanus Maurus, Liber do laudibus Sanctae Crucis: Vollständige Faksimile-Ausgabe des Codex Vindobonensis 652 der Oster. Nationalbibliothek.* 2 vols. Comm. Kurt Holzer. *Codices Selecti,* vol. 33. Graz: Akademische Druck, 1973. I, fol. 7v.

---. *Liber de Laudibus Sanctae Crucis.* Migne. Vol. 107.

Mengaldo, Pier Vincenzo. *Linguistica e retorica di Dante* Pisa: Nistri-Lischi, 1978. 223-46.

Migne, J.P., ed. *Patrologiae Cursus Completus: Series Latina*. Paris: J.P. Migne, 1858.

Miller, Edmund. "'The Late Massacre': Milton's Liturgical Sonnet." *Concerning Poetry* 17 (1984): 43-50.

Milton, John. *The Poetical Works of John Milton*. Ed. Helen Darbishire. Oxford: Oxford UP, 1958.

Motto, Marylou. *«Mined with a Motion»: The Poetry of Gerard Manley Hopkins*. New Brunswick, N.J.: Rutgers UP, 1984.

Nardi, Bruno. *Saggi e note di critica dantesca*. Milan: R. Ricciardi, 1966.

Nicholas of Gorran. *In Acta Apostolorum, et Singulas Apostolorum . . . Canonicas Epistolas, et Apocalypsin Commentarii*. Antwerp: John Keerberg, 1620.

Primasius. *Commentaria super Apocalypsim*. Migne. Vol. 68.

Prudentius. *Poema*. Migne. Vol. 59.

Reeves, Marjorie, and Beatrice Hirsch-Reich. *The Figurae of Joachim of Fiore*. Oxford: Oxford UP, 1972.

Roberts, Alexander, and James Donaldson, eds. *The Ante-Nicene Fathers*. New York: Christian Literature Co., 1896.

Samuel, Irene. *Dante and Milton: The Commedia and Paradise Lost*. Ithaca: Cornell UP, 1966.

Singleton, Charles S., ed. *The Divine Comedy*. By Dante Alighieri. Princeton: Princeton UP, 1970.

Sir Gawain and the Green Knight. Ed. J.R.R. Tolkien and E.V. Gordon. 2nd ed. rev. Norman Davis. Oxford: Oxford UP, 1967.

Svendsen, Kester. "Milton's Sonnet on the Massacre in Piedmont." *Shakespeare Association Bulletin* 20 (1945): 14-55.

Swain, Kathleen M. "Some Dante and Milton Analogues." *Renascence* 37 (1984): 43-51.

Tertullian. *Opus Tertulliani* II. *Corpus Christianorum: Series Latina.* Turnhout, Belgium: Brepols, 1954.

Tondelli, Leone, ed. *Libro delle Figure dell' Abate Gioachino Da Fiore.* 2nd ed. 2 vols. Torino: Società Editrice Internationale, 1953.

Valeriano, Piero. *Hieroglyphica.* Basil: Thomam Guarinum, 1556.

Van Doren, Mark. *Introduction to Poetry.* New York: Sloane, 1951.

Hopkins as Teacher:
The English Years

Understanding the Man by Watching Him Work

Joseph J. Feeney, S.J.

Gerard Manley Hopkins dedicated more of his life to teaching than to any other work. Leaving Oxford in 1867 with twenty-two years to live, he devoted nine years to his Jesuit studies and spiritual development, and three to parish work in England and Scotland. He spent ten years, though, in various classrooms of England and Ireland and thus gave the largest part of his working life to teaching and to his students.

Hopkins' classes were diverse in both age and geography. He first taught in September 1867, when, fresh from Oxford, he spent seven months in Birmingham as a junior master at John Henry Newman's Oratory School. Five years later and a Jesuit, he spent six days in the early summer of 1873 substituting for a master at Stonyhurst College in Lancashire, and then during the academic year 1873-74 taught young Jesuits at Roehampton in London. Years later, after his ordination in 1877, he spent three terms in Derbyshire with the schoolboys of Mount St. Mary's College. He returned to teaching in 1882, to prepare older students--the "secular philosophers" at

Stonyhurst--for the External B.A. degree from the University of London. Finally, in February 1884, he was sent to University College, Dublin, as Professor of Greek, to lecture to university students and conduct examinations for the Royal University of Ireland. He remained there until his premature death in June 1889, seven weeks before his forty-fifth birthday.

Various and conflicting reports of his teaching have survived: that he taught well, that he was eccentric, that (in his later Dublin years) he conducted his classes in an uproar and assiduously avoided covering examination material. In his own letters, journals, and poems Hopkins also commented on his teaching experiences, frequently stressing the great weariness his work brought him. Several poems also grew out of his work in the schools; a minimal list would include "The Elopement" (135), "Brothers" (54), "The Blessed Virgin compared to the Air we Breathe"(60), and surely the Terrible Sonnets (64-69) of his Dublin years.

To understand Hopkins, then, it is important to study his years of teaching, especially his English years (1867-84) which prefigure the anguished dark years in smoky Dublin. What sort of teacher was he? Was he ever happy in the classroom? What were his relationships with his students and his reputation as a teacher? What happened as Hopkins moved from class to class and school to school? And--a question rarely asked--did his experiences and reactions as teacher show any patterns of continuity or change as Hopkins grew from a young convert in Birmingham to a depressed teacher at Stonyhurst? Some surprises emerge from this study: (1) Hopkins' recurring complaints about teaching began before he became a Jesuit; (2) Hopkins was at times quite happy as a teacher and was even recognized as one who "teaches well"; (3) despite his great talent as a classical scholar, he might well have been happiest with younger students; and (4) Hopkins' depression, so debilitating in his Dublin years, predated his assignment to Ireland. But such conclusions depend on a careful and systematic examination of historical data, year by year and period by period.

The Oratory School, Birmingham, September, 1867--April, 1868

Hopkins and Newman at first misunderstood each other on the question of an appointment to the teaching staff of the Oratory School. In 1866 Newman had been kind and helpful when Hopkins was coming to a decision about entering the Roman Catholic Church, and he had received Hopkins into the church on October 21, 1866 (*F* 100). The following January, Hopkins, then in his last year at Oxford, went to the Birmingham Oratory for a retreat, and at that time he and Newman discussed teaching as a possible career or at least as a temporary occupation. Hopkins himself seemed uncertain about whether he would like, be called to, or even be fit for, a career of teaching--"schooling," as Newman put it--and consequently Newman dropped the subject. About four weeks later, though, Hopkins wrote to ask Newman's advice about a teaching position recently offered him by a Mr. Darnell. This letter resolved the misunderstanding, and on February 22, 1867, Newman sent this gracious invitation:

> When you said you disliked schooling, I said not a word. Else, I should have asked you to come here for *the very purpose* for which Mr. Darnell wishes for you. . . .
>
> I think you would get on with us, and that we should like you:
>
> Since then it was only delicacy which prevented my speaking when you were here, I have no hesitation in asking you to accept the invitation which we now make to you. (*F* 406)

Hopkins quickly accepted this invitation to teach at the Oratory School, which Newman had founded in 1859 as a Catholic equivalent of an English public school (Bergonzi 48). Newman, equally prompt, confirmed

Hopkins' appointment as a lay master only six days after his invitation: "You will not find your work hard here--the terms would be those which Mr. Darnell offered you.... I am glad we shall have you" (*F* 407). Hopkins thus decided on the Oratory after finishing Oxford. That summer he wrote to an old friend, "I go to the Oratory in September" (*F* 38); there he was to teach Latin and Greek (Lahey, *Gerard Manley Hopkins* 47).

He arrived on September 10, and spent a blissful week of peace before classes began (*F* 41, 42). Even before he met any class he was already calling his students "my boys," and he thus described his job to a friend: "My boys come back the day after tomorrow but school goes but languidly till Friday. I have got the fifth and a kind of super-sixth form, consisting of two boys who are staying to coach" (probably, at that time, for the London External B.A. degree). Then Hopkins, with both the self-doubt and the impracticality of a new teacher, went on, "The work, I think, is within my attainments and I do hope it is within my time, for I want to read almost every thing that has ever been written" (*F* 228). In that passing comment about free time and intellectual growth--while teaching teenagers!--lay false expectations, unattainable hopes of leisure, and the seeds of future depression.

After only two weeks, reality had its effect by the end of September. In one letter even the date was unsure: "Sept. 30, is it not? '67"; and he wrote another friend, "How badly you must think I have remembered my promise to write soon. If I had only done so the first week I was here it wd. have been well: ever since then I have scarcely had a minute of leisure." Then he described his room, his schedule, and his new life:

> For the first week I was in the Oratory as a guest: now I am in the house where Walford [a former master] was and do not see anything of the Oratory. Fancy me getting up at a quarter past

> six: it is however done with a melancholy punctuality nearly every morning. The boys' mass is at seven; then what they call Preparation fr. 7.45 to 8.30; then breakfast in Hall, so to speak; at 9.30 school till 12; dinner in Hall at 1; school fr. 2 to 3; then the boys and I sometimes go to their field, which they call Bosco, for a game, just now hockey but soon football; at 6 tea in Hall; from 6.30 to 8.30 school. My class is the fifth [form] but besides this my work includes two private pupils who come to me fr. 8.45 to 10 on all nights but Saturday and fr. 5 to 6 on the half-holidays Tuesday, Thursday, and Saturday. With reading the class books and looking over exercises (which takes a long time) I find all my time occupied. Today however is Sunday and the boys are playing fives like good ones: I wish they wd. play all the other numbers on the clock all the other days of the week.

Hopkins clearly felt harried, but then, without realizing the irony, he added a practical count of his fifth form and of his private students: "The fifth, the head class, has only five boys: thus I have seven." (Newman, perhaps, may have been right when he commented that "you will not find your work hard here.") More positively, the new teacher also showed a care and even affection for his students and their innocence: "I feel as if they were all my children, a notion encouraged by their innocence and backwardness. They never swear beyond Con-found you, you young fool, and that only one of them" (*F* 43-44). At this early stage Hopkins had even learned his students' politics: one was a nobleman's son but many were "Radicals" (*F* 45).

His colleagues at the Oratory School did not inspire a similar affection, and before the end of September he wrote, "The masters' table appears to be the dregs of Great Britain." He immediately added, "When I say dregs I only mean that they come fr. all quarters indiscriminately and I include myself: it is sweepings, not dregs I mean. They are nice souls and one of them, a very young man, I like particularly." He had other complaints: no newspapers, no letters from family or friends, no time for private reading. He did enjoy some pleasures--hearing a string quartet, walking the nearby countryside ("really very good for so near Birmingham")--and had asked Fr. Ambrose St. John, Newman's close associate, to arrange more time for reading. Yet all was not good, and at this early date--September 30, 1867--Hopkins first uttered what would become a repeated complaint: "I wonder if there is anything I cd. do, though the income were less, wh. wd. give me more time, for I feel the want of that most of all" (*F* 44).

One month later, on October 26, Hopkins was still enjoying his students even though one had injured him at football. He was jocular and lighthearted: "I am very fond of my 'spiritual children,' which fondness the fattest and biggest has repaid by laming me at football." And one of his students later remembered him "even catching frogs and newts" for the "lusty delectation" of his students (Lahey, *Gerard Manley Hopkins* 47). Other experiences, though, evoked more complex responses: Hopkins found Newman's preaching good, felt reasonably close to him, was delighted that his old Oxford friend H.W. Challis had joined the staff, looked forward to the visit of another friend, yet still found the Oratory disorganized and the food sometimes sparse, even for guests (*F* 45-46). And on November 1 he renewed his complaint about the lack of time: "I am so hard at work I have scarcely any leisure at all" (*B* 18).

Hopkins' work, or his weariness, grew more intense in November, and he did not make any journal notations from November 4 to January 1 (*J* 158-59). But he still seemed to like the students: "At the beginning of December there was about a week of sharp weather and the boys flooded the ball-court and slid and skated on it." December also brought welcome news from Oxford, especially about the examination results for his friends, and he twice went to the Oratory for special Expositions of the Blessed Sacrament. Then, after speeches and prize-giving on December 19, both the boys and Hopkins went home for Christmas.

Renewing his journal at year's end, he reviewed the past months: "I began my school work with the fifth form and Sparrow and Bellasis [his two special pupils]. Presently I gave them to Challis and had the fifth and fourth. Occasionally, when Stokes [another master] was away, I had the second too. I did a great deal of work, clinched with the exam. papers, and am much tired" (*J* 158-59). Such was Hopkins' first term as a teacher. And, despite comments on his students, his weariness, and his lack of time, he never once in letter or journal mentioned either teaching or any classroom experience.

Returning to Birmingham on January 21, 1868, Hopkins assiduously kept up his journal during the next term but devoted most of his comments to the weather (*J* 159-64). As early as February 12 he renewed his complaints and began to seek some new occupation:

> I must say that I am very anxious to get away from this place. I have become very weak in health and do not seem to recover myself here or likely to do so. Teaching is very burdensome, especially when you have much of it: I have. I have not much time and almost no energy--for I am always tired--to do anything on my own account. I put aside that one sees and hears nothing and nobody here.

Only two things pleased him: Challis' presence and his own students ("I ought to make the exception that the boys are very nice indeed"). He was also trying to make a decision about the rest of his life--painter? writer? priest?--and was worried about his mother's pain if he should choose the priesthood. "The general result is that I am perfectly restless about things that I shd. otherwise care about, uncertain as I am." He even asked a friend about a private tutorship for the next term: "Do you happen to know of any tutorship I cd. take for a few months after Easter? as I am anxious to leave this place then" (*F* 231-32).

The rest of term was equally dull, with but few diversions: an "instrument concert," some lovely crimson nut-buds on a hazelbush, Newman's 67th birthday, a rare trip, letter, or visitor, and an occasional sign of spring (*J* 160-63). He even began to learn the violin (*F* 231). Hopkins also contributed a poem, "The Elopement" (135), to a handwritten student magazine, with his poem followed by a parody, "The Robber," written by his two former special-students, R. Bellasis and W. Sparrow (*P* 309). Hopkins' poem suggests that escaping was much on his mind:

>All slumbered whom our rud red tiles
>Do cover from the starry spread,
>When I with never-needed wiles
> Crept trembling out of bed.
>Then at the door what work there was, good lack,
>To keep the loaded bolt from plunging back.
>
>When this was done and I could look
>I saw the stars like flash of fire.
>My heart irregularly shook,
> I cried with my desire.
>I put the door to with the bolts unpinned,
>Upon my forehead hit the burly wind.

Escape finally came; after the troubled and dull term he seemed relieved to write in his journal, on April 4, "School over."

The next day, Palm Sunday, a retreat began at the Oratory-- probably for the school's old boys--which was given by a Jesuit, Fr. Henry Coleridge,

S.J.[1]   During this retreat, which ended on Maundy Thursday, April 9, Hopkins probably consulted Fr. Coleridge about his future. Soon afterwards, on April 15, Hopkins departed from the Oratory School with Newman's blessing (*J* 163, 381; *F* 408).

Hopkins thus left his first teaching position before the year ended. It had been a difficult time, especially during the unsettled second term. And several themes emerged that would characterize Hopkins' teaching career: weariness and lack of energy, distaste for the tiring task of grading examinations, desire for leisure, affection for his students and their innocence, and reticence (or lack of interest?) in talking about teaching and the classroom.

Stonyhurst College, June--July, 1873

Hopkins' second stint as teacher was short: it lasted six days. In the early summer of 1873 Hopkins, by then a Jesuit scholastic, had just finished his three years of philosophical studies at St. Mary's Hall, next to Stonyhurst College. After his examination he was called over to the College to instruct the School of Rhetoric during a master's absence.[2] Perhaps because of his experience at the Oratory School Hopkins was brought in, and his journal records the circumstances: "June 30--I went to teach the School of Rhetoric at the College in Mr. Sydney Smith's absence, while he was with some of

---

[1] On Fr. Coleridge, whom Hopkins called his "oldest friend in the Society" (*F* 138), see *J* 381-82, and his obituary in *Letters and Notices*. It was he who, as editor of *The Month*, rejected "The Wreck of the Deutschland" for publication. He was also a close friend of Newman.

[2] The regular master, Mr. Sydney Smith, S.J., taught both rhetoric--at Stonyhurst the sixth form (Roberts, "Notes" 210)--and a group of older students who were preparing for the External B.A. degree (*Catalogus* (1873) 7).

his boys who were gone to Manchester to matriculate, and I taught six days." The journal records nothing about his classes; the only experience that impressed him was a curious word-usage by the College's watchman who said to Hopkins, "I'll put on my shoon and let thee out" (*J* 232).

Characteristically, Hopkins later remembered at least one of these students. This young man, James Scanlan, had entered the Society of Jesus on September 7, 1873, and lived in the Jesuit community at Roehampton where Hopkins was teaching; he died a few months later, on January 1, at the age of nineteen (*Catalogus* (1874) 15; (1875) 40). At his death Hopkins noted in his journal, "Br. Scanlan, who was a pupil of mine that six days I was at the College at Stonyhurst, died lately at Brighton." Having heard of young Scanlan's devotion to his Jesuit vocation and his religious garb, Hopkins added, "He insisted on wearing his gown to the last" (*J* 241).

Manresa House, Roehampton, September, 1873--July, 1874

On finishing his studies in philosophy Hopkins expected to teach in one of the English Jesuits' schools "at Stonyhurst or elsewhere" (*F* 58). He would teach "one of the higher classes," he thought, and "the year's teaching was given as a rest" from his studies. "I think," he noted, "this is as good an arrangement as could have been made" (*F* 122). Instead of schoolboys, however, he was sent to teach young Jesuits--the "Juniors"--at the novitiate and juniorate at Roehampton.[3] He had twenty-three Juniors to teach, plus five novices who also followed the Juniors' course. Although they were just beginning their Jesuit training, they were mature students, their ages ranging from 17 to 27 and averaging 22 years (*Catalogus* (1874) 13, 14, "Index"). Divided into two groups, they had separate year-end examinations; Hopkins,

---

[3] For a thorough account of this year, see Thomas, *Hopkins the Jesuit* 129-49.

it thus seems, had two separate courses and two separate preparations (Thomas, *Hopkins the Jesuit* 146). He was expected to teach them Greek, Latin, and most of their English.

For an extra but light task he was also named house-historian, which involved writing an account of the events--usually minor ones--at Manresa House. Like his students, Hopkins had full holidays on Sundays and Thursdays, and a half-holiday on Tuesday afternoon. Important feasts, too, like that of the Jesuit St. Francis Xavier on December 3, also meant a holiday. Despite the multiple preparations it does not seem a heavy schedule or onerous job; according to Alfred Thomas, S.J., the assignment was "probably regarded as a 'cushy berth' in the Province, as compared with the more hectic rough and tumble of teaching in one of the large schools" (Thomas, *Hopkins the Jesuit* 131, 135-36).

On the evening of August 27, 1873, Hopkins received his assignment; arriving at Roehampton the next day he happened to meet the Provincial "who spoke most kindly and encouragingly" to the new teacher (*J* 236). From the evening of August 30 to the morning of September 8, he made his annual eight-day retreat (*J* 236). Then, to see how much Latin and Greek his students knew, he gave a "trial examen" on September 9, covering Virgil's *Georgics* and a speech of Aeschines. September 22 brought the start of classes (*J* 238); however, the academic year did not officially begin until October 1 with the singing of the "Veni Creator Spiritus" before the Community Mass (Thomas, *Hopkins the Jesuit* 130-31).

Aside from the phrase "Sept. 22--The schools begin" (*J* 238), neither Hopkins' journal nor published letters mentioned teaching; from September to December his journal dealt only with nature-observations, the weather, a family wedding, some Jesuit news, his retreat (with its "great mercy" about his friend Dolben's salvation), unusual words, a nightmare, and visits to the

"Kensington Museum" (the Victoria and Albert Museum), to the Jesuits' Beaumont College, and to his family in Hampstead for Christmas week (*J* 236-40).

One further comment might be added: in his nightmare of September 18, the day of his visit to the Kensington Museum, he

> thought something or someone leapt onto me and held me quite fast: this I think woke me.... This first start is, I think, a nervous collapse of the same sort as when one is very tired and holding oneself at stress not to sleep yet / suddenly goes slack and seems to fall and wakes, only on a greater scale and with a loss of muscular control reaching more or less deep.... The feeling is terrible: the body ... seems to fall in and hang like a dead weight on the chest. (*J* 238)

Given that classes were to begin in four days, and given his words "very tired" and "stress," this nightmare may perhaps have been evoked by the prospect of a year's classes and by memories of his weariness at the Oratory School.

The new year, 1874, brought Hopkins a new hobby: "I myself am learning the piano now, self-taught alas!" He was, though, not learning for performance, he wrote his Oxford friend Robert Bridges, "but to be independent of others and learn something about music." Surely such self-teaching and practice took time, but right after mentioning his piano-playing he added, "I have very little time though. I am professor of rhetoric here since last September" (*B* 30). As in the past, he never mentioned his teaching but rather commented on nature, politics, trips to museums and elsewhere (sometimes with his students), a bit of Irish dialect, an occasional visitor, and news of his community, family, and friends. He even noted a "great famine in Bengal" (*J* 240-49). But nothing on teaching or his classes, even though during this period[4] he composed his "Lecture Notes: Rhetoric" (*J* 265-90).

These "Lecture Notes: Rhetoric" merit a few comments, since they seem to deal with Hopkins' personal interests rather than with his students' understanding of Greek and Latin rhetoric. Did he, without intending any disadvantage for his students, design his lectures more to understand recondite questions of rhythm than to meet the educational needs of his Jesuit students? His lectures had so many examples and such unstressed topic sentences that a young English Jesuit student would likely have been either bored or confused.

During this year Hopkins' only mention of his educational work came, as before, at the end of term. In late July he wrote, "Our schools at Roehampton ended with two days of examination before St. Ignatius' feast the 31st."[5] And one ominous old theme recurred:

> I was very tired and deeply cast down till I had some kind words from the Provincial. Altogether perhaps my heart has never been so burdened and cast down as this year. The tax on my strength has been greater than I have felt before: . . . I feel myself weak and can do little."

Then he put his weariness in a religious context: "But in all this our Lord goes His own way" (*J* 249-50).

Hopkins continued to feel a personal care for, and interest in, his students. He sometimes spent a day's outing with one or two of them, going on trips "to Kew Gardens with Br. [Archibald] Campbell the High-

---

[4] According to the best scholars (House xxvii-xxviii; Storey xxvi-xxvii; Thomas, *Hopkins the Jesuit* 134).

[5] For details of this examination, and for the two separate classes, see Thomas, *Hopkins the Jesuit* 146.

lander," to the Royal Academy with Joseph Bampton, and again to the Kew Gardens with John Dobson.[6] Towards the end of the year, in July, he twice accompanied a larger group of his Juniors to Parliament, once to the House of Lords and once to the House of Commons. On the second occasion, July 14, Hopkins commented in his notebook on the quality of the oratory; perhaps this expedition had been a "field trip" to offer his students some practical examples of the art of rhetoric (*J* 248-49; Thomas, *Hopkins the Jesuit* 145).

During this year he also maintained contact with some former students. On March 24, for example, he welcomed his student from the Oratory School, R.G. Bellasis, for whose schoolboy magazine Hopkins had written "The Elopement" and who had co-authored the subsequent parody. (A year earlier he had sent Bellasis greetings through a friend.) On this visit Bellasis was accompanied by Hopkins' Oxford friend, H.W. Challis, his former colleague at the Oratory School; both visitors had become barristers. Bellasis would return to Roehampton for a retreat from March 29 to April 3 and for another visit with Hopkins on April 11. Since Beliasis was later to become an Oratorian and a priest, his vocation might well have entered their discussions.[7]

Hopkins again remembered his students when they died. At Roehampton he noted, "April 25 . . . Br. Alexander Byrne died of rapid consumption. He was a novice but had been one of my pupils" (*J* 243). A

---

[6] *J* 243, 244, 248, 430-31, 435. As the *Catalogus* (1874) shows(13-15), there were two Dobsons at Roehampton at that time (see also *J* 435). It is likely that Hopkins' companion was John Dobson, the Junior, rather than Joseph Dobson, the novice; a Junior would have been much freer than a novice to go on a trip into the city.

[7] *P* 309; *J* 377-78; *F* 238; Thomas, *Hopkins the Jesuit* 140-41.

few months later another pupil died, Richard O'Neill, S.J., and Hopkins remembered him both in a letter to his own mother--"one of my late pupils has suddenly died"--and in his journal:

> This day my late pupil Br. Richard O'Neill died at Stonyhurst of (most likely typhus) fever brought with him from Roehampton. There was, I now remember, a sad wistful look he had, a sort of mark of early death stamped on him: I interpret this after the event. (*F* 128; *J* 260)

In late summer 1874, his year at Roehampton finished, Hopkins arrived at St. Beuno's College to begin his study of theology in preparation for the priesthood. Only months later, with the perspective of distance, did he comment on his work with the Juniors. Writing Bridges on February 20, 1875, he recalled the year's boring routine and, quite atypically, evaluated his performance in the classroom: "If you had sent me such an invitation last year, when I really was at Roehampton, what a pleasure it would have been and what a break in the routine of rhetoric, which I taught so badly and so painfully!" (*B* 30). One of the students, however, kept kinder memories, and fifty years later told an interviewer "how much he enjoyed Hopkins' course and how mightily he profited from it" (Lahey, "Hopkins In his Years").

Mount St. Mary's College, October, 1877--April, 1878

In the summer of 1877 Hopkins finished his third year of theology at St. Beuno's and was preparing for ordination to the priesthood in September. He assumed that he would remain there after ordination for a final year of theology in the four-year "Long Course" of studies (*B* 30; *F* 122, 242). What he did not anticipate, however, was that he would fail in his third-year examination for the Long Course. When this happened, he automatically fell into the "Short Course," although he received a sufficient grade for ordination. Thus, following the English-Province pattern of that time, he became available for work in the Province's schools and parishes.[8]

With Hopkins suddenly and unexpectedly ready for assignment, one of his contemporaries, recently named Prefect of Studies at Mount St. Mary's College, saw an opportunity to gain a needed classics master. The new headmaster, John Clayton, S.J., knew Hopkins well, for had spent three years with him at St. Beuno's and had been ordained the year before him. Arriving at "The Mount" on September 10, Fr. Clayton seemed quickly to have recognized the school's need for a classical scholar. Finding that Hopkins was available, he probably discussed the question with the Provincial on October 5 (he made a special trip to see him at Wakefield) and asked to have Hopkins on his staff. Hopkins arrived at Mount St. Mary's on October 19, 1877 (Keegan 11, 13), and found a school of about 150 students, mostly boarders, and a Jesuit community "moderately small and family-like" (*F* 148).

Before his arrival Hopkins was unsure about his precise duties, and he had written his mother, "The work is nondescript--examining, teaching, probably with occasional mission [parish] work and preaching or giving retreats attached: I shall know more when I am there" (*F* 148). He was right to put examining and teaching in first place, for though he was officially listed as "subminister" (a minor administrator of physical facilities), he taught religion, the classics, and English, and sometimes took over the classes of a sick master. He also helped with the school plays, writing a

---

[8] For the complexities and results of Hopkins' third-year examination, see: Feeney, "Grades"; and Feeney, "Hopkins' 'Failure.'"

comic prologue for *Macbeth* and possibly directing a play during the normal director's illness.[9]

Hopkins' year at Mount St. Mary's provides one of the rare records of Hopkins' performance in the classroom, for years later one of his students remembered both his gentleness and his naive trust in the students:

> Another and more fugitive temporary master was Fr. Gerard Hopkins, young and newly ordained, with a well deserved reputation for scholarship. He taught my class for some weeks during Mr. Hepburne's absence, a welcome interlude after our usual fierce ragout [Hepburne's reproofs to the students were often severe]. On the occasion he gave us, to put into Latin verse, that hoary chestnut 'The Assyrian came down,' at which we were delighted, as we had the whole of it turned into flawless elegiacs. . . . I remember I had included two or three verses of the crib amongst my native productions. Fr. Hopkins' lead pencil had been very busy among the latter, but under the former were his firm wavy strokes of commendation and the side note 'extraordinarily good.' He had found the wheat among the tares, but was too trustful to have suspected me of borrowing, and I feel ashamed to have deceived him. My only wonder now is whether the rest of the class availed themselves of the same tap and if Fr. Hopkins found any similarity of wording. (Lee, cited in Keegan 19)

Hopkins, it seems, was a likeable but gullible teacher.

---

[9] Keegan 13, 15, 17, 19, 22. Keegan quotes a contemporary report on the content of Hopkins' religion course: "The treatises de Principiis, de Religione Christiana and de Religione Revelata, together with Church History down to the reign of Constantine" (15).

The second view of Hopkins as teacher comes from his own desk, for in a letter Hopkins once made fun of his students' writing. The group in question, assigned to Hopkins in their regular master's absence, was younger than his Latin elegists, probably between 11 and 13 (Keegan 22). Here is his account:

> The little charges thrown on me by their master's illness have written me an account of the Earthquake of Lisbon. "It was a fine bright day" they say "when at ten o'clock a picture of extreme suddenness came on." After the earthquake "an old ruffian of a mob ran about killing everyone he met." Finally "this catastrophe has left many a mark on the minds of learned men." A batch of copybooks lies before me with no doubt more of the same sort on the Earl of Nithsdale's escape. (*F* 149)

One might note that at this stage Hopkins was not pulled down by the prospect of grading examinations--a sign that he greatly enjoyed both Mount St. Mary's and his young charges.

Though he could laugh at their work Hopkins again showed an affection for his students. "I have," he wrote in April, "become very fond of the boys I have had to do with as pupils, penitents, or in other ways. I think they lead a very happy life with us, though discipline is strict." In the years to come, too, Hopkins continued his contact with at least one of the boys, and fifty years later John Ashton, having become a Jesuit, recalled, "I knew Fr. G. Hopkins at Mount St. Mary's . . . when I was one of his penitents. He afterwards wrote to me, but unfortunately I have not kept his letters" (Ashton).[10]

---

[10] For hospitality and permission to publish I thank Rev. Francis Edwards, S.J., former Archivist of the British Province.

The boys at the Mount reciprocated his esteem, and invited him for day-trips as spring blossomed in late April. Hopkins recalls:

> Some of them got me to take them on Monday to Clumber Park the Duke of Newcastle's seat . . . and we had a very pleasant day; also the next day a party of ourselves went there driving and managed to see Steetly chapel, the most beautiful little Norman ruin you can imagine, on our way and Cresswell Crags, a cleft between cliffs with water between. (*F* 150)

The enthusiastic prose itself communicates Hopkins' delight.

He took a particular interest in one of his most talented pupils, Herbert Berkeley. A tutorial student of Hopkins--"my particular pupil" (*F* 49)--Berkeley had won several prizes that year and, in addition, was a talented actor (Keegan 15, 17). "My pupil Herbert Berkeley," he wrote his mother,

> lately carried off an 'Intercollegiate' prize, for which several of our schools compete. I was more pleased than I should have thought possible, but he is clever and hardworking and I had not much to do with the result. I shall not easily have so good a student again. He is eager to take down everything I say and repeats it with minute accuracy long afterwards. (*F* 150)

In that year, incidentally, the subject for the English-verse prize was the "Loss of the Eurydice"; it is not known which prize Berkeley won, but it is probable that while Berkeley (and perhaps other students at the Mount) were working on this topic, Hopkins was writing his own poem "The Loss of the Eurydice" which is dated "Mount St. Mary's, Derbyshire, April 1878."[11] Hopkins may even have drawn Robert Bridges into the competi-

---

[11] Keegan 17; *P* 270. The topic of the contest was announced in "Inter-Collegiate Competition. 1878," *Letters and Notices* (London), 12 (1878-79), 106-11.

tion, for shortly later he asked Bridges about the progress of "your own ode on the Eurydice" (*B* 54).

Berkeley also performed a comic prologue which Hopkins had written for *Macbeth*. He was

> a born actor, a very amusing low comedian and still better in tragedy; his Lady Macbeth, in spite of being turned into "Fergus"[,] Macbeth's younger brother,[12] was quite a "creation." I wrote them a prologue to Macbeth: it was a scene of farce and consisted in the speaker seeming to forget all the points, but Berkeley did it so naturally that he overshot the mark and most of the audience thought he had forgotten in earnest and that his strange behaviour was due to "refreshments" behind the scenes. (*F* 149)

Interesting here is the tone of the comments: Hopkins was laughing *with* his students and making fun of the audience.

Hopkins also took an interest in the dramatic productions of other students. At Christmas time,

> on Twelfth Night they had a mumming, which is the custom. . . . Our boys gave two performances [of plays] in aid of the poor schools, the country people came, laughed prodigiously at the jokes and sometimes at the wrong places and wept freely at the pathetic scenes. (*F* 149)

He might also have adapted a comic play for the young actors--"A Model Kingdom"--but the text has been lost (Keegan 22-23).

Hopkins' interest in the students' plays and his friendship with the student-actors also gave rise two years later to his poem "Brothers." That

---

[12] In this period in Jesuit schools "boys were not allowed to impersonate female characters, so every play had to be adapted for an all-male cast" (Keegan 22).

poem, dated August 1880, tells of an older brother's pride and worry as he watches his younger brother Jack appear on stage. The poem, when read as a portrait of Hopkins, shows several aspects of Hopkins the teacher: the students' ease in his presence ("Henry, by the wall / Beckoned me beside him"), his own interest in the character and reactions of the boys ("I came where called, and eyed him / By meanwhiles; making my play / Turn most on tender byplay"), and his admiration of the older brother's fraternal love ("fond love") and innocent kindness[13] ("Ah Nature, framed in fault, / . . . Nature, bad, base, and blind, / Dearly thou canst be kind") (54, *P* 279). It is clear that Hopkins enjoyed his year at Mount St. Mary's with its amateur dramatics, outings with students, unintentionally humorous essays, generous and innocent young boys, and one unusually talented student and actor.

From time to time, Hopkins' weariness and depression reappeared. In gloomy February he complained to Robert Bridges, "Write me an interesting letter. I cannot do so. Life here is as dank as ditch-water and has some of the other qualities of ditch water: at least I know that I am reduced to great weakness by diarrhoea, which lasts too, as if I were poisoned" (*B* 47). In April, too, he hinted at depression: "My muse turned utterly sullen in the Sheffield smoke-ridden air and I had not written a line till the foundering of the Eurydice the other day [24 March] and that worked on me and I am making a poem" (*B* 48). But these two passages were the only signs of depression, and his exhaustion seemed due to

---

[13] Hopkins' respect for and love of the innocence of children--the "innocent mind and Mayday in girl and boy" (33)--is one of his recurring themes; see, e.g., "Spring," (33) "The Handsome Heart" (47), "The Bugler's First Communion" (48), and "On the Portrait of Two Beautiful Young People" (157). Surely Hopkins' schoolteaching experiences, especially with the younger boys at the Mount--the youngest students he ever had--helped to develop this admiration for innocence.

physical rather than psychological causes. Even his loss of weight during the Lenten fast, he wrote, "has left me no worse" (*F* 150).

Nor did he complain about his lack of time for himself. Though he wrote in January that "I am so fallen into a mess of employments that I have given up doing everything whatever but what is immediately before me to do" (*F* 148-49), that statement was followed not by a complaint or moan but by hearty comments on the Christmas festivities and on his young writers' essays on the Lisbon earthquake.

This year at Mount St. Mary's was one of Hopkins' happiest years as an active Jesuit and clearly his happiest year as a teacher. In contrast to the Oratory School and to his later teaching, his exhaustion and depression were less; pleasure, enthusiasm, even exhilaration and laughter predominated. This mood may not have lasted; perhaps it was just a newly ordained priest's first enthusiasm. Or perhaps Hopkins might have continued to find joy and contentment in teaching the younger, innocent boys at Mount St. Mary's or elsewhere. (His brilliance in the Classics, for better or worse, drew his superiors to send him higher). Whatever the case, during his months at Mount St. Mary's Hopkins was clearly and notably happy.

As spring came to the Mount, Hopkins received two new assignments, one temporary and one apparently permanent. On April 24 he wrote the details to his mother:

> My news will surprise and probably please you. I am going to leave this place on Saturday for Stonyhurst, where I am to be till July, coaching some people, I suppose they are students of our own, for their degrees at the London University. After that I am to be stationed in town at Mount Street: Fr. Gallwey has some time asked to have me.

Hopkins' Jesuit community at Mount St. Mary's also was surprised by his sudden reassignment (Keegan 11). To the Jesuit provincial both assignments probably seemed a more sensible and better use of Hopkins' talents. But near the end of his letter Hopkins wrote, "I am leaving Mount St. Mary's College, Chesterfield just when its neighbourhood is gayest and prettiest, as vermilion tiles and orchard blossoms make it" (*F* 150-51). Many years later a Jesuit historian added, "If he had been left at Mount St. Mary's he might have been much happier: its charm was already beginning to work on him" (Keegan 30).

Stonyhurst College, April--July, 1878

In going to Stonyhurst Hopkins returned to a place he knew well, both from his three years of Philosophy at St. Mary's Hall and from his six days of teaching Rhetoric at the College in 1873. His new students, called the "Secular Philosophers" to distinguish them from the Jesuit philosophy students at St. Mary's Hall, were several years older than his students at the Mount and were preparing for the External B. A. degree from London University. Hopkins, it seems, was being called "higher" to teach older students as befitted his talent and his Oxford training.

In this temporary appointment Hopkins stayed for the full summer term of 1878, though precisely why he was needed and sent there cannot be determined (Roberts, "Jaded" 35; letter).[14] Nor, during his ten weeks there, did he comment greatly on his teaching, and his two letters to Bridges--long and with postscripts--dealt mostly with poetry (*B* 49-55). During this short period, though, he began his correspondence with R. W. Dixon and in his first two long letters he reminisced about his own schooldays at Highgate

---

[14] I am grateful to Mr. Roberts for his search of the records at Stonyhurst.

School where Dixon had been a master (*D* 1-9); perhaps some incident at Stonyhurst or Hopkins' sense of the school's antiquity brought him to return to his own schoolboy past. During this period Hopkins' only new poem was "The May Magnificat" (42; *P* 272); in mid-May, too, he told Bridges that "The Loss of the Eurydice" (written at Mount St. Mary's) had been rejected by the Jesuit journal *The Month* (*B* 50).

Among the few comments that touched on teaching, Hopkins returned to his old complaint of a busy schedule and lack of time. Probably wounded by the rejection of "The Loss," Hopkins told Bridges, "I shall never have leisure or desire to write much" (*B* 54). Two weeks later he wrote Dixon that "this letter has run to a greater length than the little time at my disposal makes justifiable" (*D* 8). One might note, too, that Hopkins' worry about time now involved a moral dimension--"makes justifiable"--that had not previously been obvious. His earlier complaint lamented his inability to do leisure-things; now his use of time seemed to involve guilt. And, anticipating his parish work in London, Hopkins even began to *expect* this problem: "I shall have, no doubt, little time when in London" (*B* 55). The old worry, absent from his letters at the Mount, had again come to trouble him.

When Hopkins arrived in London he was clearly conscious of his recent and frequent changes of assignment; within nine months he had moved from St. Beuno's to the Mount to Stonyhurst to London. Perhaps, too, he was emotionally reacting to his premature departure from two places he had greatly loved, St. Beuno's and Mount St. Mary's. Shortly after arriving in London he wrote Bridges that "I am, so far as I know, permanently here, but permanence with us is a ginger-bread permanence; cobweb, soapsud, and frost-feather permanence" (*B* 55).

An Interval: Parishes and Tertianship, 1878--1882

Hopkins' three years in the parishes of London, Bristol, Oxford, Bedford Leigh, Liverpool, and Glasgow, and his final year of spiritual training in the tertianship at Roehampton, add little to a portrait of Hopkins the teacher. Yet in one sermon at Bedford Leigh, his favorite parish, Hopkins twice spoke about teaching. He mentioned first the blessed role of parents in teaching their children about Christ:

> Children as soon as they can understand ought to be told about him, that they may make him the hero of their young hearts. . . . It is at the father's or the mother's mouth first the little one should learn. But the parents may be gossiping or drinking and the children have not heard of their lord and saviour. Those of you, my brethren, who are young and yet unmarried resolve that when you marry, if God should bless you with children, this shall not be but that you will have more pity, will have pity upon your own. (S 35)

Shortly afterwards he preached about Christ's effectiveness as a teacher. Mentioning how people were spellbound by his eloquence, he said,

> No stories or parables are like Christ's, so bright, so pithy, so touching; no proverbs or sayings are such jewellery; they stand off from other men's thoughts like stars, like lilies in the sun; nowhere in literature is there anything to match the Sermon on the Mount: if there is let men bring it forward. (S 37)

Parents, he thought, should be the first teachers and Christ was the best of all teachers. In both cases teaching was a blessed and holy task.

Stonyhurst College, October, 1882--February, 1884

On August 31, 1882, renewed in spirit and refreshed in body after his tertianship at Roehampton, Hopkins returned to Stonyhurst for his new and presumably stable assignment--again to teach the "Secular Philosophers." Since classes did not begin until October 2, he left a few days later for a brief visit to Mount St. Mary's where he had taught so happily (Roberts, "Jaded" 35). On returning to Stonyhurst, he described his tasks:

> My appointment is to teach our "philosophers" (like under-graduate students) Latin, Greek, and perhaps hereafter English (when I know more about it) for the London B. A. degree.[15] . . . The Provincial further added that what time was left over I might employ in writing one or other of the books I had named to him. But very little time will be left over and I cd. never make time. Indeed now, with nothing to do but prepare, I cannot get forward with my ode. But one must hope against hope. (*B* 150)

Such a letter shows that Hopkins' condition had worsened: he had not even *started* to teach and he already presumed a lack of time. He presumed, too, that somehow he "cd. never make time." Before even starting, he had come to admit defeat. And one may wonder what the provincial actually said to him. Was it, as Hopkins heard it, "What time is left over you can employ in writing," or perhaps something more like, "With

---

[15] Hopkins was more specific the following January, and he compared his work to the Oxford program: "I am here to coach classics for the London University Intermediate (say Moderations) and B. A. (say Greats) examinations" (*F* 251). For perspective on the English Province's methods of assigning their men in that era, see Feeney, "Grades" 26-28, and Feeney "Reassignments." I mention again that neither the English bishops nor the Jesuit General (at Fiesole, in exile from Rome) approved of the English Province's pattern of changing Jesuits from place to place with excessive frequency.

this assignment, you should have a fair amount of time for writing"?[16] Hopkins, it seems, was at this point ready to presume the worst, perhaps wounded by his past experiences in the colleges and parishes.

In this same letter he praised Stonyhurst College with enthusiasm. "I wish I could show you this place," he wrote Bridges; "it is upon my word worth seeing. The new college, though there is no real beauty in the design, is nevertheless imposing and the furniture and fittings are a joy to see," and he went on to describe the College and its surroundings (*B* 151-52). And it was indeed an important school and place. Founded on the continent in 1594 by exiled Jesuits and designed to educate the sons of English Catholics also exiled under Elizabeth I, it counted martyrs among its old boys. The college was later moved to an Elizabethan country house in Lancashire, and at Hopkins' arrival housed nearly 300 boys and was recognized as the ancient and emotional home of the English Province. Its teaching had a high reputation. Politically, its mood was that of intelligent Toryism, and its headmaster, John Gerard, S.J., and a number of its Jesuit staff would likely have been appealing colleagues for Hopkins (Roberts, "Jaded" 35-38, 41-42).

---

[16] Christopher Devlin, S.J., in his "Introduction" to the "Isolated Discourses" in *The Sermons*, offers a different and starker reading of the provincial's words, though he admits it is a "supposition": "Confronted with the perfect neatness of the Provincial's mind, with his massive and smoothly-moving deliberation, a wave of diffidence amounting almost to despair seeped up in Hopkins. It was borne in upon him that he must look on his poetic genius as an amiable weakness which a hard-working Jesuit might indulge for an hour or two occasionally. And he grasped, half-consciously but once and for all, that the secret 'wildness' of his inspiration could never be channelled in that manner" (*S* 215). When Fr. Devlin wrote that, however, he had just been reassigned (at his partly-witting request) from a happy teaching assignment at Roehampton to the Rhodesian mission. Since he could barely finish his edition of *The Sermons*, his comments may well reflect his own personal (and only temporary) pain in leaving his editorial work to labor on the foreign missions (see Madeleine Devlin 94-95, 101-09; and *S* viii). In these circumstances I suggest at least the possibility of *eisegesis* on Devlin's part.

What were Hopkins' experiences as a teacher during his eighteen months at Stonyhurst? Teaching, of course, limited his leisure. Before classes began he was working on "The Leaden Echo and the Golden Echo," writing a bit of music, and studying musical harmony, but in early October he wrote Bridges, "I want to go on with the study of harmony, but now my scholastic work is beginning and at first at all events I fear I shall not have time even for necessities, let alone luxuries or rather bywork" (*P* 282; *B* 152-53). But he still continued to make personal contact with the students, and even asked one--George Fitzpatrick, who later became a Jesuit--to write an accompaniment to an air Hopkins had written (*B* 152; Roberts, "Jaded" 39). Six years later in Dublin Hopkins still wrote of "George Fitzpatrick, a dear young friend of mine but now not seen for 5 years" (*B* 289).

Hopkins was quite right about an initial press of work (he was teaching a new course to older students) but between October 1 and Christmas he managed to write Bridges nine letters (some quite long) with detailed discussions of poetry (*B* 152-68). He even celebrated teaching in a letter to Dixon: "My own experience is that any teaching, any literary work is good for the mind provided that it be literary, by which I include philosophy & exclude mathematics" (*D* 105). And, becoming practical, he recommended to Bridges "the gelatine process" for copying a poem. It was used "by all our masters here" to reproduce notes for students, and for a poet "secures one against irretrievable loss by the post" (*B* 158). Between September and the end of December he also conceived and completed "Ribblesdale" and probably at least one of "The Trio of Triolets" (*P* 281).[17] This first term, though busy, seems to have been a time of peace, and at

---

[17] On dating the "Trio" see Thomas, "Unpublished Triolet" 184, 186-87. Hopkins let these verses be published in *The Stonyhurst Magazine*, 1 (March, 1883), 162 (*P* 312).

end of term Hopkins felt quite elated: "I seem to be in a griggish mood; it must be because holidays have begun" (*B* 167). It was the last truly happy term he would ever enjoy.

After such gaiety a change of mood overtook and surprised him, and brought him to write on January 4, "Since our holidays began I have been in a wretched state of weakness and weariness, I can't tell why, always drowzy and incapable of reading or thinking to any effect" (*B* 168). What is unusual here is that the depression came upon him during the holidays. And it continued into mid-January:

> I fall into or continue in a heavy weary state of body and mind in which my go is gone (the elegance of that phrase! . . .), I make no way with what I read, and seem but half a man. It is a sad thing to say. I try, and am even meant to try, in my spare time (if I were fresher or if it were anyone but myself there would be a good deal of spare time taking short and long together) to write some books; but I find myself so tired or harrassed I fear they will never be written. (*F* 251-52)

He was deeply depressed, surely, and he had also found something new to worry about: In saying "if it were anyone but myself there would be a good deal of spare time" Hopkins realized, and verbalized for the first time, that his anguish and debility lay in himself and not in his schedule or work.

He did have a few consolations: epistolary discussions of poetry with Bridges and of Greek drama with Baillie, some piano-playing ("I try to get a bit of strumming every day now"), and meditation on St. Paul's view of Christ (*B* 168-78; *F* 250-53). Once again he enjoyed his students: "I like my students and do not wholly dislike the work" (*F* 251). But the winter was long ("atrociously so" by late March) and his weariness continued. "I am always jaded," he wrote on March 26; "I cannot tell why, and my vein [of poetry] shews no signs of ever flowing again " (*B* 178). At the same time he spent "much time" completing an exercise in musical counterpoint (*B* 178). Then, in mid-April, he was driven to *beg* Bridges for a letter: "Dearest Bridges,--I wish you would write; it makes me disconsolate punctually every morning to get no letter" (*B* 178). His depression had settled in from later December, and in this case it seemed to grow out of himself rather than from his teaching or workload.

May, though cold, was less depressing, and Hopkins was completed his Stonyhurst May-poem for Mary's month, "The Blessed Virgin compared to the Air we Breathe" (*B* 179; *P* 283). On May 18 he even sounded perky, waxing enthusiastic about music, the weather ("fine day, with a solar halo"), a school-holiday, and even student sports ("our boys to have a match") (*B* 180). He was also continuing his lessons in musical counterpoint (*B* 182; *D* 109).[18] Depression returned with the end-of-term work of late June, but this time (as in mid-January) Hopkins recognized that his inability to work and his lack of time were due to his own weakness: "My time, as I have said before this, is not so closely employed but that someone else in my place might not do a great deal, but I cannot, and I see no grounded prospect of my ever doing much not only in poetry but in anything at all." Worn down as poet, teacher, and man, he concluded, "It is God's will and though no change that I can foresee will happen yet perhaps some may that I do not foresee" (*D* 108-09). During June he also worried about death, for he told his sister Grace, "I have also warnings sometimes of an approaching death: I had such a one lately, but it was slight and I paid little attention to it." And probably about this time he began to compare himself to such

---

[18] Gerald Roberts offers an explanation: "One suspects that it was the barrenness of his own poetic invention that was driving him to try his hand in another art form, where he was perhaps deceiving himself about his potential" ("Jaded" 39).

very productive Jesuits as Stonyhurst's Fr. William Forbes-Leith, S.J., "who never lets a minute go idle and after his teaching-work at once returns to his own studies" (*D* 119). Hopkins thus found himself simultaneously facing both his own barrenness and the productivity of others.

In this first year of his return to teaching Hopkins repeated some old themes: joy in his students, need for an occasional escape from teaching duties (by correspondence, reading, nature-walks, poetry, and piano-playing), a rare comment on teaching, his expectation that *some* problem would inevitably appear, and often a debilitating weariness. As at Mount St. Mary's he could sometimes enjoy his work, but at Stonyhurst his pleasure lasted only one term. And new dimensions appeared: his depression came on him during the Christmas holidays, his moods oscillated perhaps more frequently, and he realized that when he had leisure time he was unable to use it. He recognized, too, that others could manage a similar schedule while he was unable to, and he saw that teaching was not the cause of his problem. Fearing that his poetic vein was drying permanently, he began to believe that he would *never* accomplish anything in his life. And he was reduced to begging for a letter. This first year at Stonyhurst had brought him to realize--it seems for the first time--that the source of his weariness and sense of ineffectiveness was internal: his problem was himself.

Thus understanding Hopkins' new and painful insights into himself, we can more deeply feel the pathos of his letter to Bridges on July 26, 1883. Hopkins had somehow convinced himself that he would be transferred from Stonyhurst--moved yet once again as in his parish work--and he cried out to Bridges,

> It seems likely that I shall be removed; where I have no notion. But I have long been Fortune's football and am blowing up the bladder of resolution big and buxom for another kick of her foot.

> I shall be sorry to leave Stonyhurst; but go or stay, there is no likelihood of my ever doing anything to last. And I do not know how it is, I have no disease, but I am always tired, always jaded, though work is not heavy, and the impulse to do anything fails me or has in it no continuance. (*B* 183)

From September 1882 to July 1883 Hopkins had suffered a terrible loss of confidence and of verve. Despite his weariness he had come to realize that the "work is not heavy" and that he himself constituted the problem. And, poignantly, Hopkins liked Stonyhurst.

His fear of a transfer proved ungrounded, and only ten days after his worrisome letter he wrote Bridges, on August 5, that "My appointment is renewed" (*B* 185). Seven days later he expressed his pleasure to Dixon: "I am reappointed for the ensuing year, I am happy to say" (*D* 112). (One may ask was there ever an indication to the contrary other than Hopkins' own worry?) In any case, his next year--or, as it turned out, only his next six months--would be stable.

One happy event, and perhaps another reason for his change of mood between July 26 and August 5, took place on July 29, 1883. On that day Hopkins, asked by the Stonyhurst rector to host a distinguished visitor, first met the poet Coventry Patmore who had come to Stonyhurst for the end-of-year "Great Academies," the speechday which concluded the College's year (*F* 295; *D* 111). After that meeting Hopkins entered into a new, rewarding friendship with Patmore. Their correspondence continued until a year before Hopkins' death in 1889.

Soon it was time for the school year to begin again. During his annual retreat in early September Hopkins recalled a wise Jesuit's advice that "a great part of life to the holiest of men consists in the well performance, the performance, one may say, of ordinary duties" (*S* 253). Yet within two weeks Hopkins, facing the prospect of ordinary work, again began to worry about lack of time. By September 23 he felt that "time presses" and five days later he wrote that "I shall very soon be in the thick of my work" (*F* 300, 313). But when classes began he still managed fairly regular letters to Patmore, including a gentle and kind letter of sympathy on the death of Patmore's son Henry (*F* 335-38).

For this second year at Stonyhurst there is little information about Hopkins' teaching. One letter shows that he expected students to work hard and did not countenance prize-winning without labor (*F* 337-38). He continued to maintain contact with his students, and by October 1883 he knew the tastes of one pupil well enough to lend him Dixon's book *Mano* (telling Dixon about this, he again complained about his lack of time) (*D* 116-17). He also had enough time to compose essays for the scientific journal *Nature*; on November 12, 1883, and December 21, 1883, he recorded careful observations of unusual sunsets (as he had also done in November 1882) (*D* 161-66). It is likely, too, that sometime during 1883 he wrote what later became known as the "Author's Preface" to his *Poems* (*P* 253). During these months at Stonyhurst he also made a lasting friend among the students, an Irishman named Bernard O'Flaherty. Such was their friendship, in fact, that while teaching in Dublin in 1887 he still maintained contact with O'Flaherty and called him "one of my best friends"(*F* 180).[19] Hopkins, usually shy and retiring, even visited him in County Wexford during Easter week of 1887 (*F* 182). O'Flaherty must have been a valued friend.

To this chronicle of Hopkins' eighteen months at Stonyhurst three unusual bits of data should be added, one on his health and two on his performance as a teacher. All come from Jesuit administrators and offer

---

[19] On O'Flaherty, see Roberts, "Jaded" 36-37, 40.

212 G. M. Hopkins: New Essays

a different (and sometimes puzzling) perspective on Hopkins' own statements during this period. The first, dealing with his health in 1883, comes from the handwritten "Catalogus Primus" of the English Province.[20] This "Catalogus," written in Latin, describes a Jesuit's health--his "vires" ("strength" or "power")--by applying an adjective to the word "vires." In the case of Hopkins in 1883 his "vires" were described as "sat firmae" ("strong enough" or "adequate"). His physical health, then, was seen as habitually solid at some point in the year 1883. (Hopkins himself had written Bridges, a medical doctor, on July 26, 1883, "*I have no disease*, but I am always tired" (*B* 183, emphasis mine).)

The two other documents, written during the Stonyhurst years when he was being considered for an appointment to University College, Dublin, deal with his teaching. The first evaluation, dated November 5, 1882, appears in a letter from George Porter, S.J., to William Delany, S.J., the Irish Jesuit who was trying to form a Jesuit staff for University College.[21] After mentioning another man as "a first class teacher," Porter continued, "Hopkins is clever, well trained, teaches well but has never succeeded well:

---

[20] In the late nineteenth century Jesuit provinces were asked every three years to collect some basic information about every Jesuit: age, place of birth, education, degrees received, years in the Society, etc. It was composed probably by each house's rector, or by the minister (the "prefect of health"). The ms. is in the Archivum Romanum Societatis Iesu (ARSI), Rome, vol. #1801. Not all of these "Catalogi" are extant. (For hospitality and permission to publish I thank Rev. Edmond Lamalle, S.J., and his staff.)

[21] At the time Fr. Porter was acting English Assistant to the Jesuit General, Peter Beckx, S.J., then in exile in Fiesole. On Fr. Porter, see his obituary in *Letters and Notices* (London), 20 (1890) 121-30. A Scotsman, he had been Prefect of Studies at Stonyhurst, Professor of Theology at St. Beuno's, Rector of the college and parish in Liverpool, Master of Novices, Rector of Farm Street, acting Assistant for the English Assistancy, and from 1887 Archbishop of Bombay. On Fr. Delany, see Morrissey.

his mind runs in eccentric ways" (Porter, Letter to Delany).[22] Two points stand out: Hopkins *could* and did teach well, but was often carried away by eccentricities.

The second letter, written to Delany a year later, came from the English Provincial, Edward I. Purbrick, S.J.[23] After mentioning some English-Province Jesuits who were "just the cream of the Province, and absolutely not to be spared" for University College, he went on, "Fr Hopkins is very clever and a good scholar--but I should do you no kindness in sending you a man so eccentric. I am trying him this year in coaching B. A. at Stonyhurst, but with fear and trembling--This *inter nos* [between us]" (Purbrick, Letter to Delany, 10 Nov. 1883). One final letter, though not mentioning Hopkins' teaching ability, completed this exchange. After--and perhaps despite--Purbrick's letter, Delany requested Hopkins for his staff, and on November 29 Purbrick replied,

> As far as I am concerned I have no objection to your inviting Fr Gerald [sic] Hopkins to stand as a Candidate for a Fellowship. He is the only man *possible*. You know him. I have the highest opinion of his scholarship and abilities--I fancy also that University work would be more in his line than anything else. Sometimes what we in community deem oddities are the very qualities

---

[22] For hospitality and permission to publish this letter, I thank the late Rev. Fergal McGrath, S.J.

[23] On Fr. Purbrick see his obituary in *Letters and Notices* (London), 32 (1914), 565-68. Like Fr. Porter, Fr. Purbrick was a well-known and successful administrator: Rector of Stonyhurst, Provincial of the English Province, Tertian Instructor, Superior of the college and parish at Wimbledon, Provincial of the Maryland-New York Province, Tertian Instructor in New York. In his obituary he was called "one of the most distinguished--in his prime and later life indeed *the* most distinguished member--of the English Province" (566).

which outside are appreciated as original and valuable.
Then he added, with a graceful touch, "I have not said anything to Fr Hopkins because I thought an invitation direct from you with my sanction more complimentary and appetizing to him" (Purbrick, Letter to Delany, 29 Nov. 1883).

To finish this study of Hopkins at Stonyhurst, two points need comment: Porter's statement that Hopkins "teaches well" and the characterization of Hopkins as "a man so eccentric" (Purbrick) and a man with "eccentric ways" (Porter). I have found no way of defining Porter's phrase "teaches well," and my comment here is simple: Porter's words, in a private and frank letter from one Jesuit administrator to another, deserve to be believed. Hopkins could, at least in some circumstances, teach well. Thus Hopkins' own comment that he taught "so badly and so painfully" at Roehampton cannot be taken as the sole evaluation of his classroom performance, and one of his students remembered that he had "mightily . . . profited from the courses" in that year (Lahey, "Hopkins In His Years").

With regard to Hopkins' eccentricity in the classroom, a letter of his classmate, Joseph Rickaby, S.J. offers a helpful clue. Writing to his biographer nearly forty years after Hopkins' death, Rickaby concluded, "I cannot say he was a success . . . as a teacher. He was too whimsical." I interpret this to mean that Hopkins was accustomed to jump from topic to topic as his enthusiasm and interest might dictate, instead of engaging in a systematic or organized presentation. Confirmation, I think, is offered in Hopkins' "Lecture Notes: Rhetoric," where he seems so caught up in his own interests that he offers his students his speculations on poetry and rhythm (brilliant but inappropriate) rather than coherent lectures based on their educational needs. These notes, in my judgment, are important for scholars interested in Hopkins' views on poetry and rhythm but, as notes for teaching, they involve unexpected leaps and overdetailed digressions which well merit the adjectives "whimsical" and "eccentric."[24]

Like many original artists and thinkers, Hopkins seemed unable to understand another person's perspective; limited by his originality, he could not enter his students' minds to determine what they knew, how they thought, and how he could systematically build on their knowledge and needs. No wonder he later concluded that he had taught them "so badly and so painfully." Like many an ineffective teacher, he knew he had not succeeded but could neither explain why he failed nor change his approach.

The English Years: Patterns and Perspectives

Though happiness and depression mixed together during Hopkins' five years of teaching in England, his students usually brought him joy. In his letters and journals he commented on their games and ice-skating, and he sometimes joined them in their sports, trips, and poetry-contests. He lent them books, wrote and attended their amateur plays, admired their generosity, and remembered them when they died. As teacher, he carefully read their assignments, commending their felicities, laughing gently at their mistakes, and never suspecting their use of cribs. Like many other teachers he preferred the brighter students. Over the years he taught many different levels--his students' ages ranged from roughly 11 to 22--and he particularly admired the innocence and simplicity of the younger boys. After his students left school, he would exchange letters and visits with some of them, and showed a special interest in those who had become Jesuits. For his

---

[24] Fr. Thomas also sees a problem in Hopkins' approach: "As to what his pupils made of them [the 'Lecture Notes: Rhetoric'] one hardly dares to think. One hopes that they occasionally saw a text as well" (*Hopkins the Jesuit* 135).

students he showed a magisterial affection and, happily, some of them returned this affection both in school and in later life.

While teaching in England he found pleasure, too, in leisure activities. Indeed, except for the students, Hopkins' interests lay outside the classroom. He wrote long and splendid letters to family, friends, and fellow Jesuits, and was especially open with two close friends, R. W. Dixon (the Anglican priest with whom he shared his Christian faith), and Robert Bridges (the longstanding, agnostic friend from Oxford to whom he could say almost anything, no matter how personal). In his teaching years in England Hopkins also created poems (though not his greatest), read widely, and discussed literature with Bridges, Dixon, and Patmore; he also commented on their poems and listened to (and argued with) their comments on his work. He also loved to hear news from his family or old friends at Oxford, and enjoyed the strange dialect-words or foreign sounds of Lancashire, Ireland, Malta, or Arabian lands. He taught himself to play the piano, attempted the violin, and as a fledgling composer wrote music and tried to learn counterpoint. He visited art exhibitions and museums, often (while at Roehampton) with another Jesuit. And he took long, delightful walks, alone or with a companion or group, in city and country--to London's Kew Gardens, for example, or to the fields of Lancashire and the pools of the Ribble near Stonyhurst.

He even had some pleasures specifically as a teacher: exploring poetic rhythms with his Jesuit rhetoricians; instructing a few unusually bright students; living (without complaint) a busy, tiring life at Mount St. Mary's in the midst of boarding students. As teacher, too, he gradually came to love the schools and their surroundings: the Oratory, Mount St. Mary's, Roehampton, and Stonyhurst. And he gladly dealt with diverse academic disciplines--Greek, Latin, English, and religion, at various levels--and (especially at Mount St. Mary's) willingly served as substitute-teacher for an ailing or absent master. Reflecting on teaching, he could realize and affirm that "teaching . . . is good for the mind" (*D* 105). And during all his years of teaching he prayed each morning,[25] and tried to relate his life and work to the life and work of Christ.

As his teaching career progressed, though, the darker side of Hopkins appeared, waned, and then gradually dominated his days. Even from his earliest days at the Oratory School he began to complain about a lack of time. (Did Hopkins, one might ask, have excessive expectations of leisure, from both his days at Oxford and from watching his father write history, verse, and fiction after his office work was finished? (Bergonzi 1)) Furthermore, as a Jesuit teacher, he continued to complain about time, began to consider himself overworked, and often felt a bone-deep weariness. Only at Mount St. Mary's did his complaints grow quiet, and after his first year at Stonyhurst, he came to admit that his "work is not heavy" (*B* 183). And, one must note, the accomplishments of Hopkins' leisure time--poems, letters, music, walks, visits--imply that the shortness of time existed more in Hopkins' consciousness than in his external circumstances.

Still more ominous was Hopkins' growing, debilitating weariness. It had afflicted him from his days at the Oratory, but in 1874, as he ended his year of teaching at Roehampton, Hopkins first established the link between weariness and depression. At this time he was consoled only by "some kind words from the Provincial" and by the realization that "in all this our Lord goes His own way" (*J* 249-50).

---

[25] In Dublin he concluded that he should *not* engage in mental prayer for fear of madness, and it is clear from Hopkins' notes that this was a change of custom. For his normal pattern, see *S* 254-60; for his decision to break from this practice see *S* 262.

At Mount St. Mary's, in 1878, his depression was briefer, the creature of dim February, when life was "as dank as ditchwater" and Hopkins was weak from diarrhea (*B* 47). Far more serious was the situation at Stonyhurst, when depression came upon him at the beginning of his Christmas holidays. Starting his period of rest, he was "always drowzy and incapable of reading or thinking," and three weeks later he would still "continue in a heavy weary state of body or mind" (*F* 251-52). By March he was "always jaded, I cannot tell why" (*B* 178). And, despite a good May, he was again deeply dejected in June: "I see no grounded prospect of my ever doing much.... No change that I can foresee will happen" (*D* 108-09). By July he cried out, "There is no likelihood of my ever doing anything to last. ... I do not know how it is, I have no disease, but I am always tired, always jaded, though work is not heavy" (*B* 183).

At this point some larger patterns become clear. The periods leading up to Hopkins' bouts of depression, it seems, fall into a pattern and usually progress from (1) lack of time, to (2) feeling overworked, to (3) deep weariness, to (4) depression, and then to (5) a sense of personal inadequacy. In his early days of schoolteaching the problem seemed mainly a question of time and hard work; the cause was usually end-of-term examinations or the weather of January and February. Later, at Roehampton and especially at Stonyhurst, his condition indicated true depression, sometimes for no apparent reason. He became unable to work or write, and at Stonyhurst, watching other Jesuits at work, he realized that his difficulty lay not in his work but in his own body and psyche. From December 1882 Hopkins was the victim of recurring depression and melancholia, which seems to have been brought on, at least in part, by the burdens of teaching and examining.

During Hopkins' last years of teaching in Dublin--1884 to 1889--the depression and pain were even greater. In May 1885 he told Bridges about "fits of sadness [that] . . . resemble madness" (*B* 216). But this greater depression of the Dublin years, recorded (among other places) in his Terrible Sonnets, was, I believe, a continuation of his Stonyhurst condition rather than a malady developed in Dublin. To be sure, the Dublin weather, the politicized students of University College, and the examination duties of the Royal University exacerbated his collapse as teacher and person. But even before he came to Dublin all the sad symptoms were in place, and were discernible in the story of his teaching. The symptoms were clear, the collapse had started, and the pattern had begun to destroy him even while he was back home in England teaching the students of Stonyhurst College.

Works Cited

Ashton, John, S.J. Letter to G.F. Lahey, S.J. 30 November 1928. Archives of the British Province of the Society of Jesus, London, Lahey Papers, 1/4/5/1.

Bergonzi, Bernard. *Gerard Manley Hopkins*. New York: Collier, 1977.

"Catalogus Primus" (1883). Archivum Romanum Societatis Iesu (ARSI), Rome, vol. #1801.

Catalogus Provinciae Angliae Societatis Jesu. Roehampton: S. Josephi, 1873; 1874; 1875.

Coleridge, Henry, S.J., Obituary of. *Letters and Notices* (London) 22 (1893-94): 214ff.

Devlin, Madeleine. *Christopher Devlin*. London: Macmillan, 1970.

Feeney, Joseph J., S.J. "Grades, Academic Reform, and Manpower: Why Hopkins Never Completed His Course in Theology." *The Hopkins Quarterly* 9 (Spring, 1982): 21-31.

---. "Hopkins' 'Failure' in Theology: Some New Archival Data and a Reevaluation." *The Hopkins Quarterly* 13 (1986-87): 99-114.

---. "Hopkins' Frequent Reassignments as a Priest." *The Hopkins Quarterly* 11 (1984-85): 103-06.

Hopkins, Gerard Manley. Letter to Grace Hopkins. 9-10 June 1883. Hopkins Collection of the Humanities Research Center, University of Texas, Austin.

---. *Selected Prose*. Ed. Gerald Roberts. Oxford: Oxford UP, 1980.

---. "The Trio of Triolets." *The Stonyhurst Magazine* 1 (March, 1883): 162.

House, Humphry. Preface. *The Notebooks and Papers of Gerard Manley Hopkins*. Ed. Humphry House. London: Oxford UP, 1937.

"Inter-Collegiate Competition. 1878." *Letters and Notices* (London) 12 (1878-79): 106-11.

Keegan, Francis, S.J. "Gerard Manley Hopkins at Mount St. Mary's College, Spinkhill, 1877-1878." *The Hopkins Quarterly* 6 (1979): 11-34.

Lahey, G.F. *Gerard Manley Hopkins*. London: Oxford UP, 1930.

---. "Gerard Manley Hopkins In His Years of Training." Unpublished Typescript (1935). Archives of the British Province of the Society of Jesus, London, Lahey Papers.

Lee, William Francis. From *The Mountaineer* (1926). Quoted in Keegan 19.

Morrissey, Thomas J., S.J. *Towards a National University: William Delany SJ (1835-1924)*. Dublin: Wolfhound, 1983.

Porter, George, S.J. Letter to William Delany, S.J. 5 November 1882. Archives of the Irish Province, Dublin, box Delany I: letters O-S, in Porter file.

Porter, George, S.J., Obituary of. *Letters and Notices* (London) 20 (1890): 121-30.

Purbrick, E.J., S.J. Letter to William Delany, S.J. 10 November 1883. Archives of the Irish Province, box Delany I: letters T-Z [sic], under Purbrick.

---. Letter to Rev. William Delany, S.J. 29 November 1883. Archives of the Irish Province, box Delany I: letters T-Z [sic], under Purbrick.

Purbrick, E.J., S.J., Obituary of. *Letters and Notices* (London) 32 (1914): 565-68.

Rickaby, Joseph, S.J. Letter to G.F. Lahey, S.J. 29 February[?] 1927. Archives of the British Province, Lahey Papers, 1/4/5/1.

Roberts, Gerald. "The Jaded Muse: Hopkins at Stonyhurst." *The Hopkins Quarterly* 6 (1979): 35-47.

---. Letter to Joseph J. Feeney, S.J. 26 July 1983.

---. "Notes." In Gerard Manley Hopkins, *Selected Prose*.

Storey, Graham. Preface. Gerard Manley Hopkins, *Journals and Papers*. Ed. Humphry House and Graham Storey. London: Oxford UP, 1959.

Thomas, Alfred, S.J. "G.M. Hopkins: An Unpublished Triolet." *Modern Language Review* 61 (1966): 183-87.

Thomas, Alfred, S.J. *Hopkins the Jesuit: The Years of Training*. London: Oxford UP, 1969.

Of Miracles, Martyrs, and Prayer Gauges

Tom Zaniello

Teleologists will yet "baptize" Darwin, as they baptized Aristotle in the thirteenth century, and classical literature in the sixteenth. They will accept as much evolution as is capable of proof, and glorify God Who planned the germ and primitive potentiality. They will yet, as Kingdon Clifford once dreaded they would, seize all the glories of modern science and weave them into a crown for the Creator and Redeemer of men. (Joseph Rickaby, *Evolution Run Wild* 8)

The roll-call of female martyrs and saints Hopkins celebrated in verse is short: Thecla of Asia Minor, Winefred of Wales, and Margaret Clitheroe of York. To this day, the reputations of Clitheroe and Winefred command significant attention in their home areas (See Caramon, Charles-Edwards, and David); Thecla in Konya (southern Turkey) may not. Presumably only the readers of Hopkins' poetry or students of Catholic hagiography are familiar with the details of their lives. Nonetheless this group of long-suffering women marks a significant counterpoint to the strong and quietly heroic men Hopkins celebrated in "Felix Randal" (53) and "Harry Ploughman" (71).

Hopkins' interest in these saints, especially Winefred, represents his distinctive but publicly silent contribution to an important campaign waged by his friends and colleagues in the Society of Jesus after the first Vatican Council ended in 1870. Hopkins pursued miracles at St. Winefred's Well in northeastern Wales for many years. Besides writing pieces of a verse drama which celebrated the heroine of this shrine (59, 152), he was even willing to document alleged cures as a means of convincing his father, a statistician and marine claims investigator, of the efficacy of the miraculous water. His friends and colleagues, Herbert Lucas and Richard Clarke, actively walked similar paths, Lucas at St. Winefred's Well and Clarke at Lourdes. The Rickaby brothers, John and Joseph, wrote essays which attempted to reconcile a belief in miracles and contemporary scientific ideas. Michael Maher, another Stonyhurst Philosopher (but not one of Hopkins' associates), announced in 1895, just six years after Hopkins' death, that the London press had finally found its way to the tiny Welsh village and had begun to treat the "cures" with greater respect, even going so far as to drop the quotation marks around "cures" (Maher 154).

Why this pursuit? Why, besides the normal Catholic respect for the miraculous, were Hopkins and his fellow Jesuits especially keen to document not simply divine intervention into everyday lives but such intervention in England specifically?

There are at least three good reasons for their pursuit of the miraculous. Two of the reasons have to do with the spiritual leadership of the Catholic Church. First of all, there was the authority and leadership of John Henry Newman, perhaps best described as an informal but powerful intellectual force, especially among such recent converts as Hopkins and some of his colleagues. Secondly, there were the promulgations of the Vatican Council of all the bishops of the Church in 1869-70. This Council was prescriptive in terms of dogma, explicitly referring to contemporary issues involving evolution and skepticism towards miracles. The third reason reflects developments which preceded and to a certain extent overtook the meetings of the Vatican Council. These developments, which gave an urgency to the Jesuits' mission among not only its own believers but the public as well, were the work of three leading British scientists who--in the wake of the impact of Darwinian science--took time out from their laboratories to mount a public campaign against miracles. I will consider each of these reasons in turn.

Although Newman's reputation as a keen rationalist is deserved, Hopkins and his associates knew a man who was passionately attached to miracles. "Miracles are not only not unlikely," he wrote in "The Present Position of Catholics in 1851," "they are positively likely." "I firmly believe," he added, that "saints in their lifetime have before now raised the dead to life, crossed the sea without vessels, multiplied grain and bread, cured incurable diseases, and superseded the operation of the laws of the universe in a multitude of ways." He described the Catholic Church "from east to west, from north to south," as "hung with miracles." In Italy, Newman went on, painted Madonnas would often "nod" at visitors who came to admire an artifact but remained as witnesses to a minor miracle; equally dramatic was the liquifaction of the dried material of the relic of St. Januarius' blood, a miracle which happened as often as eighteen times a year (Newman 375). His English disciples would have learned Newman's appreciation of St. Winefred's Well as "the scene of wonders even in our unbelieving country" (Newman 371-72). The water which sprang up at the site of the martyrdom and subsequent resurrection of this Welsh princess had cured pilgrims to the site since the seventh century.

Newman's vehement defense of miracles was in part based on his experiences in the Oxford Movement. After the mid-1840's, with many Anglicans on the brink of Catholicism, Newman organized a project later called *The Lives of the English Saints*. Such a collection would emphasize the national and medieval church of *England*, and demonstrate that British soil was no stranger to the miracles celebrated in Catholic Europe. Newman's intentions were circumspect: "Doctrinal questions need not enter" into saints' lives, he wrote to one of the contributors. "As to miracles, I think they may be treated as matters of faith--credible according to their evidence" (Holmes 529).

The project attracted a reasonably strong cadre of writers, although Newman's interest in specifically English matters waned as he made his final approach to Rome by 1845, the final year of publication of the *Lives*. One of the writers, Mark Pattison, the Rector of Lincoln College, Oxford, did not become a Catholic; in fact he became a well-known skeptic. But his role in the project reveals how--in Cardinal Manning's phrase describing trends in English Catholicism--it was "more Roman than Rome." Before beginning work on his share of the *Lives*, Pattison travelled to Paris in 1843 in quest of intellectual Catholics "who might be of a better mental stamp" than those he encountered in England. He had visited Newman's headquarters in Birmingham but found there "a lurking fondness for stories of miracles." He succeeded no better in France, where there was a "spirit of credulity so vulgar" that the "religious people believed every miraculous story which was brought in, and simply because it was miraculous" (Pattison 211-12).

Perhaps Pattison's frustrated search simply mirrored his own equivocation on the issue of miracles evident in his life of St. Ninian, the fifth-century apostle of the Southern Picts. Since, in Ninian's lifetime, *everyone* believed in miracles, Pattison wrote rather plaintively, we should not worry about the "physical facts" in a miraculous case, but just take them "as things expected." St. Ninian's religious community had a reputation for "sanctity" and that reputation should suffice. We should also, Pattison added, in an aside which indicated his growing skepticism on the miraculous, not concern ourselves too much about the unusual finds of sea shells on mountaintops. "Recent investigations" indicated that they may not have been left there after the "deluge" receded (A.W. Hutton V 322-23).

Newman's attitude towards miracles, unlike many of his later positions which sometimes brought him into conflict with some members of the Catholic hierarchy, placed him in accord with one section of the program which Pius IX brought to his papacy. Skeptics like Mark Pattison, it would turn out, had probably more effect on creating an educational system, like Oxford, which became known, at least among serious Anglicans and devout Catholics, as a center of unorthodoxy.

The conflict of the miraculous and the doubtful was highlighted by the important doctrines which characterized the long tenure (1846-78) of Pius IX as Pope. The first major doctrine was the Immaculate Conception of Mary, which Pius promulgated in 1854. Papal infallibility (on matters of church dogma, the Pope cannot err) was the second and more controversial of the two doctrines. The convening of a Vatican council, the first such meeting of all the bishops of the Church since the Council of Trent in the sixteenth century, was primarily a means of having papal infallibility ratified by the collective body of the Church. The Jesuits were part of the Ultramontane or pro-Roman majority of the Catholic hierarchy who argued that both of Pius IX's doctrines had been part of Catholic tradition for centuries, a view contested by the minority or liberal wing of the Church, represented in England by Newman (not yet a cardinal), his supporters, and kindred spirits, and in Europe by the "Gallican opposition"--the strong, independent French Church. The fact that a select number of the Jesuits took a fourth vow of direct obedience to the Pope meant that they had a special duty to defend the decisions of Vatican I.

One of those decisions, about miracles, did not quite gain as much publicity as the Council's attack on evolution or its support for papal infallibility, but it was clearly part of the presiding spirit of the age, at least as far as the Catholic hierarchy was concerned. The Council reaffirmed the central role of miracles:

> If any one shall say that miracles are impossible, and therefore that all the accounts regarding them, even those contained in Holy Scripture, are to be dismissed as fabulous or mythical; or that miracles can never be known with certainty, and that the divine origin of Christianity cannot be proved by them; let him be anathema. (Manning 202)

The struggle between the miraculous and the doubtful in post-Darwinian England, a struggle from which Hopkins was never isolated, took the form of an on-going emphasis on miracles within the Church, while outside the Church advocates of skepticism increased. In fact the first Vatican Council in part reflected but in part generated the investigations of scientists who were either atheists or agnostics. Often it was not enough that Darwin had disrupted very traditional views among scientists; his followers applied the concepts of "chance" or "random" happenings from his theory of natural selection to *all* human affairs. Huxley went so far as to state publicly that it was the Catholic church which was the principal enemy of science (John Rickaby 197).

Within ten years of Pattison's nervousness about the miracles of St. Ninian, Victorian scientists at first slowly and then very aggressively began to tackle the question of miracles. Three major scientists--leaders in the fields of psychology, biology, and physics--began to test various hypotheses about miracles. Francis Galton, T.H. Huxley, and John Tyndall were regarded by many of their orthodox contemporaries as some three-headed monster of materialism, skepticism, and atheism. They began to investigate claims of "theocratic intervention," as Galton called the general class of phenomena in the first edition (1883) of his *Inquiries into Human Faculty and Its Development*. All three, despite their different fields, emphasized what Huxley in the *Fortnightly Review* in 1869 called "the physical basis of life." And since miracles often interrupted the "physical basis" of death, they felt compelled to intervene on the side of the doubters.

Galton, as a physiologist, had asked his own cousin (Darwin) some difficult questions in *Nature* in 1871 about what we would call today the "genetic" difficulties in Darwin's theory of natural selection. Galton, as a psychologist, asked some more difficult questions in an essay, "Statistical Inquiries into the Efficacy of Prayer," which appeared in the *Fortnightly Review* in 1872. If prayers really work, why don't insurance companies charge ministers less? Why do banks with pious stockholders sometimes fail? Why do Quakers, "who are the most devout and most shrewd men of business," not rely on prayers to make themselves even more successful (Galton "Statistical Inquiries" 123-34; 127-28)? His colleague, Tyndall, was one of the first to help answer Galton's questions. By expanding on Galton's offer to classify fractures and amputations into two classes, those of the "markedly religious and piously befriended" and those who were "remarkably cold-hearted and neglected"--medical sheep and goats, as it were--in order to see who would walk first. Tyndall proposed a "prayer gauge" which would test "the efficacy of prayer on a selected hospital ward" (R.H. Hutton 181). Tyndall's offer, however tongue-in-cheek, moved Huxley to remark that scientific investigators "jealous" of their time simply could not bring themselves to chase after the verification of miracles both "sparse and rare" (R.H. Hutton 183-84).

Huxley nevertheless did not let the issue drop. By 1870 Darwinism had strong supporters everywhere. Huxley was able to turn on occasion from Darwinian struggles to religious analysis. He took on Moses first, establishing him as an intriguing character of mainly (90%) fictional composition. He carried his statistical drive onwards through the Bible and reported that the world is not "haunted by swarms of evil spirits." He chopped at dogma and miracles alike in *Science and the Christian Tradition* (1892; reprinted in his *Collected Essays*), the summation of his career as critic of the pseudo-miraculous. Perhaps his strongest essay was "The Value of Witness to the Miraculous" which studied miracles associated with Charlemagne's court. Eginhard, ninth-century abbot of that court, had recorded some remarkable goings-on. His peasant parishioners really did believe that the dusty bones of Roman martyrs could sweat blood and heal the lame. But Eginhard discovered that the very bones achieving these miracles were not those of saints but literally old bones dug up by unscrupulous merchants of relics. So great had the demand been for relics to consecrate new churches, that the clergy were being tricked time and time again. Huxley's conclusion was inexorable. Christians would have trouble believing in the miracles skeptically recorded in a tenth-century copy of Eginhard's ninth-century manuscript. How could they ever "profess to believe in stories of like character, which are found in documents as uncertain as the Gospels and the Acts of the Apostles" (*Essays* V 185)?

Both as a reaction to the publicity generated by these three anti-miracle workers and as support for the Vatican Council decisions, Hopkins' friends and associates wrote and lectured on the official Catholic position on miracles. Their work, which in many cases paralleled Hopkins' own interests, was carried out by the men who came to be known as the Stonyhurst Philosophers--John and Joseph Rickaby, Richard F. Clarke, and Herbert Lucas. These men, like Hopkins, had been nicknamed "Stonyhurst Philosophers" as students in the second stage or "philosophate" of their Jesuit training at St. Mary's Hall at Stonyhurst. In their mature years a number of them not only became professors of philosophy at Stonyhurst but they also launched the "Stonyhurst Philosophical Series" of texts on theology, logic, and epistemology. In hundreds of articles and books they vigorously defended the liberal nineteenth-century Catholic position on matters of science and faith, typified by Joseph Rickaby's remark (quoted as epigraph to this essay) that teleologists "will accept as much evolution as is capable of proof."

Hopkins' reaction to all these controversies was private. Unlike his fellow Stonyhurst Philosophers who entered into public debate with the scientists in the pages of the Jesuit magazine, *The Month*, and elsewhere, Hopkins exerted his efforts quietly. His poems about St. Thecla in the first century A.D. and Margaret Clitheroe in the sixteenth century celebrated the steadfast courage of the two women--Thecla's decision to forego marriage because "the world was saved by virgins" (136) and Margaret's resolve to sew her own shroud (145). But while the martyrdom of the two women clearly moved Hopkins, his more substantial interest was in Winefred.

During his "theologate" or final stage of religious studies at St. Beuno's College in Wales, Hopkins learned of the miraculous cures associated with St. Winefred's Well, in the town now called Holywell, about ten miles from his college. Hopkins read about the details of Winefred's dramatic career in Alban Butler's *Lives of the Fathers, Martyrs and Other Principal Saints*, an enormous and well-known eighteenth-century encyclopedia, still popularly known in Hopkins' day as "Butler's *Lives of the Saints*."

The story Hopkins learned from Butler was one handed down in oral tradition and occasionally in print since the seventh century. Caradoc, son of a local Welsh prince, visited Winefred one day when it chanced that no one was with her at home. She had already refused to marry Caradoc and, realizing that his request for refreshment was leading to more physical liberties, she attempted to escape to the church of her uncle, Beuno. Caradoc caught her and chopped off her head. When her uncle reached her, he put her head back on her body and she recovered. At the spot where her head fell, a spring arose; into another nearby crack in the earth Beuno sent Caradoc directly to his doom. The spring remained constant, with many miraculous cures to its and Winefred's credit. She became a nun in a nearby community and soon her well became a focus of pilgrims and others in search of cures. When Butler visited the well in the eighteenth century, he saw "pebble stones and large parts of the rock in the bottom" which were "stained with red streaks, and with moss growing on the sides under water, which renders a sweet fragrant smell." Butler quoted an eighteenth-century doctor who told of "the green-scented moss" which was "frequently applied to ulcerated wounds with signal success" (*Butler* XI 68).

In 1874 Hopkins and a fellow "theologian," Clement Barraud, travelled to the Well and bathed there. "The sight of the water in the well," Hopkins wrote, "as clear as glass, greenish like beryl or aquamarine, trembling at the surface with the force of the springs, and shaping out the five foils of the well quite drew and held my eyes to it." Hopkins was charged with the realization of how a "sensible thing" like the Well is capable of "uttering the spiritual reason of its being" (*J* 261). It was at this time that he wanted his father--who was certainly no soft touch--to accept evidence of such an "alleged cure of a case of rupture" caused by the water from the Well. Hopkins sent the young man involved "searching questions," but received no answers. When he "heard of another cure having just been worked in London by the moss or water," he vowed to inquire about that (*F* 132).

St. Winefred's story became very important to Hopkins. His reaction to the miracles associated with her story may have been his quiet part in the Jesuits' campaign for the defense of Vatican I's position on miracles. On a more down-to-earth level, Hopkins was certainly attracted to the natural elements of the scene at St. Winefred's Well. It was situated in-- by the 1870's--a lovely little valley, yet before the miraculous spring erupted in the seventh century the vicinity was known as Sechnant or Sychnant (Welsh for a "dry valley" or "dry riverbed"). Winefred's uncle, Beuno (the namesake of Hopkins' theologate college) was such a "mythological center to the Welsh," Hopkins explained to a skeptical Bridges, that any "odd marks on cattle were called Beuno's marks" (Bridges 40). Hopkins wrote fragments of an extended closet-verse drama about Winefred's struggle with her attacker, Caradoc, whom Hopkins portrayed at Byronic: "Henceforth / In a wide world of defiance Caradoc lives alone." Her miraculous valley was described thus:

> As long as men are mortal and God merciful
> So long to this sweet spot, this leafy lean-over,
> This Dry Dean, now no longer dry nor dumb, but moist and musical
> With the uproll and the downcarol of day and night delivering
> Water, which keeps thy name.... (152.II)

Within five years of Hopkins' death in 1889, two Stonyhurst Philosophers continued his interest in St. Winefred. Herbert Lucas provided in *The Month* an interim report on her legend, emphasizing that although her story was as yet "not proven," "one day" may bring "some unlooked-for confirmation of the story." Lucas was especially taken, as was Hopkins, with the original name of the valley--Sychnant--and argued, in terms of etymology, for the accuracy of some of the details of Winefred's miraculous spring (Lucas 437). A lesser-known Stonyhurst Philosopher, Michael Maher, who was not Hopkins' friend (having joined the group as Professor of Psychology in the 1880's), also argued in *The Month* that 1894 had, in "the number of cures wrought and of pilgrims who have visited the Well" exceeded "any decade during the last two hundred years." Even the London press, Maher noted, has found its way to the tiny Welsh village and has treated the "cures" with greater respect, even going so far, in the end, as to drop the quotation marks around "cures." His enthusiasm matched Hopkins: "The paths to the Well through the vale of Sechnant had been worn bare by the feet of British and Celtic saints before either Norman or Dane landed in England" (Maher 153-55). To this day the Well has visitors seeking cures. Guidebooks, at least through the 1960's, reported a "fine reddish moss," *Byssus iolithus*, growing on the steps of the Well: the moss "appears like splodges of blood" (Hammond 49; Metcalf xxi).

Hopkins' interest and support of miracles and martyrs was characteristic of his strong peer group, the Stonyhurst Philosophers. And their importance in the Society of Jesus would alone justify Hopkins' relationship to the miraculous. Another explanation is possible, however, and it is based on a reminiscence and interpretation of Hopkins offered by Bridges, Hopkins' Oxford friend and eventually the poet laureate.

Long after Hopkins had died, Bridges wrote of an incident *fifty* years earlier, when Hopkins, then a young Jesuit in training, refused a peach from Bridges' hands, because Hopkins (in Bridges' words) "feared the savor of it." Bridges' analysis of that incident appears in his pretentious but occasionally fascinating long poem, *The Testament of Beauty* (1929). The *young* Bridges could almost accept that refusal, for he said that he was "no stranger to fear of pleasure" then. But now, as an older and wiser man, he has "grown fearful of that fear." He describes Hopkins and his contemporary Jesuits as keenly aware that their "sheer asceticism" is justified, despite the appearance of "self-holocaust," because the very "bent and native color of mind" that leads them to asceticism is in fact the "very delicacy of sense" which could easily distract them wholly from their high pursuit." As a result they attempt to "fly" from nature, "God's garden" corrupted by Satan, but to little avail. The power of nature is so great that "these mystics" like Hopkins "find no language but to echo again the psalm of her captivity." In fact, Bridges shrewdly concludes, Hopkins the novice knew very well that poets like him inevitably sing of nature because it is "the reincarnation of their renounced desire" (Bridges 149-51).

Bridges may have been wrongheaded in many of his reactions to Hopkins; even this analysis, which strikes me as having an important truth about Hopkins, his love of nature, and even his emphasis on miracles and martyrs, has the stiff and pompous attitude of a know-it-all about it. Nonetheless we know Hopkins was an amateur scientist, that he was conversant with most major trends in Victorian science, and that he held a liberal Catholic's view of Darwinian evolution (Zaniello). Yet he believed and sought verification for miracles, the very subject a number of prominent scientists regarded as a litmus test for scientific objectivity. Perhaps, to paraphrase Bridges, Hopkins sang of miracles because they were exactly the embodiment of everything that science could not explain.

Works Cited

Bridges, Robert. *The Testament of Beauty*. Oxford: Clarendon Press, 1929.

Butler, Alban. *The Lives of the Fathers, Martyrs, and Other Principal Saints*. 12 vols. Dublin: James Duffy, 1866.

Caraman, Philip. *Margaret Clitherow*. London: Catholic Truth Society, 1977.

Charles-Edwards, T. *St. Winefride and Her Well*. London: Catholic Truth Society, 1971.

Clark, Richard F. "Modern Miracles." *Nineteenth Century* 12 (1882): 766-80.

---. *Lourdes and its Miracles*. London: Catholic Truth Society, 1886.

David, Christopher. *St. Winefride's Well: A History and Guide*. Slough: Kenion Press, 1971.

Galton, Francis. "Pangenesis." *Nature* 4 May 1871: 5-6.

---. "Statistical Inquiries in the Efficacy of Prayer." *Fortnightly Review* 1 Aug 1872: 125-35.

---. *Inquiries into Human Faculty and Its Development*. 1st ed., 1883; rev. ed, 1907. Rpt. London: J.W. Dent, 1911.

Hammond, Reginald J.W. *The Complete Wales*. London: Ward Lock, 1966.

Holmes, J. Derek. "Newman's Reputation and *The Lives of the English Saints*." *Catholic Historical Review* 51 (1962): 528-38.

---. *More Roman than Rome: English Catholicism in the Nineteenth Century*. London: Burns and Oates, 1978.

Hutton, A.W., ed. *The Lives of the English Saints Written by Various Hands at the Suggestion of John Henry Newman*. 6 vols. London: S.T. Freemantle, 1901.

Hutton, R.H. "The Metaphysical Society." *Nineteenth Century* 19 (August 1885): 177-96.

Huxley, Thomas Henry. "On the Physical Basis of Life." *Fortnightly Review* 1 Feb. 1869: 129-45.

---. *Collected Essays.* 9 vols. London: Macmillan, 1893-1894.

Lucas, Herbert. "The Bollandists and St. Winefride." *The Month* 79 (November, 1893): 421-437.

Maher, Michael. "Holywell in 1894." *The Month* 83 (February, 1895): 153-82.

Manning, Cardinal Henry Edward. *The Vatican Council and Its Definitions: A Pastoral Letter to the Clergy.* London: Longmans, Green, 1870.

Metcalf, Philip. *The Life of Saint Winefride* (1712). Ed. Herbert Thurston. London: Catholic Truth Society, 1917.

Newman, Cardinal John Henry. *Characteristics from the Writings of John Henry Newman.* Ed. William Samuel Lilly. 5th ed. London: C. Kegan Paul, 1880.

Pattison, Mark. *Memoirs.* London: Macmillan, 1885.

Rickaby, John. "St. Augustine and Scientific Unbelief." *The Month* 28 (October, 1876): 195-204.

Rickaby, Joseph. *Evolution Run Wild.* London: Catholic Truth Society, 1886.

Zaniello, Tom. *Hopkins in the Age of Darwin.* Iowa City: University of Iowa Press, 1988.

The Final Act

Hopkins' Last Sonnets

David Anthony Downes

Gerard Manley Hopkins' last poetry includes ten poems which, taken together, form a remarkable pattern of religious experience. For the most part Hopkins wrote poetry that expressed what he called "news of God," poems which discover through the formalities of Ignatian spirituality and biblical parable spiritual encounters that dramatize the soul's opening up to new and sometimes transcending religious experiences. In these last poems, Hopkins wrote of those experiences which St. Ignatius called "The Discernment of Spirits"[1] by which he meant those forces and powers both within and without the soul that radically reorder its spiritual composure. These poems are in their deepest sense about personal reality, ways of experiencing the self in states of spiritual nakedness, justified and unjustified before the Almighty.

Because these last poems are such powerful expressions of the psychology of Christian love and sacrifice that emanates from Hopkins' faith

---

[1] For further discussion of this, see Downes, *Great Sacrifice*.

in Jesus and belief in His promises, and because the formalities of textuality through which he expressed his own "great sacrifice" are in the main radically different from his earlier celebratory poetry of Christian proclamation, readers have paid them greater attention. In this essay I wish to offer readings of these poems that will show that they are very much within the religious tradition of the Bible as well as central to Hopkins' finalized commitment to love and obey God in the person of Jesus Christ.

The most notable change in the poetic pattern in these last poems is that Hopkins moved from the poetic parable form of faith-witnessing in the earlier poems to the drama of faith-testing. Unsurprisingly, the poetic form he used reflects this transition. Instead of the narrative richness of description (the *Mythos* of Nature), perception (brimming religious consciousness), and exuberant action (seeking, finding, celebrating, prophesying, teaching, warning, exhorting, praying) of the earlier religious poems, in the last sonnets we are confronted with astringent monologues of crisis (self-assessments, struggles, distemper, fearful wonderment, feelings of failure, and flirtations with despair and suicide). The general dramatic situation of these last poems is that of the final act (I am not construing these last poems formally as five dramatic scenes but this critical approach has some interpretive merit); the plot (God's plays and man's ploys) is about to reach its denouement; the characters are deeply embattled, the conflict is mortality and immortality. The apocalyptic moment is at hand. The New Testament ricochet is The Revelation of John: "For the hour of fulfillment is near." Discussing Jesus' dialogues in the New Testament, Amos Wilder observed: "The issues in these confrontations are fundamental to the new message and way. Life or death, weal or woe, hang upon the response" (61). Years earlier, in "The Wreck of the Deutschland," Hopkins himself wrote about this coming of Christ: "Thou heardst me truer than tongue confess / Thy terror, O Christ, O God" (28, st. 2).

Very much like a prologue to these last poems, "As Kingfishers," "The Leaden Echo and the Golden Echo," and "Spelt from Sibyl's Leaves" (57, 59, 61) are poems which set the terms of the conflict coming after. Each poem in its own way is a parable poem that reveals an aspect of the mystery of "The Kingdom of Heaven." They also function much as does the Prologue in The Book of Job. As in the prose story in Job in which is set forth the conflict over divine wisdom and justice between God, Job, and his associates, so in these sonnets, Hopkins wrote about these subjects as he saw them in his own spiritual life reflecting the message of the Gospels. "As Kingfishers" is about the question of justice in its most fundamental terms: "Each mortal thing does one thing and the same; / Deals out that being indoors each one dwells; . . ." The poet tells us, using the actions of the self-naming in non-human subjects, that the very constitution of being this or that individual involves enacting thisness or selfness, a self-proclamation that is justly due each individual nature. The higher the nature, the higher the justice: "the just man justices." Original self-justice was perfectly ordered in Paradise. But, as we recall from Hopkins' sermons on the commonwealth of God's "first Kingdom" (*S* 53-58), the original order of justice was broken because Eve and Adam pridefully took it upon themselves to assert their own creaturely order in violation of the Divine order of justice. Henceforth earthly justice and Divine justice became the battleground between God and mankind: "the Divine 'I' and the human 'I.'" The enactment of identity, whether human or Divine, is expressed in the poem as a metaphor of natural and supernatural justice.

But how can human justice be rectified? Inevitably the pride of human righteousness would collide with God's justice unless some mediation be found. In the first four lines of the sestet, the poet explains how human justice is reconciled with God's order. Having acknowledged the existential status of everything in Creation, the natural order without any divine dimensions, Hopkins goes on: "I say more." He then simply states the transformation of human justice into grace through the Incarnation. The implications are vast. Because of Christ the selving of self as an existential condition becomes "justicing" on an entirely new plane. Selving is changed from egocentric selfness (self-love) to charity (self-interest raised to self-less love) because Jesus elevated human pride into the paths of humble obedience and love of God; hence human self-justice in justicing "keeps grace." And grace builds on nature: "that keeps all his goings graces." Now human identity is Christ identity; Christ co-inheres in the natural self because of His Incarnation. It follows that every human act of justicing is grace elevating the act in God's eye to co-participation of Christ and the actor at the natural and divine levels: "Acts in God's eye what in God's eye he is-- / Christ." The justifiable pride of creaturehood as expressed in our selving natures is through the saving grace of Christ harmonized with the "pride" of the Creator and therefore is again human destiny: "To the Father through the features of men's faces." But the fruits of this mysterious union of justice and grace are not automatic; there must be in human self-enactment a faith consciousness that is ready and willing to turn over natural egoism to God as an act of love. This is the "catch." The issue is clear: with Christ humanity is "in God's eye"; without Christ humanity inevitably drowns in the waters of wounded self-pride, "Selves--goes itself." The octave and the sestet of this sonnet are a parable about Creation, the Trinity, the Incarnation, and the Fall from Eden, justice and charity--all subjects full of theological mystery and moral paradox.

But the reconstitution of original justice through faith is not without difficulty. The new "Kingdom of God," as Jesus expressed in His parables, is a mystery to be penetrated. Finding faith is a dark voyage into religious consciousness. Does the Creator provide any aids for such discovery in Creation? For example, will any of His infinite attributes reflected in Creation lead back to Him? Hopkins took up this question in his parable poem about beauty, "To what serves Mortal Beauty?" (62). He cites music (Purcell) from the world of art and the natural beauty of humanity, instancing the beauty Pope Gregory saw in the Angles as potential intermediators for bringing the justice of Christ to England. Does such beauty only affirm earthly pride (music), and when natural beauty is transformed into grace (Angles), how does this come about? The poet offers three dispositions about these matters, each of them open to interpretation: the beauty that abounds in Creation should be openly received for what it is, splendid natural order; such beauty should be left to be itself without any undue attachments; but such a respectful dismissal should be positive, thereby honoring the Divine original of beauty: "wish all, / God's better beauty, grace." This sonnet is about the question of how Creation through beauty is a salvific path that one can follow depending on how one settles (recognize, sacrifice, celebrate) the moral conflict between egocentrism identified with natural and artificial beauty and sacrificial love elevated by grace. From the critical perspective of poetic parable, again the narrative pattern is that of seeking "God's Kingdom," the focus being upon the mystery of the finding, most of which must be left to God's providence.

In each of the poems discussed thus far, we have seen that Hopkins proffers a solution to seeking and finding "the Kingdom of God," even though the solution is hidden in the mystery of Jesus' faith and faith in Jesus. Hopkins changed the metaphor for faith in "The Leaden Echo and the Golden Echo." Using the figure of sounds emanating from a leaden instrument and a golden horn as tollers of our choice to follow Jesus or merely to echo the entropic cycle of Nature, Hopkins dramatizes the belief crisis in the human predicament. How do we hold back dissolution, not only of our material nature but all that upholds it? Is our restless desire for the preservation of our selfness, a desire fixed deep in the well of our being, never to be fulfilled? In the humanistic spirit of Classicism, Hopkins asks and answers whether there is any way to search or any place to find any other than the leaden answer of death: "O there's none; no no no there's none: / Be beginning to despair, to despair." However in the plaintive echo to this somber question, the poet hears the tones of a different reply. Seek to find a new sound buried in this old song of death, he suggests, by opening the ears to a new transcending sound, a golden one which will reveal the sweet melody of Christian reprieve for all that haunts the human heart. The leaden dirge of destruction and death will turn to the golden, heavenly music of salvation--"fond keptness." Again the parable poem leaves us with the metaphor of music expressing the mysteriousness of faith--that transformation of lead into gold which only the Master Alchemist can accomplish, thereby producing a new sounding of hope in the world. But we aspirants must want to hear the new music by trading back the leaden music of our selfness, and all selfness we encounter; God will receive our gifts and change our little music. While the mystery of faith surrounds both the giving and the getting, the narrator tells us, our joy will be like turning lead into gold, dirge into joy, sad music into happiness. Hopkins' sonorous poem of faithlessness / faith is in the poetic tradition of Milton's famous mood poems, orchestrated so that sound and rhythm are the very sense of the poem.

But if pride is not humbled through obedience that is part of the mystery of faith, then the personal tragedy that will be forthcoming will be unimaginable. "Spelt from Sibyl's Leaves" is Hopkins' "Revelation" poem.

The signs and wonders he foresees through a careful astronomical observation of the heavens are apocalyptic sightings. The poet describes sunset as Nature's daily ritual portraying in prologue the ominous beginnings of the end of the world on a cosmic level and the opening of the funeral service of every living thing. The movements of the heavenly signifiers are, Norman MacKenzie tells us, from light to dark, from shining distinctiveness to blackened masses of indistinctiveness. Life--consciousness, intelligence, sensibility--all lose their discriminating powers to experience because, like the universe once perceived about them, they contrast into no-thingness (159-163). Hopkins expressed this as "Disremembering, dismembering all now." The octave evokes the primordial chaos of the Behmoth of Job and the darkness that covered the earth when Jesus died: "Óur evening is óver us; óur night / whélms, whélms, ánd will énd us."

The poet-narrator records the decoded message in his heart ("Heart, you round me right / Wlth"): the day of Judgment is coming, and when it does, the soul's earthly pilgrimage will be dramatized in God's theater as drama in black (sin) and white (grace). The echo from the New Testament is the Son of Man separating the sheep from the goats (Matt. 25. 31-46). Hopkins chose to dwell upon the dark curse of damnation, focusing upon the doom of those who did not seek and find the "Kingdom of God." The poem in turning oracular, as the title suggests, warns of the finders / losers predicament that our daily choices fix upon our spiritual destiny. The last lines most graphically represent the painful exposure of the human soul and the powerfully abrasive self-reproaches that will be experienced: "Where, selfwrung, selfstrung, sheathe-and shelterless, / thoúghts agáinst thoughts in groans grínd." The eternal verdict self-produced and self-inflicted, as depicted in the narrative of this parable poem, expresses the sorrowful, dark tale of faithlessness, moral relativism, and religious indifference.

In these "prologue" poems to his "dark sonnets," Hopkins approached his Christian faith in terms of moral conduct, right and wrong, and Divine justice which underlie the mystery of faith. His poetic parables strikingly emphasize the ultimate implications for individual destiny in the seeking and finding of Christ. Finding Jesus involves, he makes clear, intimations of Him in Nature, in the heart's core, and in the volitional intellect, for all of these are doers of the drama of the mystery of faith sought, found, and lived, or ignored and lost. Such personal episodes are part of the test and torments of dealing directly with God in the very pieces of experience of our lives.

The subtexts to these poems, indeed to all of Hopkins' major poems, is the spirituality of St. Ignatius. The shaping spirit and methodological approach to Hopkins' lived and preached Christianity devolves around the spiritual psychology which Ignatius put into his *Spiritual Exercises*. In this document and its surrounding commentaries, Ignatius centered spiritual growth on meditations of the Kingdom of Christ and the Two Standards of service which constitute the moral and spiritual quality of Christianized human life. From Christ we learn why and for what ends we were created, and from Christ we have been given the standard of loving service befitting God. We can elect this sublime standard by answering Jesus' call, or we can languish in Satan's camp. *The Spiritual Exercises* organize our insights so as to see how Christ is in all Creation, how He co-inheres in our very being, and once truly seen, we will elect in the fullness of our spiritual desires to give all of ourselves to honoring and serving God. Hopkins, as a Jesuit, lived this Ignatian spiritual life, and, as a religious poet, his imagination was profoundly shaped by Ignatius' chivalric call: "What should I do for

Christ?"[2] All of Hopkins' great religious poetry is centered around the answer to this question.

I do not wish to explore the biographical contexts of the last sonnets here. They have been explored extensively elsewhere.[3] Nor do I wish to argue here which are the "terrible" sonnets or in what order they should be placed.[4] What I wish to focus on is their biblical subtexts and their dramatic contexts. These poems represent a unique version of New Testament speech (especially those instances in which Jesus confronts or is confronted about the ultimate implications of His message) and Old Testament dialogue in which figures like Job or Moses directly exchange with God as if in a collective negotiation. The language of all of these speeches is dramatic because it is rooted in conflicts that divide persons in fundamental ways--the manner in which they conduct their lives. The drama of these poems is not that of presenting the main actions of the plot. Rather the actions depicted are strategic pieces of the main plot through which we can infer the *Mythos* of the entire drama. Thus the speech is often cryptic, sometimes fragmentary, and nearly always in the form of the dramatic monologue (God, of course, is the identifiable but mysterious Presence in each poem). As exponents of the dire implications of the main plot--the faith crisis of winning or losing the "Kingdom of God"--these poems are speech acts in which the main character, Gerard, "This Jack, joke, poor potsherd," expresses his exasperation, torments, sorrows, and sufferings at having discovered that, put to the test by God (whose dominating Presence

---

[2] See Downes, *Great Sacrifice*.

[3] See Downes, *Great Sacrifice* 81-114.

[4] See Downes, *Hopkins' Sanctifying Imagination* 123-124.

permeates each scene), he must, like Job, renounce even the righteousness of true discipleship before the Almighty if He demands it. This is to say that to restore original justice, God does ask at times that His subjects acknowledge that there is sinful pride of self even in the true righteousness of dedicating all of one's life and talent to His service--a very hard lesson, indeed.

Though his enactments (the poet's seeking and finding and in their doing spinning his choices as the web of his life "on two spools") expressing the main plot are off-stage, the moral pivots on which conflict turns are made clear in the "prologue" poems previously discussed. Each sonnet, then, read in this dramatic critical context, is a part of the monologue of part of a scene which we can only partially surmise though we can discern its dramatic texture. Also these poems taken together form the climactic parts of scenes of the play which might be called, "Gerard."

"Carrion Comfort" (64) is the poem in these last poems which has the strongest biblical ricochet. Gerard, like Job ("My days have been swifter than a runner . . . swift as vultures swooping on carrion") has been doing mortal battle with the forces God has permitted to assault him. The portion of the scene that the poem depicts is the aftermath of a major struggle in which Gerard has been nearly defeated. He is delirious so that his report is narratively disordered. The second half of the octave reports the battle that has taken place, while the first half is the speech of the defeated Gerard barely holding out. Like Job, Gerard refuses to give in to the torments that God has sent him. Punished like Job as an evildoer that neither was, and baffled to the point of resentment over his treatment, Gerard bolsters his courage to hang on to his being, his selfness, "these last strands of man / In me." In the second half of the octave, the dialogue moves from "talking out loud" to talking with the Master of his assailants.

Like Job's, Gerard's complaint is directly to God who visits him as a voracious beast devouring him body and soul. The language is accusative, confronting, questioning. In effect Gerard is asking why he, a true and faithful servant of God, is being cursed, and why God, who is the perfect judge and the author of perfect justice, has become the curser. Like Job in his complaint to God, this questioning carries with it some rashness if not a counter curse. The dialogues make clear that the conflict is an ultimate combat, the combatants, while totally mismatched, nevertheless are battling to "master" the other. These dialogues suggest that the battle is in its last stage, God is winning (Gerard still loves Him and His service), but has not won. (The tensive symbols of Cross and Resurrection form the theological subtext here as they do in all of these poems.)

The sestet opens with the word "Why?" The speaker is addressing himself primarily, though God is not excluded. This inquiry, which haunts the story of Job no matter how interpreted, is a mystery in this poem as well. Did Job curse God in his complaint as one bold interpreter (Robertson 36) suggests? Is Job really innocent? Is his punishment truly out of proportion to the "sin" of being a finite creature whose righteousness must be less than perfect? Is God truly allowing punishment out of "pride" in the total devotion of His servant? Though God is all-powerful and thus undefeatable, nevertheless has the combat turned against Him by putting His justice and His mercy on trial? And if His faithful servant is less than perfect, why can He not forgive him? Is He testing whether His servants truly love Him, or whether their worship is really selfish--to get what they can? Job is not told, nor does Gerard, I think, ever find any answers to these questions. Unlike most other readers, I do not think that the speaker answers his question in the line, "That my chaff might fly; my grain lie, sheer and clear." I take this as an apparent pious justification, but it is really a rationalization for God's behavior. The speaker has no answers for the spiritual violence he has suffered. Only read in this Job-like way does the rest of the sestet make full sense. The remainder of the poem is a declaration of victory by Gerard, not in the sense of defeating God, an impossibility in any case, and never the object of his struggle, but in the sense that out of his spiritual battles, his physical sufferings, his priestly service, he affirms the integrity of his discipleship, the wholeness of his Christian righteousness. This is why he can "cheer," why Gerard dare consider cheering himself as the hero "that fought him," while admitting that he was beaten flat, pinned by God, now depicted as the overpowering wrestler. But this is only the first combat, round one. Gerard's reference to "now done darkness," we learn as the dialogue of the next scene tells us, is to be undone by his opponent as the battle goes on.

"No worst, there is none" (65) and "I wake and feel" (67) remind us of Job's complaint to God in Chapter 3, and in Chapter 7 Job cries,

> When I think my bed will comfort me,
> that sleep will relieve my complaining,
> those doest terrify me with dreams
> and affright me with visions. I would rather be choked outright;
> I would prefer death to all my sufferings.
> I am in despair, I would not go on living;
> leave me alone, for my life is, but a vapour.
>
> (7.13-16)

Gerard tells us that he too experiences an inconsolable grief that is like an ear-bursting sound. Like Job he complains that he is not receiving any attention from God, or any intercession on his behalf from the saints like Mary. Like Job he feels his griefs to be so overwhelmingly intense that they aggregate, gain even more intensity from "herding" and "huddling," so that they seem to begin to fill the whole world with sorrow, as if his heart through some terrifying judgment of God becomes the anvil whereon God strikes the strokes of punishment producing the horrible voice of a Fury shrieking vengeance. In the sestet Gerard replies to the grief shrieking in him. His words are strangely calm considering the level of feeling that had poured out of him as if unbidden in the first part of the speech lament. Now he attempts to respond with some assessment of the destructiveness of his grief. He envisions himself as an alpine climber clinging for dear life to some sheer cliff, unable to go up, unable to go down, stuck on the sheer face of the mountain, waiting to be flicked off by the wind. Just before he is about to fall into the abyss, he is able to creep onto a ledge and rest, but the respite is a kind of death trance. The terrain here is spiritual and psychological--sin and sanity. The sleep that comes is a presage of death, a mime of rigor mortis. Job says, "When I lie down, I think, / "When will it be / day that I may rise?"; Gerard says "all / Life death does end and each day dies with sleep."

In "I wake," the morning poem that dramatically follows "No worst," Gerard awakens to a morn whose light is shrouded in gloomy murk. Job felt so aggrieved that he called on the day (his birthday particularly but every rebirth of his life that each day is) to die: "May darkness sully it, and murk and gloom, / cloud smother that day, swift darkness eclipse its sun" (3.3-7). He wanted no more of sleep: "When that I think that my bed will comfort me / that sleep will relieve my complaining, / thou does terrify me with dreams / and affright me with visions" (7.13-14). Gerard too can find no healing rest in his sleep nor any solace in the morning's light. He talks about time as "black hours" which in his dispirited consciousness becomes an endless darkness, living-death. Trapped in time's labyrinthian cave, his cries and his calls disappear into the empty darkness. God will answer neither Job nor Gerard, nor will He take them out of their misery. Is it because both are sinners?

Unlike Job who, while accepting his moral frailty as a human being ("What is man that thou makst much of him / and turnest thy thoughts towards him, / only to punish him morning by morning / or to test him every hour of the day?" (7.16-18)), Gerard in the sestet speech exhibits a much greater sense of creaturehood. Job's language suggests in his talk with Eliphaz about his human finitude, that his is less than a whole righteousness which is the lot of being human, though he does describe his human condition in physical terms similar to Gerard's self-derogation: "My body is infested with worms, / and scabs cover my skin" (7.5). Gerard, being mindful of his sinfulness in its most particular individuation as being an expression of his unrighteousness, in the incarnation of his identity is an incarnation of imperfection. The resultant imagery expressing this state depicts a soul sensing its moral ugliness through experiencing the body as a bitter and sour bile flooding every rift of its being. From this overpowering sense of unworthiness before God, Gerard has an intimation of the damned in hell punished by an eternity of tasting their sins as a sweat oozing from their bodies. The dramatic predicament of Gerard's statement is an enigma. For either as another Job suffering the desolations of a faithful servant being severely punished for unknown wrongdoing, or as a disobedient servant made to suffer for his rebelliousness, Gerard's hell is only slightly better than the very worst--being condemned to hell's fires. In this dialogue of self and soul, Gerard has awakened to a darkness in which the only illumination is that of the fires in his rancid blood burning, burning.

Just where these two poems fit into the full context of the last scenes of Gerard's drama is unclear. But whether they preceded or succeeded the battle with God makes little difference. They are poems in which the speaker expresses extreme physical suffering and great spiritual agony. Faith in "God's Kingdom" seems a contradiction. Gerard, like Job, is placed in perhaps the most difficult moral conundrum of all, that of being a true seeker after the higher righteousness, finding it, bidding and buying it, only to have the seed die, the treasure decay, the pearl become worthless. Indeed, they all become a plague upon his soul and body. These dialogues are speeches about experiencing the fires that Jesus told about, that burning inferno that those who are separated from God will suffer. With these poems, Gerard is pitched into the pit of despair, the "Kingdom of God" unreachable and impossible, faith nightmarish and incredible. Job stated the dilemma exactly: "I tremble in every nerve; / I know that thou wilt not hold me innocent. / Why do I labour in vain?" (9.28-29)

Who will still Gerard's heart? "Patience, hard thing!" and "My own heart let me more have pity on," (68, 69) are monologues[5] which evoke the beginnings of spiritual recovery. Like Job who suffered the anguish of seeing his family destroyed by a divine whirlwind, Gerard has been plunged into a spiritual crisis over feelings of God's belligerent abandonment. As in Job where we are surprised how angry he becomes in arguing his innocence, the unfairness of the punishments he is being sent, so Gerard in his interior dialogue about Patience astonishes us by talking about his much needed state of soul in belligerent terms. Mention patience and the attributes that come to mind are serene quietness and graceful perseverance. Gerard tells us that patience is a "hard thing," therefore, asking for it is a "hard thing" because what we are asking for is "war," "wounds," pervasive weariness over being denied, being put down, while still obeying. Moreover, he explains

---

[5] I realize that all of these sonnets can be read as soliloquies, but I prefer to read them as monologues because they take on much more poetic and dramatic power supposing that God is a participant presence.

that these are the only ground out of which patience grows, and when it does, it masks severity with serenity like ivy covering a ruin. From a distance patience looks stately, disguising the ruin on which it grows, and as it flutters in the breeze, it is easy to mistake the violence ("There she basks / Purple eyes") of decay hidden beneath its "seas of liquid leaves all day.")

Gerard describes his feelings about patience, about asking for patience, how it hurts ("Hearts grate on themselves," that is scrape bruise on bruise). Then the shocker in the speech. It is not war, weariness, and wounds that hold back the bid for patience; it is pride, pride of selfness, pride of creaturehood, still being justified before the "pride" of God, the Creator. Still he must bid for patience to be granted. In the final tercet, Gerard gives us another shock. He who bids for the warfare of patience deserves at least kindness, he asserts, and true kindness is that peace of soul that comes only from God. And where is that dispenser of "Delicious kindness"? Why he is being patient with his disciple! Gerard explains what this Divine patience is by using the metaphor of the honey comb as the collector of that most sought after "Delicious kindness." God, like the bee, comes to fill the comb of the heart in his own due time, but He comes only when the comb is prepared, that is shaped to His liking, a shaping that comes from bidding for torment and toil that bends the will (comb) into the proper shape. Thus Gerard explains the huge irony that is at the center of Christian spiritual advancement. In this bit of dialogue between self and soul surfacing from the grand battle of wills, the main conflict of this drama, Gerard, like Job, states the situation of trying to bid for "God's Kingdom": to have holy obedience one must demonstrate patience, which means to accept unexplained punishment, indeed, to ask for such punishment in hope that in His own good time, God will send the kindness of His grace. This is to say that serving God means more than being submissive, more than being duly righteous; God sometimes asks that His true servants "destroy" themselves for His sake--("Our ruins of wrecked past purpose"). And even if we "bid for" this self-destruction, we must wait amid all our wounds and weariness for His blessing. What a terrible revelation Gerard has discovered about admittance to "God's Kingdom"! In this monologue, he has put in a few words all the bitter and terrible irony of Job's case against God as well as God's answer about the status of a "poor Jackself." No wonder that Gerard's next dialogue poem is about pity for his "sad self." The subtext in these poems is Jesus in the Garden and on the Cross. Ignatius wrote of such spiritual anxiety, "When one is in desolation, he should strive to persevere in patience" (*Spiritual Exercises* 143).

In his seeking to find the "Kingdom of God," Gerard has found that God is imperial even to His most faithful of servants. No matter what the urgency born out of love shown through service, God's mastery (approval and acceptance) comes to His faithful servant in His own time and manner. Ignatius wrote, "God alone can give consolation to the soul without any previous cause" (147). Perhaps no spiritual circumstance as that of pleading for the gift of an "elevating" grace brings the realization of the "highness" of the Divinity and the "lowness" of humanity. Thus the war of patience must go on without respite. Gerard now understands that he is left to pity himself in trying to submit his entire will to God's mastery. Not to offer himself self-pity is to either become angry with God, really a show of pride, or to continue to berate himself for not finding and receiving any "quickening" or "corrective" graces through his choices and his desires, truly a path to spiritual self-destruction. The paradox of seeking "God's Kingdom" cuts both ways. What else is there to do but submit to God's will? This admittance of human finitude with its accompanying ontological evils is a devastating realization, especially difficult to one whose sense of "selfness" was elemental to his vision of Creation, his notion of Divinity, his exercise of service and devotion. Yet Gerard must acknowledge that in "God's eyes" he signifies nothing. This emptying out of the self leaves only self-pity. So Gerard calls on himself for more tenderness, more kindness, more caring ("My own heart let me more have pity on") by giving over any more struggle that results only in more torments, "not live this tormented mind / With this tormented mind tormenting yet." In the second speech he notes the futility of finding any self-comfort. Comfort is out there in God's providence, but to him it seems as impossible to obtain as light to a blind man or a drink in a world drenched with water. The latter statement, of course, dramatizes how absolutely comfortless he felt, and how impossible it was for him to be a comfort to himself. Abject, denied, reduced, humiliated, he has become prostrate in all of his spiritual ambitions. Has he come to the end?

The opening speech of the sestet marks a powerful change in his predispositions towards himself. Before he would struggle, he would lament, he would complain, he would even admit to his sinfulness, but he still held on to that last shred of pride, his identity, which is to say God's recognition of him. Now he must give that over. A new voice arises in him to address the burnt out case: "Soul, self," that is, the identity you have been clinging to out of pride of "selfness." Admit that you are in your Creator's consciousness nothing more than a moment in an infinity of moments: "come, poor Jackself, I do advise / You, jaded, lét be." The acquiescing voice counsels retreat. Maybe in the disengagement of defeat some comfort might come by, even some happiness born of accepting one's self as is. Anyway it is up to the Master to decide where and when to give His peace, but He will not be forced ("wrung"). His consolation will come, if it comes, unexpectedly, and if He sends light and happiness into Gerard's life, it will manifest itself dramatically by changing the climate of the overcast self instantly, like a burst of dappled sky breaking through the stormy gloom showing a beckoning sunny path between two mountains. This dialogue implies a scene of momentous change in Gerard. He pleads *nolo contendere* and leaves the case up to the jury of God's will. He doesn't know what God will do, but he has faith that in his own self-pity, forged out of humility and patience, God will speak, send a grace, shed a light on his way. Here Gerard's humble faith parts significantly from Job who holds on to his case of self-justification to the very end so that God has to put him in his place when he finally speaks to him.

"That Nature is a Heraclitean Fire and of the comfort of the Resurrection" (72) is the final speech in the final scene of this religious drama. It is important to notice that the poetic form is no longer a monologue but rather it is an epilogue of the drama. The speaker[6] mysteriously experiences an incredible flash of spiritual light that leads to a transcendent religious experience--the grace of a direct comfort from God which floods his mind and heart so fully that he has an intimation of the joy of religious glorification. One cannot help but think of St. Ignatius' sickbed effusion of loving desire to serve his Lord (Rahner 37). Gerard's voice is at first steady, assured, and his words confident, but it soon becomes anxious and threatened when suddenly it is raised to jubilation. Why this dramatic change? Gerard now views himself differently. He is no longer fighting to preserve his own identity before God and, therefore, he is not so "pitched into grief." He has admitted his sinful nature, whether because of his being less than wholly righteous or because of his own lifetime of failures, his "lonely began," and misdeeds, his "sweating self." His battle now is the

---

[6] I, of course, am assuming that the speaker is Gerard, whose spiritual composure is one of suffering patience, and that he and Christ, who suddenly graces Gerard's heart, are the *dramatis personae*.

warfare of patience, his field equipment is complete submission, his battle hymn, St. Ignatius' oath: "Take, O Lord, and receive all my liberty, my memory, my understanding and my whole will. Thou has given me all that I am and all that I possess; I surrender it all to Thee that Thou mayst dispose of it according to Thy will. Give me only Thy grace; with these I will be rich enough, and will have no more to desire" (102). Gerard is ready to encounter the finitude of natural existence as well the mystery of Jesus' faith in the mystery of the "Kingdom of God."

The scene is set on a day that is bright but windy between days of torrential rain. Gerard is gazing at the sky, watching the clouds. He reflects that he is watching a beautiful dance in the heavens ("heaven-roysters, in gay-gangs"), a dance full of movement and transformation the patterns of which never reach any permanence because their orchestra, the wind, billowing and blowing like a fire, never lets them come to a full stop except momentarily. The wind music drives the clouds here and there, up and down, gathering them and separating them, then condensing them downwards from the heavens towards the earth ("Down roughcast, down dazzling whitewash"). Now the earth enters the scene as the antagonist to the wind that makes its "light show" entry to this new stage. The earth is then swept around by the wind and, as their dance swirls about, the earth's costume is transformed because the wind is changing its coat from wet to dry, gathering up all its licors for transfer back to the heavens. Gerard stops and looks at his own footprint in the soft, wet earth. He realizes that Nature's great drama, which he is witnessing with such admiration because of the magnitude and beauty of its self-enactment, in fact has engulfed him, absorbed him into its plot, and hence into its finale. His awe of Nature is transformed into that of a witness to a murder in his realization that the descending and ascending fire of Nature (sun and wind recapturing the moisture from the flooded earth), which he has seen and heard in all its beauteous splendor and enveloping power ("the bright wind boisterous"), will snaffle him and all mankind up into its indifferent cyclic process ("Million-fuelèd, / nature's bonfire burns on"). Selfness will be "dried up" into the basic elements for a chance reformation into some "thing" else. More than the natural body will be gone. The great exploits of human accomplishment and the wondrous creations of the imaginative intelligence will disappear ("his firedint, / his mark on mind is gone!"). The insight is inescapable: everyone's spark and mark, ordinary or extraordinary, is doomed in Nature's entropic fire.

If this is a true insight, then, the dream of human nature as "star material," that is, beyond the transforming flux of sun and wind, is a delusion; mankind's feats and faculties, "Both are in an unfathomable, all is in an enormous dark / Drowned." The disproportion between aspiration and destiny is so great that the joyous voice that opened the poem now becomes sad and plaintive.

O pity and indig | nation! Manshape, that shone
Sheer off, disseveral, a star, | death blots black out; nor mark
    Is any of him at all so stark
But vastness blurs and time | beats level.

More than depressing, this conclusion rocks the speaker beyond endurance ("Enough!"). The thought of an absolute personal oblivion is so contrary to all of his being that he must immediately seek and find a saving resolution. We come now to the most difficult part of the poem.

The poet suddenly has a complete change of consciousness. His dejection is blasted away by a kind of visionary intuition of the personal and religious significance of the Resurrection which is revealed to him with the penetration of "a trumpet crash." (It is here that the *Mythos* of the Bible is most evident, for the very utterance of the Resurrection Christ confers spiritual power that changes the soul.) As opposed to the destructive winds of Nature, this wind is of a different kind, one that clears away the heart's joylessness and dejection. His sinking soul is flooded with a trans-earthly light ("In a flash"). No longer does the threat of his self being wasted by Nature's diurnal swings bother him. In fact, the destruction of his physical self is gladly bequeathed to Nature's gather-all (worms and ashes) in which the "world's wildfire" burns. The poet explains why this dramatic ending to his "world-sorrow." Jesus' "great sacrifice" is the key to finding "God's Kingdom." In Him the reestablishment of the "Kingdom of God" was made real and continues to be realized in an ever greater degree. Christ is the still center. To express this Hopkins introduces a new dimension to Nature's revolving process born out of his sudden spiritual realization: Before the onslaught of Nature and the majesty of God throned behind it, he, like any Jack human, is but a joke-self who is gradually being reduced to a shard, a scrap, a piece of kindling, ready for Nature's fire, but because Jesus entered human flesh, joined Himself with mankind, offered Himself in loving sacrifice in order to establish "God's Kingdom" anew in the mind and heart of all human kind, an awesome happening has taken place. For those who have eyes to see and ears to hear, the Incarnation changes everything. Northrop Frye explains this transformation of soul through the biblical Christ ("it makes good sense to call the Bible and the person of Christ by the same name"): "But what the Bible gives us is not so much a cosmology as a vision of upward metamorphosis, of the alienated relation to man to nature transformed into a spontaneous and effortless life --not effortless in the sense of being lazy or passive, but in the sense of being energy without alienation" (76).

The only way the poet can describe this change in his spiritual prospects in "the Kingdom of God" is through a symbol which reminds us of Jesus' parables about the treasure and the pearl of great price--"immortal diamond." Diamond, a product of the earth (a crystallized coal), becomes in the poet's surcharged religious consciousness a natural symbol for the spiritual transformation that the Incarnation, and its corollary, the Resurrection, brings about. This precious natural gem, representative of all the beauty of Nature and the richness of human culture, but in itself little more than a very hard stone, goes through a kind of transubstantiation to become "immortal," that is, becomes a medium for some spiritual state that is beyond Nature. This "New being" is the union of Christ and each human being that is the religious mystery of the Incarnation. Mankind (ordinary diamond-coal) becomes the precious treasure of the "Kingdom of Heaven" (immortal), the symbolic equivalent of Christ becoming man and man becoming Christ: "I am all at once what Christ is, since he was what I am." The secret treasure of faith in the "kingdom of God" has been "found," that is, his faith has been surcharged with a new trust and confidence because of a refreshed internalization of faith in Christ: Jack-Gerard is Christ because Christ took on a human nature, took on the finitude of the human person, suffered and died out of love for humanity, and in His own Resurrection raised mankind up from the dead to "being energy without alienation"--the "Kingdom of God."

Hopkins dramatized the transformation of his spiritual consciousness through his use of light and sound language in his sonnet. (There are fourteen action verbs depicting Nature's womb to tomb cycle--from "chevy" to "burns.") In the beginning the poet-persona "sees" Nature's lights in the sky, lights which are in constant change from brightness to blurriness and back again. "Mankind-lights" similarly spark into intensity out of darkness but soon go out, "dark/Drowned." The sound of grace is dramatic as well. From "boisterous" Nature to muffled mankind, sound expresses the ever-changing flux that "beats level" all that is "Manshape," until a new light flashes and a new sound breaks out--"an eternal beam" and a "heart's-clarion." The powers of faith dramatically overcome the powers of Nature's doom.

This movement from the "trash" of Nature to the "flash" and "crash" of faith telegraphs a momentous change of spiritual possibility--death to resurrection. What accounts for this extraordinary change of heart? How has Gerard been rescued from personal obliteration, Nature's rubbing out" of everything? The answer is an alteration of individual consciousness in which an identity that brings change, chance, and death to an end for the essential self by uniting this self to a divine self: "I" = Christ; Christ = "I." The emotional impact of this incredible realization, the revaluation of human possibility that this change of destiny implies, the transubstantiation of human nature that this union causes, the poet powerfully and graphically expresses as "Immortal diamond" that suddenly and inexplicably occurs in the series of lowly epithets he applies to the human animal. And to reinforce his perception of how the mystery of the Incarnation changes human fortune, he repeats the alteration: "Is immortal diamond." "Is" is the comforting permanence of the "Kingdom of Heaven" that lies hidden in Jesus' faith and faithfulness, the persevering "is-ness" that overrides Nature's formless flux. David Tracy remarks of such classic religious disclosures, "The proclamation's questioning, provocative, confronting, healing word of address discloses another possibility of self-understanding recognized in the Christ-event as the power that it happens" (281).

This sonnet completes Gerard's drama. In the beginning, he started dialoguing with God who seemed to be disappearing from his spiritual consciousness, then he plunged into the descending discourse of self and soul until he reached the bottom, the pit of the lonely self. Here he faced the fearful limits of humanness beyond which lay the darkness of "otherness." God did not stir. There he waited and watched, at first in an irritated impatience, but then with an acquiescing humility that led to pity and charity. With no forewarning came the call, the light, and the joyful comfort of the mystery of faith in Christ Jesus.

Echoes from the New Testament abound. In all of Jesus' dialogues, the central issue being addressed is what needs to be done to inherit eternal life. The purpose of such talk about this subject is a personal challenge of the most fundamental nature: "Tell me, Lord, the answer to this question, I am listening. I want to know." And as we believe, Jesus answered in one way or another, "Hear me, you are invited to enter the Kingdom of Heaven. In my faith and through your faith in me, I promise you that you will be with me. But it won't be easy, so be prepared to work for it, even suffer; you won't know when or how your faith in me will reveal the fruits of my promises." This is heart to heart talk at a most radical level, talk that demands a response in the core of each self. Again David Tracy, speaking of such "proclaiming narratives," in Jesus' story: "[They] disclose what an authentic life can be by narrating who Jesus was, the Crucified and Risen One" (281). Hopkins' closing sonnet is one of these "proclaiming narratives" issuing out of the hard reality of authentic religious encounter of the most radical character.

Another critical attitude from the perspective of the New Testament towards this climactic ending to one of the most powerfully penetrating series of religious poems is that of a new parable. Read as a parable, this sonnet with its intricate pattern of images of sound and light, its orchestrated rhythms reflecting the workings of Nature, the tragic reactions of human nature, and the surge of grace culminating in a grand coda of the comfort and task of personal resurrection, opens up the mystery of the

"Kingdom of God" as do the parables of Jesus. There is that same intensity of language conferring grace, the same incisive location of the basic human predicament, the same focus upon the ultimate resolution being a trust from afar--mysterious, unpredictable, final, glorious. Hopkins' poem is parable of Jesus' basic parable-story: "Believe in what I tell you and choose to follow Me to the Kingdom of my Father. Time is short; the end is near. Hear Me!" And like Jesus' parables, we are given an intimation of the internalization of His message through a richly suggestive metaphor revealing the joy and consolation of entering into a spiritual union with Him.

Finally, this sonnet represents a new creation in an absolutely original sense, a new Christian carol of unparalleled art according to Paul Mariani: "There is an opulence, a joy in creativity, a new plumbing of the dynamic potentialities of language and melodic rhythm which constitute no less than a chant to the risen Christ" (290). In no other poem did Hopkins state with such dramatic power his evangelical vision of how the Holy Spirit expresses the love that proceeds from The Father and the Son--the ultimate reality of sanctifying grace--that is the comfort of the Resurrection.

In reading these poems I have entered the texts provoked, challenged, and vexed. I have tried to encounter the disorientation the form of the texts produces by placing them in the dramatic context of a final act. Reading these poems as extant speech-acts in the mysterious, secret drama of the deepest personal religious disconsolation--the ultimate lover's quarrel, the pattern of their historicity notwithstanding, I discover soul movements of the rarest kind of the progress of love.

Works Cited

The New World Bible with Apocrypha. London: Oxford and Cambridge University Press, 1970.

Downes, David Anthony. *The Great Sacrifice: Studies in Hopkins.* Lanham, Maryland: University Press of America, 1983.

---. *Hopkins' Sanctifying Imagination.* Lanham, Maryland: University Press of America, 1985.

Frye, Northrop. *The Great Code: The Bible and Literature.* New York: Harcourt Brace Jovanovich, 1982.

MacKenzie, Norman. *A Reader's Guide to Gerard Manley Hopkins.* Ithaca: Cornell University Press, 1981.

Mariani, Paul. *Commentary on the Complete Poems of Gerard Manley Hopkins.* Ithaca: Cornell University Press, 1970.

Rahner, Karl. *The Spirituality of Loyola.* Trans. Francis John Smith, S.J. Chicago: Loyola University Press, 1953.

Robertson, David. *The Old Testament and the Literary Critic.* Philadelphia: Fortress Press, 1977.

The Spiritual Exercises of St. Ignatius. Tr. Louis J. Puhl, S.J. Westminster, Maryland: The Newman Press, 1953.

Tracy, David. *The Analogical Imagination: Christian Theology and the Culture of Pluralism.* New York: The Crossroad Publishing Co., 1981.

Wilder, Amos Niven. *The Language of the Gospel: Early Christian Rhetoric.* New York: Harper and Row, 1964.

Contributors

Warren Anderson, Professor Emeritus of Comparative Literature at the University of Massachusetts at Amherst and Rhodes Scholar and distinguished linguist, has published *Matthew Arnold and the Classical Tradition*, and essay in *Readings of "The Wreck,"* and numerous articles on Greek and Victorian Poetry. His edition of Hopkins' Dublin notes on Homer will appear shortly.

Todd K. Bender, University of Wisconsin-Madison, is the author of *Gerard Manley Hopkins: The Classical Background and Critical Reception of His Work* (1966), and *A Hopkins Concordance*, with Robert J. Dilligan.

James Finn Cotter is the author of *Inscape: The Christology and Poetry of Gerard Manley Hopkins* (1972), and has just completed a translation of *The Divine Comedy*. His studies and poetry have appeared regularly in *English Language News, Renascence, Hudson Review, The New York Times, America*, and *Hopkins Quarterly*.

David A. Downes is a member of the Editorial Board of the *Hopkins Quarterly*, and author of *Gerard Manley Hopkins: A Study of His Ignatian Spirit* (1960), *Victorian Portraits: Hopkins and Pater* (1965), *The Great Sacrifice: Studies in Hopkins* (1983), and *Hopkins' Sanctifying Imagination* (1985). Dr. Downes has served as Chairman of the English Department, and Dean of the College of Humanities and Fine Arts at California State University, Chico.

Joseph J. Feeney, S.J., Professor of English, St. Joseph's University, Philadelphia, has written on Hopkins in *Thought, The Hopkins Quarterly, America, The Month, Theological Studies, Victorians Institute Journal*, and *Victorian Studies*. He also contributed essays to several books and to the

Catalogue of the Hopkins exhibition at the University of Texas. Essays on other topics have appeared in *American Studies*, *The Critic*, the *C L A Journal*, *America*, *The Month*, *Studies in American Fiction*, and *Thought*. In 1986-87 he held the Jesuit Chair at Georgetown University.

Peter Milward, S.J., was born in London in 1925, and educated at Wimbledon College and Oxford. He has taught English literature at Sophia University, Tokyo, since 1962. The founder of the Hopkins Society of Japan, he is the author of *A Commentary on the Sonnets of Gerard Manley Hopkins*, *Landscape and Inscape*, and editor of *Readings of the Wreck*, as well as numerous studies with special reference to Shakespeare and Hopkins.

Michael D. Moore, Professor of English, Wilfrid Laurier University, Waterloo, Ontario, was the organizer of the 1980 International Hopkins Conference in Canada. He is the author or editor of a number of studies on John Henry Newman, Hopkins and others.

Raymond V. Schoder, S.J., was Emeritus Professor of Classics at Loyola University in Chicago when he died in 1987. Well known for his photographic skills, and his studies on classical archeology, Father Schoder also co-authored *Readings of the Wreck, Landscape and Inscape*, and contributed studies to the early influential collection *Immortal Diamond* (1949), as well as to *Thought* and *Hopkins Quarterly*.

Ruth Seelhammer, Curator of the Hopkins Collection at Gonzaga University, Spokane, Washington, and member of the Board of Scholars of the International Hopkins Association, is the author of *Hopkins Collected at Gonzaga*, as well as studies on Hopkins' poetry and literary reception. Besides providing regular bibliographies for the *Hopkins Quarterly*, she assisted Alfred Thomas,S.J. in the establishment of the Hopkins Society, and in the growth of the *Hopkins Research Bulletin*.

R.K.R. Thornton, Professor and Head of School of English, University of Newcastle-upon-Tyne, is the author of *Gerard Manley Hopkins: The Poems*, and other critical studies on Hopkins, his language and life, and editor of *All My Eyes See*, as well as works by Nicholas Hilliard, John Clare, and Ivor Gurney.

Donald Walhout is Professor of Philosophy at Rockford College, Rockford, Illinois. He received his Ph.D. in philosophy from Yale University, and is the author of *Send My Roots Rain: A Study of Religious Experience in the Poetry of Gerard Manley Hopkins*, *The Good and the Realm of Values*, and *Festival of Aesthetics*.

Tom Zaniello teaches film, literature and writing in the Literature Department at Northern Kentucky University. He is the author of *Explorations in Reading and Writing* (1987), *Hopkins in the Age of Darwin* (1988), and *Cinematic Perspectives* (due out in 1989).

Index

"A Model Kingdom" 198
A Portrait of the Artist as a Young Man 89
"A Voice from the World" 80
Abandonment 59, 104, 253
Aboriginal calamity 91
Academy 192
Achilles 131
Acrostic 160
Action 7, 11-13, 15-24, 27, 28, 48, 54, 100, 131, 132, 134, 135, 140, 158, 240, 261
Active life 11, 13, 17, 25, 26
Acts of the Apostles 230
Adam 147, 151, 155-158, 165, 169, 241
   New, 155, 169
Adam's 156
Adamas 169
Advent 70, 171
Adversus 170, 175
AEIOU 154, 158
Aeolian measures 117
Aeschines 189
Aeschylus 113, 125
Aesthetic 2, 7, 14, 47, 49, 51, 65, 69, 81, 95, 116, 120
Aesthetics 6, 7, 45, 47
Affective will 100
Agnostics 228
Ahern 154, 173
Ajax 129
Alacoque 77
Alchemist 60, 244
   Master, 244
Alcuin 149, 169, 173
Alexander's Feast 119
Alice in Wonderland 51
Alienation 57, 260, 261
Alliteration 50, 115
Alliterative 52, 55

Alliterative (cont.)
   pattern 52
Allusions 25, 162, 163
Almighty 239, 248
Alms 22, 100
Alpha 8, 147-152, 155, 156, 160-167, 169, 170, 172, 174
   -compass 161
   -Omega 150, 152, 160-164, 170, 172
Ambiguity 14, 57, 59, 64, 68, 69, 102
Ambivalence, psycho-sexual, 4
Americans 32
AMO 61, 151, 168
Amor 152
Amore 148, 152
Analogue 40, 42
Analogy 33, 48, 89, 100, 102, 104, 107, 111
Ananias 147
Anderson, Warren, 8, 127
Angles 243
Anglican 90, 92, 93, 107, 216
Anglican Difficulties 93
Anglicans 112, 226, 227
Anglo-Saxon 109, 110
Annus mirabilis 86
Antiphons 171
Antistrophe 116, 123
Apocalypse 148, 152, 157, 160, 162-165, 169, 170, 172, 174
Apocalyptic 164, 168, 174, 240, 245
Apollo 135, 136
Apologeticus 163
Apologia 89-91, 96, 112
Apologia Pro Vita Sua 89, 91, 112
Apostle 147, 150, 227
   fifth-century, 227
Apostles, Acts of the, 230
Apothegm 163

Aquinas 159, 173, 175
  Thomas, 159, 173
Arabian lands 216
Archbishop of Bombay 212
Architect 161, 162
  sovran, 162
Archive, computer, 71
Aristotle 48, 65, 132, 223
Arnold 1, 138
  Matthew, 1
  Thomas Kerchever, 138
Art 5, 6, 23, 24, 48, 49, 55, 56, 59, 88, 115-118, 132, 134, 137, 154, 155, 161, 165, 192, 208, 216, 243, 264
  Christian, 155, 161
Artifex Verbum 161
Artificial beauty 243
Artist 5, 18, 89, 120
Artists 26, 215
"As Kingfishers Catch Fire" 26
"As Kingfishers" 26, 241
Asceticism 85, 235
"Ashboughs" 54
Ashton 196, 220
  John, 196
Assonance 115, 152, 156, 160, 162-164, 168-170
  internal, 115
Asti, Bruno of, 149
"At the Wedding March" 24
Atheism 89, 90, 229
Atheists 92, 228
Athene 135
Augustine 33, 158, 172, 173, 237
Augustodunensis 149, 173
  Honorius, 149
AUIEO 153-155, 158-160
Aumann, J. 14
"Author's Preface" 81, 211
B.A. Degree, External, 180, 182, 187
Babel 158, 160
Baillie 59, 117, 118, 207
Balthasar, Hans Urs von, 4
Bampton, Joseph, 192
Baptism 79, 107
Barraud, Clement, 232
Baruch 159
Beatrice 147, 148, 159, 176
Beatus vir 159
Beaumont College 190
Beauty 3, 6, 7, 14, 15, 21, 24, 35, 37,

Beauty (cont.)
  40, 43, 47-49, 51-53, 55, 59, 60, 62, 63, 85-89, 92, 94-96, 98-105, 107-111, 121, 144, 164,165, 205, 235, 236, 243, 258, 261
  artificial, 243
  brute, 37, 43, 94, 98, 105
  mortal, 24, 52, 55, 87, 88, 92, 107-111, 243
  natural, 85, 86, 88, 89, 94-96, 101, 102, 104, 105, 111, 243
Beckx, Peter, 212
Bede, Ven., 149
Bedford Leigh 54, 203
Beggar 19
Belief, Christian, 8, 89
  orthodox, 89
Bellasis 185, 186, 192
  R.G., 192
Bender 7, 67, 71, 84, 120, 123, 125, 134, 146
  Todd, 7
  Todd K., 67, 84, 146
Bennett 171, 173
Bergonzi 4, 181, 217, 220
  Bernard, 4
Berkeley 125, 197, 198
  Herbert, 197
Beuno 32, 34, 36, 44, 193, 194, 202, 212, 231-233
Bible 3, 161, 164, 165, 173, 230, 240, 259, 260, 265
Bible Moralisèe 161
Biblical parable 239
Biglietto speech 90
Binsey 32, 54, 68
"Binsey Poplars" 54, 68
Biography 5, 6
Biology 229
Birmingham 179-181, 184, 185, 226
Bischoff 127, 146
Bishop of Shrewsbury 25
Bishops 204, 225, 227
Blacksmith 166
Blessed Sacrament 93, 185
  Expositions of the, 185
Blessed Virgin 89, 100, 105, 106, 136, 180, 208
Bluebell 95
Bluebells 94, 104
Bombay 212

Book of Job 241
Bosco 183
Bottom, Shakespeare's, 148
"Boughs being pruned" 57
Bowra 125, 143, 146
  C.M., 143
Boyde 147, 174
Boyle, Robert, 3
Bride 24
Bridges 2, 5, 9, 33, 57, 59, 85, 87, 111, 117, 119, 120, 123, 144, 190, 193, 197-199, 201, 202, 205-210, 212, 216, 219, 233, 234, 235, 236
  Robert, 2, 9, 85, 190, 197, 199, 216
Brighton 188
Bristol 203
Britain 109, 183
British scientists 225
Browne, Henry, 127
"Brothers" 165, 180, 198
Bruise 56, 254
Bruno of Asti 149
Brute beauty 37, 43, 94, 98, 105
Buckle 37, 39, 40, 43, 58, 60, 63, 64
Bugler 18, 22, 199
Bump 12, 29, 164, 173
  Jerome, 12
Burdensome 185
Busnelli 154, 173
Butler 90, 232, 236
  Alban 232
Byrne, Alexander, 192
Byronic 233
Calamity, aboriginal, 91
Calvinist 27
Campbell the Highlander, [Archibald], 191
Campion 119, 122, 128
  Edmund, 119
  Hall 119, 122, 128
    Master of, 128
Can Grande 133
Caradoc 55, 60, 232, 233
Caraman 236
Cardinal Manning 226
Careers 17, 26
Carlyle 90
"Carrion Comfort" 22, 53, 56, 58, 166, 248
Carroll 50, 51, 58, 66
  Lewis, 50, 58, 66

Catalogus 187, 188, 192, 212, 220
  Primus 212, 220
Catechumen 96
Cathemerinon 170
Catholic
  Church 90, 91, 102, 181, 224, 225, 228
  hierarchy 227, 228
  philosophical tradition 87
  Roman, 90, 181
Catholicism 92, 109, 226, 236
  English, 226, 236
Catholics, intellectual, 226
Celebrating 240
Celebratory poetry 240
Celtic 234
Centenary 2, 85
Challis 184, 185, 192
  H.W., 184, 192
Chance 52, 110, 137, 228, 259, 262
Chaos 122, 162, 245
Chapel 197
Characters 198, 240
Chardin 6
Charity 24, 25, 43, 242, 263
Charlemagne 230
Charlemagne's court 230
Charles-Edwards 223, 236
Chatillon 151, 174
Chatterton Lecture 2
"Cheery Beggar" 19
Chesterfield 201
Chevalier 7, 31, 38, 40, 41, 43, 44, 167
Chiasmus 161, 168
Children 49, 51, 75, 79, 183, 184, 199, 203
  Innocence of, 49, 51, 199
Choral
  odes 118
  pattern, Dorian 116
Choruses, tragic, Greek, 118
Christ 18, 19, 26, 35-44, 50, 53, 52-54, 57, 58, 60, 77, 78, 92, 94, 99, 100, 103, 104, 106, 110, 122, 136, 148-152, 155, 157, 158, 159-162, 165-172, 174, 203, 207, 217, 240, 242, 243, 246, 247, 257, 259-264
  Kingdom of, 35, 38, 42, 246
  the Creator 161
  the King 36
  Transfiguration of, 38

274 G. M. Hopkins: New Essays

"Christ upon the Waters" 110
Christ-Omega 165-167
Christian 8, 14, 23, 38, 52, 55, 86, 87, 89, 95, 102, 109, 155, 161, 165, 170, 173, 176, 216, 230, 239, 240, 244, 246, 250, 254, 264, 265
   art 155, 161
   belief 8, 89
      orthodox, 89
   faith 86, 89, 216, 246
   proclamation 240
   viewpoint 14
Christic
   monogram 159
   theophany 156
Christmas 171, 185, 190, 198, 200, 206, 209, 218
Church 8, 25, 77, 90, 91, 99, 100, 102, 150, 156, 163, 169, 181, 195, 224, 225-228, 232
   Catholic, 90, 91, 102, 181, 224, 225, 228
   Early, 8, 169
   French, 228
   Roman Catholic, 90, 181
Circle 83, 161, 162, 165, 170
   compass and, 161
Clare, John, 56
Clarke 224, 231
   Richard, 224
   Richard F., 231
Classical 8, 24, 120, 125, 132, 138, 144, 180, 194, 223
   literature 223
   school, English, 138
Classicism 244
Classicists,
   English, 138
   German, 135
Clayton, John, 194
Clifford, Kingdon, 223
Clitheroe 8, 23, 25, 53, 77, 134, 223, 231
   Margaret, 8, 25, 53, 77, 223, 231
Cloud 11, 25, 29, 39, 99, 100, 251
Clumber Park 197
Co-inheres 242, 246
Codices Selecti 151, 175
Coleridge 92, 186, 187, 220
   E.H., 92
   Henry, 186

Collations 72
Collected Essays 230, 237
Collins, James, 4
Color 235
Colour 35, 59
Column, Doric, 116
Comedies 131, 133
"Comfort of the Resurrection" 24, 168, 257, 264
Commedia 133, 156, 159, 176
Commentaria 170, 175, 176
Commons, House of, 192
Communion 22, 61, 199
Comparison 15, 40, 48, 68, 88, 137
Compass 161, 162
   and circle 161
Complaint 184, 200, 202, 216, 249, 250
Computer 70-72
   archive 71
   generated research tools 71
Concordance 70-72, 74, 79, 80, 83, 84, 134, 146
   Dilligan/Bender, to Hopkins, 71
Concordance to the English Poetry of Gerard Manley Hopkins 71, 84, 146
Concordances 72, 73, 80, 83
Concupiscence 79
Confessional 87, 111
Confessions 158, 173
Confidence 87, 139, 210, 261
   loss of, 210
Connotation 71, 79, 80, 82
Connotations 82, 129
Conquest 25, 56
Conrad 70, 71
Conscience 91, 94, 102, 111
Consistency 48, 55, 93, 97
Consolation 255, 256, 264
Contemplation 7, 11-25, 27, 28, 90, 91
   acquired, 17
   five levels of, 14
   infused, 17
Contemplative 11-13, 15, 17, 18, 22-27
   life 11, 13, 17, 25-27
   lives 25
"Contest Between Faith and Sight" 90
Converts 224
Cook 171, 174
Corinthians 159
Corpus Christianorum 155, 163, 177
Cotter 4, 8, 121, 122, 125, 147, 168, 174

Cotter (cont.)
  James Finn, 4, 8, 147
  Council 135, 224, 225, 227, 228, 231, 237
    of Trent 227
Counterpoint, musical, 208
County Wexford 211
Cr/gr 52
Creation 68, 69, 90, 92, 115, 124, 149, 158, 161, 162, 198, 242, 243, 246, 256, 264
Creator 40, 85, 86, 98, 161, 172, 189, 223, 242, 243, 254, 256
  Christ the, 161
Creaturehood 242, 252, 254
Cremona 147, 174
Cresswell Crags 197
Crisis 240, 244, 247, 253
Critic, reader response, 63
Criticism 2, 63, 118, 138
  reader response, 63
Critics 3, 40, 41, 85, 148, 167
  Jesuit, 41
Cross 53, 61, 62, 151, 169, 249, 255
Crown prince 42
Cruciform nimbus 150, 161
Cumae 117
Cures 224, 231, 232, 234
Curse 245, 249
Curser 249
Curtail or shortened sonnets 81
Cynewulf 171, 174
Dane 234
Dangerous 7, 37, 42, 58, 77, 85, 87, 89-94, 97, 105, 107-110
Dangerousness 93, 94
Dante 3, 8, 131, 133, 147-160, 162, 164, 170-177
Dante's Symbolism 151
Dappled 86, 95, 120, 257
Darnell 181, 182
Darwin 223, 228, 229, 237
Darwinian science 225
Darwinism 230
Dauphin 36, 40, 42
David 4, 8, 29, 223, 236, 239, 262, 263, 265
Davie, Donald, 2
De Monogamia 155
De rebus Siculis carmen 171
De Sancta Trinitate 170

De Trinitate 158, 172
De Vulgari 154, 158, 173
De Vulgari Eloquentia 154, 158, 173
Defamiliarization 69
Defamiliarized 69
Degree 120, 134, 144, 180, 182, 187, 201, 204, 260
Degree, B.A., External, 180, 182, 187
Degrees 200, 212
Deistic natural theology 111
Delany 212-214, 221
  William 212, 221
Denotation 71, 73, 80, 82
Denouement 240
Depressed 180, 207
Depression 180, 182, 199, 200, 207-209, 215, 217-219
Despair 20, 62, 108, 140, 205, 240, 244, 250, 253
Deutschland 3, 12, 19, 37, 39, 53, 61, 68, 80, 89, 95, 121-123, 133, 136, 141, 165, 166, 187, 240
Devlin 9, 205, 220
  Christopher, 205, 220
Devotional writings 3, 9
Dialogues 240, 249, 253, 263
Diamond 57, 67, 168-170, 261, 262
  immortal, 57, 168, 261, 262
Diaries 3
Dichotomy 87, 104
  moral, 104
Diction 2, 116, 128, 129
Dictionary 70-72, 76, 78, 83
Dictionnaire de théologie catholique 157
Dilligan 71, 84, 134, 146
Dilligan/Bender Concordance to Hopkins 71
Diocles 143
Discourses 89, 93, 96, 98, 105, 112, 205
Discussions and Arguments on Various Subjects 91, 112
Distemper 240
Divine Comedy 148, 174, 176
Divine
  justice 241, 246
  order 50, 241
  principle in nature 85
  providence 135, 137
  stress 88
Dixon 5, 9, 118, 122, 201, 202, 206, 210, 211, 216

Dobson, John, 192
Doctrinal 93, 94, 96, 226
Doctrine 14, 89, 93, 95, 102, 172, 227
  Jesuit, 14
Doctrines 227, 228
Dogma 104, 225, 227, 230
Dogmatic faith 90
Dolben 189
Dom Wulstan Phillipson 134
Donne, John, 3
Dorian 116-118
  Bar 117
  choral pattern 116
  measure 117, 118
Doric column 116
Doublets 50
"Dover Beach" 1
Downes 8, 239, 247, 265
  David, 8
  David Anthony, 239
Downside Review 134, 146
Drama 2, 117, 118, 134, 207, 224, 233, 240, 245-247, 252, 254, 257, 258, 262, 264
  Greek, 117, 134, 207
Dramatic monologue 247
Dublin 1, 4, 5, 8, 47, 112, 117-120, 127, 128, 134, 138-140, 142, 144, 146, 180, 206, 211, 212, 217, 219, 221, 236
  Note Book 128
Duke of Newcastle 197
Duke of Savoy 164
Duns Scotus 25
Dyslogistic 70, 80
Earth 1, 17, 24, 54, 58, 60, 64, 79, 85, 86, 98-100, 102-108, 110, 115, 125, 157, 159, 163, 172, 232, 233, 245, 258, 259, 261
Easter 22, 61, 69, 186, 211
"Easter Communion" 22, 61
Easter week 211
Eccentric 135, 180, 213-215
Eccentricities 213
Ecclesiastical politics 90
Echo 48, 49, 56, 62, 108, 109, 122, 137, 160, 165, 172, 206, 235, 241, 243, 244, 245
Edda 131, 132
Eddas 131
Eden 68, 100, 157, 158, 242
Edition,

Edition (cont.)
  Fifth, 3
  First, 2, 130, 138, 229
Education 49, 175, 212
Efficacy of prayer 229, 230, 236
Eginhard 230
Egocentric 242
Eighteenth century 131, 232
Eisegesis 205
Electronic
  files 72
  library 72
Eliphaz 252
Elizabeth I 205
Elopement 180, 186, 192
Elwy 23, 32, 57, 103
Emblem 72, 105, 162
Enciclopedia dantesca 153, 174
Energy 81, 141, 144, 185, 187, 260, 261
England 32, 33, 91, 109, 123, 132, 138, 170, 171, 179, 215, 216, 219, 224, 226, 228, 234, 243
  Post-Darwinian, 228
English 2, 3, 6, 8, 71, 73, 83, 84, 89, 110, 113, 118, 119, 122, 123, 128, 130, 131, 138, 143, 146, 148, 160, 179-181, 188, 189,191, 194, 197, 204, 205, 212, 213, 215, 216, 225, 226, 236
  Catholicism 226, 236
  classical school 138
  classicists 138
  Early, 118
  ode 122
  orthography 160
  Province 204, 205, 212, 213
Enjambment 161
Entasis 116
Entropic fire 259
Environmental 13
Epic 128, 129, 131-135, 141, 160, 171
  poetry 128
Epilogue 257
Epinician odes 122
Epistemology 231
Epithets 19, 115, 120, 122, 128, 129, 141, 142, 262
  compound, 115
  stock, 128, 129, 141
Essence 18, 26, 81, 97-99
Etymologiae 154, 155, 175
Etymological 67, 69

Index 277

Etymology 68, 234
Eudes 77
Eulogistic 70, 79, 80
  value 70
Euripides 129, 133
Eurydice 19, 68, 103, 121, 165, 197-199, 202
Evangelical 264
Eve 68, 241
Evil 79-81, 117, 230
Evolution 223, 225, 228, 231, 235, 237
Evolution Run Wild 223, 237
Exhausted 68
Exhorting 39, 240
Exile 204, 212
Exiled Jesuits 205
Existential 241, 242
Exodus 156, 157, 163
Experience 7, 13, 14, 27, 33, 34, 37, 40, 53, 62-64, 69, 72, 78, 81, 82, 87, 123, 150, 165, 170, 185, 187, 188, 206, 239, 245, 246, 257
Explication 82
Expositio in Apocalypsim 151, 174
Expositions of the Blessed Sacrament 185
External B.A. Degree 180, 182, 187
Failure 82, 194, 220, 240
Faith 1, 16, 23, 44, 76, 77, 86, 89, 90, 92, 93, 96, 97, 99, 109, 145, 165, 172, 216, 226, 231, 239, 240, 242-244, 246, 247, 253, 257, 258, 261-263
  Christian, 86, 89, 216, 246
  dogmatic, 9
  -testing 240
  -witnessing 240
Faithfulness 23, 262
Faithlessness 244, 245
Falcon 31, 167
Fall 38, 43, 58, 68, 69, 72-78, 80-82, 103, 107, 157, 158, 160, 161, 163, 165-167, 190, 207, 218, 242, 251
Farnell 116, 125
Farrer 157, 174
  Austin, 157
Farrier 18, 166
Fearful wonderment 240
Feeney 5, 8, 179, 194, 204, 220, 221
  Joseph, 5, 8
  Joseph J., 179, 221
Felix Randal 20, 166, 224

Fell 20, 67-69, 166, 193, 232
Fergus 198
Fiesole 204, 212
Fifteen Sermons 89, 90, 96, 112
Fifth-century apostle 227
Files 72
Finale 258
First century 231
First Pythian ode 115, 125
First Vatican Council 224, 228
Fish, Stanley, 63
Fisher 51, 66
Fitzpatrick, George, 206
"Floris in Italy" 62
Flux 259, 262
Food 184
Forbes-Leith, William, 209
Ford Madox Ford 70
Fortnightly Review 229, 236, 237
Fortune 209, 262
Fortune's football 209
Foster 25, 147, 174
France 226
Free Will 54
French Church 228
"'Freshness Deep Down Things': Hopkins' Dublin Notes on Homer" 8
Frye 260, 265
Fugue 115
Gallican opposition 228
Gallwey 200
Galton 229, 236
  Francis, 229
Garden 69, 100, 152, 157, 173, 235, 255
  of Eden 157
Gardner 3, 9, 119, 121, 122, 125, 134
  W.H., 3
Gawain 170, 176
Gemini 159
General 3, 5, 15, 16, 20, 21, 27, 32, 42, 73, 94, 96, 103, 118, 120, 121, 128, 129, 185, 204, 212, 229, 240
Genesis 161
Gentlemen's religion 90
Georgics 189
Gerard, John, 205
"Gerard Manley Hopkins: An Idiom of Desperation" 2
German Classicists 135
Germany 132

Getto 147, 174
Gildersleeve 114, 117, 125
Gladstone 51, 139
Glasgow 203
"Glories of Mary" 89, 105
Glory 38, 44, 79, 92, 95-99, 101, 102, 105, 106, 117, 121, 136, 157, 170
Gnostic 4, 8, 170
  Teachings 170
  Victorian, 4
God 1, 3, 4, 11-27, 38, 42, 43, 49, 50, 52-54, 56, 57, 60, 79, 86-88, 90-93, 95-98, 101-110, 121, 123, 136, 137, 148, 149, 155, 156, 157, 159-161, 164, 165, 167, 169, 171-173, 203, 208, 223, 233, 235, 239-258, 260-264
  Kingdom of, 242, 243, 245, 247, 253, 255, 258, 260, 261, 264
  -Man 156, 159, 160
God's garden 235
"God's Grandeur" 1, 3, 52, 57, 165
"Golden Echo" 56, 62, 108, 109, 122, 206, 241, 243
Golden Lyre 117
Goldstein 163, 174
Gospel 38, 148, 157, 173, 265
  of John 157
Gospels 230, 241
Gow's Theocritus 138
Grace 4, 14, 15, 18, 22, 24, 25, 39, 53-55, 86, 92, 93, 96, 104, 105, 107, 110, 111, 123, 136, 137, 166, 208, 220, 242, 243, 245, 254, 255, 257, 258, 261, 263, 264
  special, 14
Graces 54, 242, 255, 257
Grammar 69, 70, 153
Grammatical deviation 69
Grandeur 1, 3, 4, 52, 57, 114, 115, 165
Gray 114
"Great Academies" 210
Great Britain 183
Great Sacrifice 169, 240, 260
Great Sacrifice 239, 247, 265
Great Vowel Shift 160
Greats 144, 204
Greek 3, 77, 94, 113, 114, 116-120, 122, 125, 127, 128, 130, 131, 134, 135, 137, 142, 146, 150, 157, 160, 165, 180, 182, 189, 191, 204, 207, 216
  drama 117, 134, 207

Greek (cont.)
  literature 113, 117, 120
  lyric poets 114
  melic poetry 122
  metres 118
  Professor of, 127, 180
  tragic choruses 118
Greeks 118, 130, 135, 143
Gregory 55, 109, 110, 243
Groom 24
"Habit of Perfection" 18
Haecceitas 141
Hagiography 223
Hail Mary 54
Haimo 149, 169, 174
  of Auxerre 149, 174
Hamlet 58
Hammond 234, 236
Hampstead 190
Hans Urs von Balthasar 4
Harmony 48, 116, 206
Harrassed 207
"Harry Ploughman" 57, 124, 224
Hartman 2, 3
  Geoffrey, 2
Harvest 3, 16, 21, 37, 50, 53, 64, 98, 99, 136
Health 20, 104, 185, 211, 212
  physical, 212
Heart 18-21, 32, 34, 36, 37, 39, 41, 44, 45, 49, 56, 64, 72-79, 86, 88, 91, 92, 95, 96, 98, 99, 101, 103, 104, 110, 121, 139, 159, 165-167, 172, 186, 191, 199, 244-246, 250, 253, 254, 256, 257, 260, 262, 263
Heathen 96, 110
Heaven 17, 22, 54, 60, 61, 86, 91, 99, 100, 105, 110, 119, 152, 172, 241, 258, 261-263
Heaven-Haven 17
Hebrew 157, 160, 174
Hector 134
Hector's body 134
Hellenic 124
Henry V 36
Hepburne 195
Hera 136
Heracles 142
Heraclitean Fire 5, 24, 54, 57, 168, 174, 257
Herbert 2, 44, 45, 57, 66, 197, 224, 231,

Herbert (cont.)
234, 237
George, 44
Hero 37, 130-132, 142, 165, 203, 250
Heroic 124, 132, 224
Heroine 224
Heywood 134, 146
Hierarchy 227, 228
Catholic, 227, 228
High frequency words 73
Highgate 6, 131, 138, 144, 201
Hildebert of Lavardin 170, 175
Hillard 154, 175
Hines 120, 124, 125
Holmes 226, 236
Holy Ghost 1, 57, 86
Holy Scripture 228
Holy Spirit 151, 165, 264
Holywell 32, 231, 237
Homer 3, 8, 127-132, 134-140, 142-146
Homeric poems 134, 138, 146
Homerists 132, 138
Homiletic 7, 67
"Homiletic and Poetic Vocabulary in Hopkins" 7
Homograph 162
Homographic 68, 69
ambiguity 68, 69
Homophone 58
Homosexual 4
Honor 5, 120
Honorius Augustodunensis 149
Honour 25, 56, 57, 124
Hopkins 1-9, 11-29, 31-36, 39-42, 44, 45, 47, 49-52, 54-72, 74-90, 92, 93, 94-113, 117-125, 127-147, 164-169, 171-176, 179, 180, 181-225, 228, 231-235, 237, 239-247, 260, 261, 263, 264, 265
"Hopkins and Pindar" 7, 113, 121
"Hopkins as Teacher, the English Years: Understanding the Man by Watching Him Work" 8
Hopkins, Gerald [sic], 213
Hopkins Research 31
Hopkins the Jesuit 188, 189, 191, 192, 215, 222
Hopkins' Sanctifying Imagination 247, 265
Horace 114-116
Horseshoe 167
House 9, 23, 31, 57, 89, 174, 182, 188,

House (cont.)
189, 191, 192, 205, 212, 220, 222
of Commons 192
of Lords 192
Hugh of St. Cher 150, 175
Human justice 241, 242
"Hurrahing in Harvest" 3, 21, 37, 50, 53, 64, 98, 99
Hutton 227, 230, 236
A.W. 227
R.H., 230
Huxley 228-230, 237
T.H., 229
I am 148, 157, 168, 250, 258, 261, 263
"I wake and feel the fell of dark" 166
"I wake and feel" 250
"I wake" 251
I wake and feel the fell of dark not day 20
IAO 157, 168
Iconography 161
Ideal 26, 48, 49, 60, 61, 159
Ideology 82
Idol-worshipping 110
Ignatian 3, 12, 239, 246
spirituality 3, 239
Ignatius 35, 38, 42-45, 191, 239, 246, 255, 257, 258, 265
IHA 47
Il Convivio 153, 173
Iliad 127-130, 132, 133, 135-146
Imagery 3, 114-116, 121, 124, 125, 127, 159, 172, 174, 252
Imaginative or sacramental synthesis 86
Immaculate Conception of Mary 227
Immanence 21, 95
Immortal diamond 57, 168, 261, 262
Immortality 169, 240
Imperial 255
In Extremity 2
"In Honour of St. Alphonsus Rodriguez" 25, 56, 57
"In the Valley of the Elwy" 23, 57, 103
In-shape 165
Incarnate 148-150, 152, 156, 159, 161, 169, 171
Son 148
Incarnation 149, 156, 159, 172, 242, 252, 260-262
Incarnational 96
Indifference 245

Individuality 32, 57, 130
Infallibility, papal, 227, 228
"Infant Baptism" 107
Inferno 147, 156, 253
Infidelity 92, 93
Infused contemplation 17
Innocence 49, 51, 69, 72, 81, 101, 158, 168, 183, 187, 199, 215, 253
  of children 49, 51, 199
Inscape 3, 11, 28, 31-33, 35-37, 39, 40, 45, 58, 95, 125, 142, 164-166, 167, 174
  poet of, 31
Inscaped 119, 167
Inscaping 86, 166
  naturalistic, 86
Instress 3, 7, 11-13, 15-17, 19, 21, 26-28, 31, 37, 166, 167
Instressed 13, 18, 19, 26, 95, 99, 121, 167
Instressing 12, 22, 24, 27, 87, 95
  religious, 87
Intellectual Catholics 226
Intelligent Toryism 205
Intentionality 15
"Intercollegiate" prize 197
Internal assonance 115
International Hopkins Association 47, 127
Interpretation 7, 24, 27, 28, 37-39, 41, 44, 52, 58, 59, 61-65, 85, 234, 243
Interpretations 40, 47, 61, 63, 111
"Interpreting the *Variorum*" 63
Intimational nature poems 86
Intuition 259
Inversnaid 32
Ion 129, 134
Ireland 5, 6, 20, 179-181, 216
  Royal University of, 180
Irenaeus 170, 175
Irish Monthly 6
Is-ness 262
Isaiah 42
Isidore 154, 155, 175
Isidore's *Etymologiae* 154, 155
"It was a hard thing to undo this knot" 58, 63
Italy 62, 225
Itinerarium Mentis ad Deum 172
Jaded 201, 204-208, 210, 211, 218, 221, 256
Januarius 225

Janus
  -word 59
  -words 7, 47, 49, 56
Jebb 114, 125, 138, 142, 146
Jebb's Sophocles 138
Jerome 12, 29, 157, 173
Jesuit 5-7, 14, 34, 36, 38, 41, 44, 45, 179, 180, 186-189, 191, 192, 194, 196, 198, 200-202, 204-206, 210-212, 214-217, 222, 231, 235, 246
  College of Stonyhurst 34
  critics 41
  doctrine 14
Jesuits, exiled, 205
Jesus 39, 45, 53, 77, 105, 128, 165, 188, 220, 221, 224, 234, 239, 240, 242, 243, 245-247, 253, 255, 258, 260-264
JHVH 157
Joachim 151, 152, 176
  of Fiore 151, 176
Job 143, 182, 189, 241, 245, 247-255, 257
  Book of, 241
John,
  Gospel of, 157
  Revelation of, 240
Johnson, Wendell Stacy, 2
Jones 4, 130, 146, 163, 175
  David, 4
Journals 3, 9, 34, 180, 215, 222
Jowett 117, 131
  Benjamin, 131
Joy 16, 21, 64, 78, 81, 86, 94, 99, 100, 102, 108, 109, 157, 200, 205, 209, 215, 244, 257, 264
Joyce, James, 89
Judge 135, 163, 249
Judgment 3, 63, 214, 245, 251
Junior master 179
Juniorate 188
Just 5, 14, 16, 18, 21, 23, 25, 33, 35, 36, 38, 41, 42, 50, 53, 55, 59, 60, 61, 79, 93, 101, 103, 155, 160, 162, 165, 183, 187, 188, 200, 201, 205, 213, 224, 227, 233, 241, 251, 252
Justice 110, 136, 151, 241-243, 246, 248, 249
  divine, 241, 246
  human, 241, 242
Justices 241
Justified 27, 235, 239, 254

Justly 241
Kant 23
Kaske 159, 175
  Robert, 159
Keating 127
Keegan 175, 194-198, 201, 221
Kensington Museum 190
Kestrel 33-35, 58, 98
Kestrels 33
Kew Gardens 191, 192, 216
King 36-38, 42-44, 103, 107
  Christ the, 36
Kingdom 35, 36, 38, 40, 42, 198, 241-243, 245-247, 253-255, 258, 260, 261-264
  of Christ 35, 38, 42, 246
  of God 242, 243, 245, 247, 253, 255, 258, 260, 261, 264
"Kingfishers" 26, 103, 241
Kitchen, Paddy, 4
Knight 35, 38, 41-44, 78, 176
Konya 223
Korg, Jacob, 2
Kossick, Kaye, 47
Labor 205, 211
Labour 43, 44, 51, 253
Lady Macbeth 198
Lahey 5, 182, 184, 193, 214, 220, 221
  Gerald, 5
Lake Poets 90
Lancashire 34, 167, 179, 205, 216
Landscape and Inscape 33, 35, 45
Landscape, poet of, 31
Language 2-4, 33, 50, 51, 66, 67, 69, 70, 73, 82, 87, 98, 99, 104, 105, 108, 110, 113-115, 119, 123, 132, 135, 148, 156, 158, 222, 235, 247, 249, 252, 261, 264, 265
"Lantern Out of Doors" 18
Laser disk technology 72
Last Sonnets 8, 239, 240, 247
Latin 67, 68, 150, 152, 160, 169, 171, 174, 182, 189, 191, 195, 196, 204, 212, 216
Latin-Italo 160
Lattimore 144, 146
Lauretus 169, 175
Law 23, 48, 111, 165
"Leaden Echo" 56, 62, 108, 122, 206, 241, 243
Leaf 75, 138, 144, 146, 152

Leaf (cont.)
  Walter, 138
Leavis 2
"Lecture Notes: Rhetoric" 191
Lee 195, 221
"Let me be to Thee as the circling bird" 56, 62
Levi, Peter, 128
Lexical items 73
Lexicon 69, 70, 72, 76, 78, 80-82, 130, 133, 146
Liber de laudibus Sanctae Crucis 150, 175
Liber Figurarum 151
Liberal-rationalist usurpations 89
Liberal wing 228
Liberalism 90, 91
Library 66, 71, 72, 161, 173
Liddell 130, 133, 142, 146
Liddell-Scott-Jones 130
Life,
  active, 11, 13, 17, 25, 26
  contemplative, 11, 13, 17, 25-27
  saintly, 25
Lincoln College, Oxford 226
Linguistic "turbulence" 7, 69
linguistics 6
Linkages 51
Lisbon earthquake 200
Literary-historical interest 88
Literature,
  Classical, 223
  Greek, 113, 117, 120
Liverpool 76, 203, 212
Lives, contemplative, 25
Lives of the Saints 232
Lives of the Fathers, Martyrs and Other Principal Saints 232
Lives, saintly, 25
Loch Lomond 32
Logaoedic 116, 123
Logic 231
Logos 161, 172
Logos-Son 161
London 9, 29, 45, 66, 112, 125, 138, 146, 174, 175, 179, 180, 182, 197, 200-204, 212, 213, 216, 220-222, 224, 233, 234, 236, 237, 265
  press 125, 224, 234
Long Course 193
Lord 5, 12, 23, 35, 37, 40-43, 49, 50, 55,

Lord (cont.)
  77, 94, 95, 100, 105, 107, 148, 155, 156, 159, 162, 163, 165, 166, 169, 171, 191, 203, 217, 257, 258, 263
Lord God 148
Lords, House of, 192
"Loss of the Eurydice" 103, 165, 197, 202
Lourdes 224, 236
Love 33, 37, 38, 43, 44, 53, 56, 58, 59, 61, 62, 77, 78, 88, 96, 98, 99, 106, 110, 111, 120, 121, 137, 147-153, 166, 167, 170, 199, 216, 235, 239, 240, 242, 243, 249, 255, 261, 264
"Love the Safeguard of Faith against Superstition" 96
Lover 23, 33, 264
Low frequency words 73-76
Lucas 224, 231, 234, 237
  Herbert, 224, 231, 234
Lucifer 42
Lütolf 170, 175
Lycidas 119
Lyre 115, 116, 129, 134
  -singer 134
Lyric poets 114, 118
  Greek, 114
"M. Notes on the Classics" 127
Macbeth 195, 198
MacKenzie 3, 9, 41, 45, 58, 66, 134, 140, 245, 265
  Norman, 3, 41, 245
Macrobius 157
Madonnas 225
Magnificat 171, 202
Maher 224, 234, 237
  Michael, 224, 234
Majesty 21, 43, 105, 260
Mallarmé 2
Malta 216
Manchester 188
Manly mould 88
Manning 226, 228, 237
  Cardinal, 226
Mano 211
Manresa 45, 188, 189
  House 188, 189
Manual of English Literature 6
Märchen 132
Marcus 170
Margaret 8, 23, 25, 53, 55, 73-80, 103,

Margaret (cont.)
  134, 223, 231, 236
"Margaret Clitheroe" 24, 134
Margaret Mary 77
Marian 106, 136
  thought 136
Mariani 122, 125, 264, 265
  Paul, 264
Marriage 24, 231
Martyr 23, 37, 77, 163
  -master 37
Martyrs 8, 163, 164, 205, 223, 230, 232, 234-236
  Roman, 230
Mary 54, 55, 61, 77, 89, 105, 107, 121, 136, 179, 187, 193-197, 199-202, 204, 208, 209, 216-218, 221, 227, 231, 250
Mary, Immaculate Conception of, 227
Mary's month 208
Maryland-New York Province 213
Master 23, 37, 123, 128, 131, 132, 134, 136, 139, 166, 179, 182, 187, 194, 195, 196, 202, 212, 217, 244, 248, 249, 256
  Alchemist 244
  junior, 179
  of Campion Hall 128
  of Novices 212
  of the tides 37, 123
Materialism 92, 229
Maur 150, 151, 175
"May Magnificat" 202
May-poem 208
McChesney 124, 125
McGrath, Fergal, 213
McLuhan, Marshall, 2
Measure, Dorian, 117, 118
Measures, Aeolian, 117
Melic poetry, Greek, 122
Mengaldo 147, 176
Mercy 110, 123, 189, 249
Merlet 114, 125
Merry 131, 138
  William Walter, 131
Metamorphosis 260
Metaphor 3, 68, 69, 114, 137, 140, 241, 243, 244, 254, 264
  in Hopkins 3
  multivalent, 69
Metaphoric vessel 78
Metaphysical 122, 236
Metcalf 234, 237

Meter 116, 123
Metre 116, 118
Metres 118, 122, 125
  Greek, 118
Metrical 116, 117, 120, 123, 129
  structure 116
Migne 150, 170, 173-176
Milky Way 99
Milroy 50, 51, 58, 66
  James, 50, 58
Milton 8, 63, 147, 160-164, 171, 172, 174-177, 244
  John, 160, 176
Milward 7, 31, 45
  Peter, 7, 31
Miracle 121, 225, 231
Miracles 8, 89, 223-231, 233-236
Miraculous spring 233, 234
Missionaries 109
Müller, Max, 50
Moan 200
Moderations 204
Modulation 50, 57
Monologue 247, 248, 255, 257
  dramatic, 247
Monologues 240, 253
Monro 133, 135, 138
Month 125, 187, 202, 231, 234, 237
Month, Mary's, 208
Moore 7, 85, 87, 112
  Michael D., 7, 85
Moral 7, 22, 23, 47-49, 51, 59, 61, 65, 88-94, 102-105, 202, 242, 243, 245, 246, 248, 252, 253
  dichotomy 104
  relativism 245
Morality 48, 49, 55, 92, 142
Morals 7, 47
"Morning, Midday, and Evening Sacrifice" 26
Morrissey 212, 221
Mortal beauty 24, 52, 55, 87, 88, 92, 107-111, 243
Mortality 169, 240
Moses 156, 157, 230, 247
Motto 167, 176
  Marylou, 167
Mount 179, 193-197, 199-204, 209, 216-218, 221, 225
  St. Mary's College 179, 193, 194, 201, 221

Mount (cont.)
  Street 200
Multilingual puns 69
Multivalent
  metaphor 69
  poetry 86
Murder 164, 258
Museum 69, 190
Music 19, 62, 88, 115, 116, 119, 122, 148, 190, 206, 208, 216, 217, 243, 244, 258
Musical 105, 116, 119, 122, 154, 155, 206, 208, 233
  counterpoint 208
Muthos 129
"My own heart let me more have pity on" 21, 253, 256
"My own heart" 56
"Mysteries of Divine Condescension" 96
Mystery 21, 37, 40, 55, 95, 97, 171, 241-244, 246, 249, 258, 261-263
Mystical 14, 39, 85, 100
  identification 39
  union 14
Mysticism 16
Mythological 233
Mythopoeic 162
Mythos 240, 247, 259
Myths 129, 132
Nardi 171, 176
National Library at Vienna 161
Natural 3, 6, 14, 18, 20, 23, 24, 85, 86, 88-96, 99, 101-106, 109-111, 121, 159, 166, 170, 228, 229, 233, 241-243, 258, 259, 261
  Beauty 85, 86, 88, 89, 94-96, 101, 102, 104, 105, 111, 243
  science 3
  selection 228, 229
  supernaturalism 90
  theology 88, 89, 111
    deistic, 111
Naturalistic inscaping 86
Nature 1, 5, 11, 12, 15, 18, 21, 24, 28, 37, 39, 54, 56, 57, 63, 67, 69, 85, 86-88, 90-92, 96, 98, 100-107, 109-111, 121, 131, 143, 145, 147, 157, 164-166, 168, 174, 189, 190, 199, 209, 211, 229, 235, 236, 240-246, 257-263
  divine principle in, 85

Nature (cont.)
  -Philosophy 91, 92
  poems 12, 86, 103, 109
    intimational, 86
  sacramental view of, 87
  -worship 111
Neo-classical 120
Neo-classical style 120
New Adam 155, 169
New Catholic Encyclopedia 14, 29
New Testament 240, 245, 247, 263
New York 29, 45, 66, 83, 125, 173, 175-177, 213, 220, 265
Newcastle 197
Newman 7, 32, 45, 85, 87-94, 96-102, 105-112, 179, 181, 183, 184, 186, 187, 224-228, 236, 237, 265
"Newman and the 'Second Spring'" 87, 112
"Newman and the Motif" 87, 112
Newman, John Henry, 7, 87, 179, 224, 236, 237
Newman's Oratory School 179
Newmanesque 104, 111
Nicholas of Gorran 171, 176
Nichomachean Ethics 48
Nimbus, cruciform, 150, 161
Nineteenth century 4, 8, 88, 89, 130, 138, 212, 231, 236
Ninth-century 230
"No worst, there is none" 20, 145, 250
Noah's Ark 150, 175
Nondum 62
Norman 234
  ruin 197,
Norwood 116, 125
Noumena 92
Novice 192, 235
Novices, Master of, 212
Novitiate 188
Nun 19, 39, 50, 53, 60, 77, 123, 136, 165, 166, 232
"O My Chevalier" 31
O'Flaherty, Bernard, 211
O'Neill, Richard, 193
Obedience 38, 43, 228, 242, 244, 254
Ode 115-117, 119, 122-125, 198, 204
  English, 122
  First Pythian, 115, 125
  Olympian
    Victory, 117

Odes 3, 114, 118, 120, 122, 125, 129
  Choral, 118
  Epinician, 122
  Pindar's Isthmian victory, 129
Odyssey 130-132, 138, 142
"Of Miracles, Martyrs, and Prayer Gauges" 8
Of the Trinity 172
Old boys 186, 205
Old Roman repertory 171
Old Testament 163, 247, 265
Olympian Ode 119
Olympians 136
Omega 8, 147-152, 155, 156, 160-167, 169, 170, 172, 174
  Christ-, 165-167
  -cosmos 161
Omnific Word 161
"Omnipotence in Bonds" 97
OMO 151, 160
"On a Piece of Music" 19
"On Personality, Grace and Free Will" 54
"On St. Winefred" 51
"On the late Massacher in Piemont" 162
"On the Origin of Beauty" 165
"On the Portrait of Two Beautiful Young People" 26, 57, 104, 199
Onomatopoetic 50, 52
Ontological 255
Oppositions 56
Orans figures 170
Oratory 179, 181-187, 190, 192, 200, 216, 217
  School 179, 181, 183, 187, 190, 192, 200, 217
  Newman's, 179
Order 13, 19, 32-34, 49, 50, 77, 108, 116, 139, 154, 156, 160, 229, 241, 242, 243, 247, 260
  divine, 50, 241
Ordination 5, 179, 193, 194
Origen 4, 157
Original sin 79, 166
ORO 151
Orthodox Christian belief 89
Orthodoxy 92, 100
Orthography, English, 160
Oxford 5, 6, 9, 32, 45, 51, 66, 89, 90, 92, 112, 117, 125, 128, 131, 138, 144, 146,

Oxford (cont.)
  151, 165, 173, 176, 179, 181, 182, 184, 185, 190, 192, 201, 203, 204, 216, 217, 220-222, 226, 227, 234, 236, 265
  Lincoln College, 226
  Movement 90, 226
  University Sermons 89
Pagan 94, 108
Painter 4, 59, 185
Paley 89, 90, 138
Paley's assumptions 89
Paling 99
Palm Sunday 186
Papal infallibility 227, 228
Parable 239-245, 263, 264
  Biblical, 239
Parables 38, 96, 203, 242, 246, 261, 264
Paraclete 79, 165
Paradise 57, 80, 151, 155, 160, 161, 172, 176, 241
Paradise Lost 160, 161, 172, 176
Paradiso 147, 152, 154, 160, 162, 173, 174
Paradox 104, 242, 255
Paray-le-Monial 77
Paris 125, 151, 174-176, 226
Parish 17, 179, 202, 203, 209, 212, 213
Parishes 194, 203, 205
Parliament 192
Parochial 91, 96, 99, 101, 107, 108, 112
Parochial and Plain Sermons 91, 112
Particularity 32
Pascal 92
Passion 44, 171
Pater, Walter, 5, 48
Patience 22, 23, 53, 56, 57, 100, 106, 121, 253-255, 257, 258
"Patience, Hard Thing!" 23, 56, 57, 253
Patmore 9, 210, 211, 216
  Coventry, 9, 210
  Henry 211
Patristic 157, 160
Pattern 13, 52, 54, 97, 116, 119, 123, 135, 165, 194, 204, 217-219, 239, 240, 243, 263, 264
Pattison 226, 227, 229, 237
  Mark, 226, 227
Paul 42, 53, 147, 153, 172, 207,
Pauline 3
Paulinus of Nola 170
Peace 23, 56, 89, 105, 182, 206, 254, 256

Penelope 131
Pentalpha 170
Perception 39, 60, 107, 164, 240, 262
Personality 4, 54
Perversion 2, 57
Peters 5, 127, 146
  W.A.M., 5, 127
Petrarchan sonnet 81
Petrocchi, Giorgio, 148
Phemius 131, 135
Phenomena 48, 89, 90, 110, 229
  physical, 90
Phillips 59, 66
  Catherine, 58
Phillipson 134, 146
  Dom Wulstan, 134
Philosophers 13, 179, 201, 204, 231, 234
  secular, 179, 201, 204
  Stonyhurst, 231, 234
Philosophical 2, 4, 13, 14, 24, 87-91, 187, 231
  tradition 87
Philosophical tradition, Catholic, 87
Philosophy 3, 5, 6, 13, 91, 92, 188, 201, 206, 231
  nature-, 91, 92
Phonology 160
Physical
  health 212
  phenomena 90
  science 50
Physics 229
Physiological 13
Piano 190, 207, 209, 216
Pick, John, 5
Picts, southern, 227
"Pied Beauty" 3, 15, 40, 49, 59, 86
Pietro da Eboli 171
Pilgrimage 32, 245
Pindar 3, 7, 8, 113-125, 129, 130
Pindar's
  Isthmian victory odes 129
  Third Isthmian 119
Pius IX 227, 228
Plague 137, 253
Plato 131, 134, 135
Plot 240, 247, 248, 258
Ploughman 18, 43, 57, 124, 224
Poems 7-9, 12, 14, 17, 21-23, 25-28, 32, 33, 40, 45, 51, 57, 59, 62, 64, 66, 67,

Poems (cont.)
   69, 85-88, 95, 102, 103, 109, 121, 122, 125, 129, 132, 134, 137, 138, 146, 180, 211, 216, 217, 231, 239, 240, 241, 243, 244, 246-249, 252, 253, 255, 263-265
   nature, 12, 86, 103, 109
      intimational, 86
   religious, 240, 263
Poesy 56, 114
Poet 2, 4, 6, 8, 12, 19, 21, 23, 27, 31, 33-41, 43, 44, 53, 56, 61, 62, 67, 68, 83, 85-88, 99, 102-104, 106, 111, 113, 116, 122, 129, 130, 132, 133, 136, 139, 144, 148-150, 152-154, 156, 157, 159, 160, 164-167, 170, 171, 206, 208, 210, 234, 241, 243-246, 248, 259-262
   laureate 234
   of inscape 31
   of landscape 31
   -priest 85, 88
"Poet of Landscape and Inscape" 31
Poetics 132
Poetry 2, 3, 6-8, 11, 13, 14, 16-18, 20, 27, 33, 37, 45, 52, 54-56, 59, 61, 64, 67, 69-71, 78, 80, 84, 86, 88, 94, 102, 104, 111, 112, 118, 120, 122, 124, 125, 128, 132, 134, 136, 137, 143, 144, 146, 148, 152, 164, 167, 170, 171, 174, 176, 177, 201, 206-209, 214, 215, 223, 239, 240, 247
   celebratory, 240
   epic, 128
   melic, Greek, 122
   multivalent, 86
Poets 3, 5, 6, 27, 90, 114, 118, 121, 123, 132, 154, 169, 170, 235
   Corner 5
   Lake, 90
   lyric, 114, 118
      Greek, 114
Politicized students 219
Politics 90, 183, 190
   ecclesiastical, 90
Pope 109, 163, 227, 228, 243
   Gregory 109, 243
Porter 18, 212-214, 221
   George, 212
Portrait of the Artist as a Young Man 89
"Portrait of Two Beautiful Young People" 26, 57, 104, 199
Post-Darwinian England 228

Posy 56
Pratt, Linda 4
Prayer 8, 14, 22, 36, 57, 100, 106, 217, 223, 229, 230, 236
   efficacy of, 229, 230, 236
   gauge 229
   gauges 8, 223
Praying 240
Preacher 78, 172
Preface to Hopkins 35, 45
Prefect of Studies 194, 212
Prelate 18
Pride 37, 134, 199, 241-244, 248, 249, 254-256
Priest 17, 85, 88, 107, 139, 185, 192, 200, 216, 220
Priesthood 185, 193
Primasius 149, 170, 176
Prince, crown, 42
Principle 41, 48, 49, 65, 85, 86, 92, 96-98, 111, 116, 119, 120
   unity of, 48, 49, 65
Pro-Roman majority 227
Proclamation, Christian, 240
Professor
   of Greek 127, 180
   of Psychology 234
   of Theology 212
Progress of Poesy 114
Prophesying 240
Prophet 107
Protestants 78, 105
Proverbs 162, 203
Providence 20, 22, 39, 135-137, 243, 256
   divine, 135, 137
Province 189, 194, 196, 204, 205, 212, 213, 220, 221
   English, 204, 205, 212, 213
   Maryland-New York, 213
Provincial 128, 189, 191, 194, 201, 204, 205, 213, 217
Prudentius 170, 176
Psalms 163
Psalterium decem chordarum 151
Pseudo-religion 90
Psycho-sexual ambivalence 4
Psychology 229, 234, 239, 246
   Professor of, 234
Puccini 76
Pun 58
Puns, multilingual, 69

Purbrick 213, 214, 221
  Edward I., 213
Purcell 3, 25, 103, 243
  Henry, 3, 25, 103
Purgatory 151, 159
  mountain 159
Pythian 115, 116, 125
  ode 115, 125
Quintilian 114
Raban Maur 150, 151, 175
Rahner 257, 265
Random 4, 21, 27, 52, 79, 152, 228
Rational 14, 148
Reader response
  critic 63
  criticism 63
Real presence 93
Rector 210, 212, 213, 226
Redemption 55, 69, 158, 165, 172
Redemptive 55
Reeves 151, 176
Relativism 245
  moral, 245
Religion 6, 40, 86, 88, 90, 92-94, 101, 109, 111, 194, 195, 216
  Gentlemen's, 90
Religious 5, 7, 8, 13-17, 21, 22, 26, 28, 38, 40, 51, 85, 87, 88, 91-96, 98-100, 102, 105, 107, 109, 111, 175, 188, 191, 226, 227, 229-231, 239, 240, 242, 245-247, 257, 259, 261, 262-264
  calling 17
  experience 7, 40, 239, 257
  indifference 245
  instressing 87
  poems 240, 263
  response 7, 85, 87
  tradition 28, 240
Repertory, Old Roman, 171
Resurrection 24, 44, 68, 69, 168, 169, 225, 249, 257, 259, 261-263, 264
Revelation 39, 97, 98, 240, 244, 255
  of John 240
Rhapsode 133, 134
Rhapsodists 134
Rhetoric 86, 111, 120, 187, 190-193, 201, 214, 215, 265
  School of, 187
Rhetoricians 216
Rhodesian mission 205
Rhyme 48-50, 56, 72, 81, 115, 164

Rhythm 31, 33, 114, 116-118, 120, 122, 123, 191, 214, 244, 264
Rhythms 116-118, 216, 263
Ribble 32, 216
"Ribblesdale" 103, 206
Rickaby 214, 221, 223, 224, 228, 231, 237
  brothers, John and Joseph 224
  John, 228
  John and Joseph, 231
  Joseph, 214, 223, 231
Riddell 131, 138
  James, 138
Righteousness 159, 241, 248-250, 252, 253
Robber 186
Roberts 155, 156, 170, 175, 176, 187, 201, 204-206, 208, 211, 220, 221
Robertson 249, 265
Robinson, John, 2
Rodriguez 25, 56, 57, 120, 124
  Alphonsus, 25, 56, 57, 120, 124
Roehampton 179, 188, 189, 191-193, 203-205, 214, 216-218, 220
Roman Catholic 90, 181
  Church 90, 181
Roman martyrs 230
Romantic theopathy 92
Rome 109, 110, 174, 204, 212, 220, 226, 236
Rosa Mystica 53
Royal Academy 192
Royal University of Ireland 180
Rules for Scholastics 43
Sacrament 15, 20, 24, 93, 185
Sacramental 86, 87
  synthesis 86
  view of nature 87
Sacramentally 137
Sacred 7, 47, 76-78, 157, 172
Sacred Heart 76-78
Sacrifice 26, 37, 38, 77, 169, 239, 240, 243, 247, 260, 265
Sacrificial love 243
Sad 193, 207, 219, 244, 255, 259
Sadness 219
Saintly life 25
Saintly lives 25
Saints 6, 99, 100, 102, 162, 164, 223-226, 230, 232, 234, 236, 250
Samuel 162, 176, 237

Satan 42, 235, 246
Savoy 164
Sayings 90, 112, 203
Scanlan, James, 188
Schoder 7, 35, 45, 113, 115, 125
  R.V., 35
  Raymond, 7, 45
  Raymond V., 113
Scholarship 8, 128, 129, 142, 144, 195, 213
Scholastic 32, 36, 44, 187, 206
School of Rhetoric 187
Science 3, 50, 223, 225, 228, 230, 231, 235
  Darwinian, 225
  natural, 3
  physical, 50
Science and the Christian Tradition 230
Scientific 211, 224, 230, 235, 237
Scientists,
  British, 225
  Victorian, 229
Scotist 12, 27, 96
Scotland 32, 179
Scott 130, 133, 142, 146, 175
Scotus 3, 25, 32
Scripture 108, 148, 150, 172, 228
"Scripture a Record of Human Sorrow" 108
Sechnant 233, 234
Secret 50, 54, 102, 169, 205, 261, 264
  name 169
Sectarian 2, 87, 92, 100, 111
Secular 7, 15, 47, 179, 201, 204
  philosophers 179, 201, 204
Selection, natural, 228, 229
Self
  -assessments 240
  -interest 242
  -justice 241, 242
  -less 242
  -love 242
  -pity 20, 255-257
  -proclamation 241
Selfness 241, 242, 244, 248, 254-256, 259
Selving 95, 110, 242
Sensory-imaginative delight 7, 85
Sensualism 85
Sermon 54, 76-79, 90, 97-102, 105, 107, 108, 110, 203

Sermons 3, 7, 9, 61, 74-77, 79-81, 89-92, 96, 97, 100, 105, 110, 112, 205, 241
  Oxford University, 89
Sermons Preached on Various Occasions 97, 112
Seventeenth century 171
Shakespeare 3, 6, 34, 119, 148, 176
Shakespeare's Bottom 148
Sheffield 199
Shepherd's Brow 19
Short Course 193
Shortened sonnets 81
Shrewsbury, Bishop of, 25
Shrine 32, 224
Silver Jubilee 25
Simile 137, 141, 143
Sin 53, 79, 80, 90, 91, 98, 156, 159, 166, 169, 245, 249, 251
  Original, 79, 166
Singleton 148, 176
Sinning 100
Sittler, Joseph, 4
Sixteenth century 227, 231
Skald 132
Skepticism 8, 89, 225, 227-229
Skeptics 227
Smith 187, 265
  Sydney, 187
Society of Jesus 45, 128, 188, 220, 221, 224, 234
Soldier 26, 41, 42, 70, 103, 165
Son
  of Man 245
  of the morning 42
Sonnet 19, 20, 39-41, 67, 81, 98-101, 123, 124, 140, 162-164, 168, 174, 175, 176, 242, 243, 248, 261-264
  Petrarchan, 81
Sonnets,
  curtail or shortened, 81
  last, 8, 239, 240, 247
  terrible, 6, 112, 180, 219, 247
Sophocles 130, 138, 142, 146
Southern Picts 227
Sovran Architect 162
Sparrow 185, 186
Special grace 14
Specialized symbolic systems 69
"Spelt from Sibyl's Leaves" 5, 51, 59, 65, 104, 140, 241, 244
Spirit 11, 12, 22, 26, 114, 119, 121, 122,

Spirit (cont.)
  124, 139, 151, 165, 169, 204, 226, 228, 244, 246, 264
Spiritual Exercises 35, 41, 42, 44, 45, 246, 255, 265
Spirituality 3, 41, 239, 246, 265
  Ignatian, 3, 239
Spools 7, 47, 59, 65, 140, 248
Spouse 100
Spring 69, 72-82, 87, 100, 101, 103, 104, 110, 112, 113, 146, 165, 166, 186, 197, 199, 200, 220, 232-234
Spring and Fall 69, 72-78, 80, 81, 103, 165, 166
Sprinker 41, 45
  Michael, 41
Sprung Rhythm 31, 118, 123
St. Alphonsus Rodriguez 25, 56, 57, 120, 124
St. Augustine 33, 158, 172, 237
St. Beuno's 32, 34, 36, 44, 193, 194, 202, 212, 231
St. Beuno's College 32, 34, 36, 44, 193, 231
St. Bonaventure 172
St. Bridget 171
St. Francis Xavier 76, 189
St. Ignatius 35, 38, 42-45, 191, 239, 246, 257, 258, 265
St. Januarius 225
St. Januarius' blood 225
St. John 77, 147, 148, 150, 152, 157, 170, 174, 184
  Ambrose, 184
  Eudes 77
St. John's 147, 148, 150, 174
  Gospel 148
St. Margaret Mary Alacoque 77
St. Margaret Mary 77
St. Mary's 179, 187, 193-197, 199-202, 204, 209, 216-218, 221, 231
  College 179, 193, 194, 201, 221
  Hall 187, 201, 231
St. Ninian 227, 229
St. Paul 42, 153, 172, 207
St. Thecla 231
St. Thomas Aquinas 159, 173
St. Winefred 23, 51, 55, 60, 224, 225, 231, 233, 234
St. Winefride's
  shrine 32

St. Winefride's (cont.)
  Well 236
Standards, Two, 246
Stimuli 13
Stock epithets 128, 129, 141
Stokes 185
Stonyhurst 6, 32, 34, 117, 179, 180, 187, 188, 193, 200-202, 204-206, 208-214, 216-221, 224, 231, 234
  College 179, 187, 201, 204, 205, 219
  Jesuit College of, 34
  Philosophers 231, 234
Stonyhurst Magazine 6, 206, 220
"Stonyhurst Philosophical Series" 231
Storey 5, 9, 35, 45, 191, 222
  Graham, 5, 9, 35, 222
Stress 12, 37, 40, 53, 58, 61, 77, 88, 118, 190
  divine, 88
Stressed 22, 95
Strophe 116, 123
Strophes 116
Structure 33, 72, 81, 115-118, 120, 123, 165
Struggles 78, 230, 240
Students, politicized, 219
Sturlason, Snorri, 132
Style, Neo-classical, 120
Subjective 15, 62, 142
Subminister 194
Suicide 240
Suitors 131
Sulloway 42, 45
  Alison, 42
Super-Pindaric 122
Supernatural 14, 16, 22, 25, 95, 96, 104, 111, 241
  grace 25, 104
  justice 241
Supernaturalism 90
  natural, 90
Supernaturalizing 104
Svendsen 163, 176
  Kester, 163
Swain 162, 177
Sychnant 233, 234
Symbol 40, 42, 92, 116, 160, 167, 260, 261
Symbolic systems, specialized, 69
Symbolism 151
  Dante's, 151

Syntactic 55
Synthesis 86
  imaginative or sacramental, 86
Tales 129, 130
"Tamworth Reading Room" 91
Teacher 8, 139, 179, 180, 182, 183, 185, 187, 189, 195, 196, 199, 200, 203, 206, 208, 211, 212, 214-217, 219
Teachers 26, 131, 203, 215
Teaching 5, 6, 8, 17, 112, 117, 137, 144, 150, 179-182, 185, 187-189, 190, 194, 200-203, 205, 206, 208, 209, 211-213, 215, 216, 217-219, 240
Technology 71, 72, 83
  laser disk, 72
Teleologists 223, 231
Tenth-century 230
Terrible sonnets 6, 112, 180, 219, 247
Tertian instructor 213
Tertianship 203, 204
Tertullian 155, 163, 177
Testament 163, 235, 236, 240, 245, 247, 263, 265
Tetragrammaton 151, 157
Teutonic 116
"That Nature is a Heraclitean Fire and of the comfort of the resurrection" 168, 257
"The Alchemist in the City" 60
"The Blessed Virgin compared to the Air we Breathe" 106, 136, 180, 208
"The Bugler's First Communion" 22, 199
The Cloud of Unknowing 11, 25, 29
"The Discernment of Spirits" 239
"The English School of Homeric Criticism" 138
"The Final Act: Hopkins' Last Sonnets" 8
"The Glories of Mary for the Sake of Her Son" 105
"The Glories of Mary" 89
The Good Soldier 70
The Great Code 265
The Growth of the Homeric Poems 138, 146
"The Handsome Heart" 18, 199
"The Hound of Heaven" 22
The Idea of a University 89
"The Infinitude of the Divine Attributes" 96

"The Invisible World" 101
The Language of Gerard Manley Hopkins 50, 66
"The Leaden Echo and the Golden Echo" 56, 62, 108, 206, 241, 243
The Lives of the English Saints 226, 236
"The Loss of the Eurydice" 103, 165, 197, 202
"The Manuscripts of Gerard Manley Hopkins" 127, 146
The Month 125, 140, 187, 202, 231, 234, 237
"The Origin of Our Moral Ideas" 48
"The Position of My Mind Since 1845" 91
"The Powers of Nature" 90, 100, 262
"The Present Position of Catholics in 1851" 225
"The Sea and the Skylark" 103
"The Second Spring" 100, 110
"The Soldier" 26, 103, 165
The Spiritual Exercises 35, 41, 45, 246, 265
"The Starlight Night" 22, 95, 99, 106
"The Tamworth Reading Room" 91
The Testament of Beauty 234, 236
"The Value of Witness to the Miraculous" 230
"The Visible Church an Encouragement to Faith" 99
"The Windhover" 7, 31, 33, 34, 37, 39-42, 58, 94, 95, 140, 144, 167
The Women of Trachis 142
"The Wreck of the Deutschland" 3, 12, 19, 37, 39, 80, 89, 95, 133, 136, 141, 165, 187, 240
"The Wreck" 21, 25, 68, 97, 137
Theban 114
Thecla 8, 223, 231
Thecla of Asia Minor 223
Thee, God, I come from 12, 22
Theocratic 229
Theologate 231, 233
Theologians 4
Theological 2, 4, 7, 14, 17, 19, 22, 24, 27, 36, 43, 76, 87, 95, 102, 111, 147, 173, 242, 249
  virtues 147
Theology 6, 27, 36, 44, 88, 89, 111, 193, 212, 220, 231, 265
  deistic natural, 111

Theology (cont.)
  natural, 88, 89, 111
  Professor of, 212
Theopathy, romantic, 92
Theophany, Christic, 156
Thirteenth century 151, 223
Thisness 32, 241
Thomas, Alfred, 5, 189
Thomist 27, 32
Thompson, Francis, 22
Thomson 116, 125
Thornton, R.K.R., 5, 7, 47
Thou art indeed just, Lord 5, 23, 55
"Thou art indeed just" 165
Thought 3, 4, 16, 23, 26, 32, 48, 53-55, 63, 75, 78, 87, 90-92, 94-96, 101, 103, 105, 108, 111, 113-115, 117, 120, 123, 132, 133, 136, 146, 148, 169, 188, 190, 197, 198, 203, 214, 215, 259
"Tintern Abbey" 62
Tired 118, 185, 190, 191, 207, 210, 212, 218
"To R.B." 5
"To seem the stranger lies my lot" 20
"To seem the stranger" 54, 55, 57
"To What Serves Mortal Beauty" 24, 87, 88, 109, 243
"Tom's Garland" 26
Tondelli 151, 177
Toryism, Intelligent, 205
Tractarian Anglican 92
Tractarianism 90
Tracy 262, 263, 265
  David, 262, 263
Tradition 23, 28, 85, 87, 123, 125, 135, 138, 146, 150, 161, 164, 168, 170, 228, 230, 232, 240, 244
  Catholic philosophical, 87
  religious, 28, 240
Tragedies 131
Tragic choruses, Greek, 118
Transcendent 24, 257
  religious experience 257
Transfiguration 38, 39
  Christ 38
Transubstantiation 261, 262
Trent, Council of, 227
Trigrammaton 157, 168
Trinity 151, 152, 159, 172, 173, 242
"Trio of Triolets" 206, 220
Trojans 135, 143

Troy 130, 134, 136
Truth 14, 22, 26, 34, 36, 57, 61, 91-93, 95, 97, 103, 104, 108, 135, 162, 235-237
Tucker, Herbert F., 2
Turbulence 7, 69
Turbulent 82
Turkey 223
Twelfth Night 198
"Two Beautiful Young People" 26, 57, 104, 199
Tyndall 229, 230
  John, 229
Typhon 117
Ultramontane 227
Ulysses 131
Underthought 123
Uniqueness 32, 33
Unison 48
Unities 56
Unity 3, 48-50, 64, 65, 85, 116, 131, 132, 151
  of principle 48, 49, 65
University
  College 4, 213, 219
    Dublin 127, 180, 212
  of London 125, 180
  of Wisconsin-Madison 71
Unjustified 239
Unorthodoxy 227
Ur-epic 132
Urquhart, E.W., 93
Valeriano 170, 177
  Piero, 170
Valley
  of the Elwy 23, 32, 57, 103
  of the Ribble 32
Van Doren 163, 177
  Mark, 163
Vanity Fair 50
Vatican 224, 225, 227, 228, 231, 233, 237
  Council 224, 225, 227, 228, 231, 237
    First, 227, 228
  I 228, 233
Vaudois 164
Ven. Bede 149
Veni Creator Spiritus 189
Vergil 133
Verse 2, 87, 104, 106, 111, 128, 131, 133, 142, 148, 149, 163, 165, 173, 195,

Verse (cont.)
  197, 217, 223, 224, 233
Vespers 171
Vice 48, 49
Victoria and Albert Museum 190
Victorian 1-4, 45, 58, 83, 119, 130, 133, 142, 229, 235
  age 119
  gnostic 4
  scientists 229
Victory ode 117
Vienna 151, 161
Violin 186, 216
Vires 212
Virgil 148, 156, 159, 189
Virgin 89, 100, 105, 106, 136, 180, 208
Virgin Mary 55
Virgins 231
Virtue 6, 11, 13, 23, 92, 94, 101, 103
Virtues 14, 15, 17, 22, 23, 82, 147
Vision 6, 35, 37-39, 87, 88, 99, 104, 121, 133, 144, 147, 151, 156, 256, 260, 264
Visitation order 77
Vocabulary 7, 67, 70, 73, 76, 114
Vocation 26, 188, 192
Vocations 26
Vow, Fourth, 228
Vowel Shift, Great, 160
Vows 22, 100
Wagner 76
Wain, John, 2
Wakefield 194
Waldenses 164
Wales 5, 32, 223, 224, 231, 236
Walford 182
Walhout, Donald, 7, 11
War 56, 110, 116, 124, 141-143, 253-255
Warning 79, 104, 240
Weak 55, 185, 191, 218
Weariness 180, 184, 185, 187, 190, 191, 199, 207, 209, 210, 217, 218, 253, 254, 255
Weary 207, 218
Weather 184, 185, 189, 208, 218, 219
Weatherby, Harold, 3
Wedding 24, 189
Wedlock 24
Weil, Simone, 141
Welsh 4, 95, 224, 226, 232-234
Westminster Abbey 5

Wexford, County, 211
White 5, 6, 51, 104, 168, 245
  Norman, 5
  stone of the Apocalypse 168
Whiteheadian 27
Wilder 240, 265
  Amos, 240
Wilkins 138, 146
  George, 138
Will,
  affective, 100
  free, 54
Willcock 143, 146
  M.M., 143
Windhover 7, 31, 33, 34, 37, 39-42, 58, 94, 95, 120, 140, 144, 167
Winefred 23, 51, 55, 60, 223-225, 231-234
Winefride 8, 32, 236, 23
Winters, Yvor, 2, 88
Word 7, 38, 40, 41, 47, 50, 53, 56-59, 62-64, 68, 71, 73, 74, 76-80, 82, 88, 90, 92, 94, 102, 114, 116, 123, 136, 141, 148, 149, 150, 152-159, 161-165, 168-172, 181, 188, 205, 212, 249, 262
  become flesh 148
  incarnate 150, 169
  Omnific, 161
Words,
  high frequency, 73
  low frequency 73-76
Wordsworth 62
Wordsworthian 92
Work-Maister 161
Working 11-13, 15, 26, 50, 73, 179, 197, 205, 206
  -class 26
Worldly joy 94
Worship, nature-, 111
Wounds 170, 232, 253-255
Wreck 3, 12, 19, 21, 25, 37, 39, 49, 52-54, 57, 60, 61, 68, 80, 89, 95, 97, 121-123, 133, 136, 137, 141, 165, 187, 240
Writer 6, 185
Xavier, Francis, 76, 189
Yeats 6
Zaniello 5, 8, 223, 235, 237
  Tom, 5, 8, 223
Zeus 115, 135, 136

STUDIES IN BRITISH LITERATURE

1. Michael E. Allsopp and Michael E. Sundermeier (eds.), **Gerard Manley Hopkins (1844-1889): New Essays on His Life, Writings and Place in English Literature**
2. Dana Grove, **A Rhetorical Analysis of** *Under the Volcano*: **Malcolm Lowry's Design Governing Postures**
3. Christopher Spencer, **The Genesis of Shakespeare's** *Merchant of Venice*
4. Oscar Wilde, ***Vera; or, The Nihilist,*** Frances Miriam Reed (ed.)
5. Rob Jackaman, **The Course of English Surrealist Poetry Since the 1930s**